The Sheriff

THE SHERIFF

America's Defense of
The New World Order

COLIN S. GRAY

THE UNIVERSITY PRESS OF KENTUCKY

Publication of this volume was made possible in part by a grant from the
National Endowment for the Humanities.

Scholarly publisher for the Commonwealth,
serving Bellarmine University, Berea College, Centre
College of Kentucky, Eastern Kentucky University,
The Filson Historical Society, Georgetown College,
Kentucky Historical Society, Kentucky State University,
Morehead State University, Murray State University,
Northern Kentucky University, Transylvania University,
University of Kentucky, University of Louisville,
and Western Kentucky University.

Editorial and Sales Offices: The University Press of Kentucky
663 South Limestone Street, Lexington, Kentucky 40508-4008
http//www.kentuckypress.com/

08 07 06 05 04   5 4 3 2 1

Library of Congress Cataloging-in-Publication Data

Gray, Colin S.
  The sheriff : America's defense of the new world order / Colin S. Gray.
    p. cm.
Includes bibliographical references and index.
  ISBN 0-8131-2315-1 (hardcover : alk. paper)
  1. United States—Foreign relations—1989- 2. World politics—1989- I.
Title.
  E895.G73 2004
  327.73'009'0511—dc22
                                2003020514

This book is printed on acid-free recycled paper meeting
the requirements of the American National Standard
for Permanence in Paper for Printed Library Materials.

Manufactured in the United States of America.

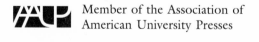 Member of the Association of
American University Presses

To Dottie with Love

Contents

Americans are "cowboys," Europeans love to say. And there is truth in this. The United States does act as an international sheriff, self-appointed perhaps but widely welcomed nevertheless, trying to enforce some peace and justice in what Americans see as a lawless world where outlaws need to be deterred or destroyed, and often through the muzzle of a gun. Europe, by this old West analogy, is more like a saloonkeeper. Outlaws shoot sheriffs, not saloonkeepers. In fact, from the saloonkeeper's point of view, the sheriff trying to impose order by force can sometimes be more threatening than the outlaws who, at least for the time being, may just want a drink.

    Robert Kagan (2002)

What seems to work best, even though imperfectly, is the possession by those states who wish to preserve the peace of the preponderant power and the will to accept the burdens and responsibilities required to achieve that purpose.

    Donald Kagan (1995)

New world orders . . . need to be policed.

    Michael Howard (2002)

Preface

Some readers may find my argument challenging, but I suspect that critics will deem it more unpalatable than incorrect. As originally conceived, the argument was to focus very heavily indeed upon defense policy, strategy, and force posture. I intended to zero in on what used to be called the Revolution in Military Affairs (RMA), but more recently has come to be known as military transformation. Books that need and want to be written have a way of all but writing themselves. My sincere intention to write a book about American defense, now that the no-name, brief post–Cold War period is over, was thwarted—not so much by events, though September 11 certainly was a factor, as rather more by the nature of the subject. I found that so much about the U.S. role in the world is coming into contention, that were I to devote most of my pages to military issues, as long intended, I would be analysing secondary issues while leaving matters of first-order significance insufficiently addressed. In practice, I have written a book that is far more about America's role in the world, and its national security policy broadly conceived, than it is about the modernization, or transformation, of its armed forces. Since my most recent book strives to marry social science and history for the purpose of unravelling the mysteries of RMAs, I was more than a little reluctant to surrender to the logic of my topic, follow Clausewitz, and give extensive pride of place to policy. Of course, the great man tersely says what he needs to say about the relationship between war and policy, and then devotes the remainder of his book to the theory of war. Would that I could have done the same.

The message in my title and subtitle is controversial, but it should not really be so. The United States has behaved, is behaving, and long will continue to behave, in the role that I name. It is a fact, like it or not. Rather less factual are the descriptive, sometimes emotive, words that we employ to give punch to our explanations. There are problems with the notion of the role of sheriff, for example. For historical reasons American culture is apt to be unduly legalistic, so I hesitate to encourage the half-truth (at best) that the country will perform as a law officer. That line of thought can lead one up some seriously unpromising canyons of international, especially UN, diplomacy. The reality is that America's authority to act in defense of its understanding of the needs of world order is born of respect for its power. Favorable nose counts in multilateral assemblies can be nice to achieve, but they are not what licenses the United States to perform as sheriff.

On balance, I prefer the sheriff descriptor to other terms popular at present. Some scholars for whom I have great respect, Eliot A. Cohen and Andrew J. Bacevich, for example, favor the concept of empire. The terms *empire* and *imperial* carry rather more historical baggage than this Anglo-American commentator finds comfortable. Also, I am afraid that Americans might fall victim to the attractions of their own theories. Notwithstanding the objective merit in the theory of a new American empire, many Americans might well take the idea more seriously than they should. I strongly suspect that a swelling public discourse on the theme of an American empire, when it is slapped down as a consequence of some rude awakening in one of the globe's rougher neighborhoods, would effect quite gratuitous damage to the vital world ordering mission. Imperial governance is not an American strength. It is culturally alien and politically unacceptable. Only time will tell whether American society has the fortitude to manage the kind of uneasy peace that its military prowess typically will deliver. Post-Saddam Iraq truly is a trial from central casting.

Many people have contributed to this book and my debts are serious and diffuse. Above all others, I am grateful to the Earhart Foundation and its trustees. They supported my research and writing in several ways that proved essential. While the argument of the book veered this way and that, I sought counsel from friends, colleagues, and even acquaintances, with what must sometimes have seemed to be a ruthless persistence. I am especially grateful to the National Institute for Public Policy in Fairfax, Virginia, for providing me with a home in the summer of 2002. Particular friends around the National Institute, namely Kurt Guthe and Steve Lambakis, made important contributions to the way my argument moved forward.

Similarly, Williamson Murray and Col. Frank G. Hoffman, USMCR (Ret.), two old friends and outstanding scholars, put in their two bits when it really mattered. I am also indebted to Washington's Center for Strategic and Budgetary Assessments, and to its director, Andrew F. Krepinevich, for allowing me to air my theories at a lunchtime seminar. Although this book is entirely my own work, warts and all, it will be readily apparent from the references that I am heavily indebted to three people in particular, all of whom I have named already. Specifically, I owe major intellectual debts of gratitude to Eliot A. Cohen, Andrew J. Bacevich, and, of course, to Carl von Clausewitz. The fact that I do not always agree with my two contemporaries does not in any way diminish the value I have found in their work.

I am in the debt of the excellent graduate students at the University of Reading, England, who were occasional, and generally willing, sounding boards for the argument as it assumed ever firmer and more contentious shape. My word-processing person, Barbara Watts, performed magnificently, cheerfully, and most competently on what I thought was often an undecipherable tangle. I am vastly in her debt. Simple justice commands that I mention my family, who—as always—suffer, albeit not without due and just complaint, when I write yet another book. Valerie and TJ, I cannot thank you enough, though I know you enjoy seeing me try!

Colin S. Gray
Wokingham, U.K.
November 2003

CHAPTER 1
The Argument

Military power is not self-validating. It should be considered preparation, or prudent investment, in anticipation of strategic demand from foreign policy. When we design, bargain over, and pursue the capabilities, declarations, and actions that comprise defense policy, we are guessing about the requirements for military support that our country may need over the years ahead. Context can be all important. A defense policy good enough for 1916, 1940, 1949, or mid-2001 looked nothing of the sort in 1917, 1941–42, 1950, or late September 2001. The narrative of U.S. defense policy is a constant trialogue among the more permanent features of the United States as a strategic player, the stimuli provided by an unruly outside world, and the somewhat undisciplined workings of the policy-debating and policymaking process. When we allow for the occasional great surprise—Pearl Harbor, the demise of the Soviet imperium in 1989 and then of the USSR itself by 1991, and September 11—on top of the conduct of defense politics as usual, it is not hard to see why books on national security policy are perhaps better left to journalists. It would seem that weighty tomes on the subject are condemned either to celebrate the authors' up-to-date detailed knowledge, though at the price of instant obsolescence, or to fly above the messy and ever-changing details on a hot-air cushion of platitudes.

I am writing so as not to abandon the field to journalists, no matter how gifted; to technophiles more interested in the equipment than in what it might mean strategically; to would-be diplomats inclined to underrate brutal military power, in their sophisticated appreciation of the added legitimacy gained by the multilateral institutionalization of American power; or to scholars of International Relations who can have such grave difficulty with the basic concepts employed here—power, world order, empire—that they tend to be professionally programmed to write largely for each other. In this opening chapter, boldly or rashly, I offer a clear argument in nine

1

parts, all of it supportive of a single, organizing vision for U.S. national security policy. The choice of clarity over complexity at this first step in the journey is made in full awareness of the volatility of defense politics and of world events. Also, as the author of a recent large book on the subject, I am nothing if not painfully aware of the many schools of thought on the controversial topic of military transformation (the RMA, or Revolution in Military Affairs, concept of yesteryear).[1] Similarly, I do not deny the importance of coalition building and maintenance—at least I do not deny it too vehemently or frequently. Finally, as a card-carrying professor of International Politics and Strategic Studies, I can play definitional word games as argument arresters as well as the next scholar. The book's title could fuel hours, if not days, of fairly futile deconstructive endeavor by my academic peers.

This is intended as a scholarly, but not intrusively academic, work. It is both descriptive and prescriptive. The message about America's role is hardly original, indeed it would be a political irrelevance if it were, but hopefully it is set forth in these pages in a way that is more easily understood than is generally the case. My intention is to help Americans, and their friends and foes, understand just what they are about in the world. Journalistic commentary, virtually by definition, lurches breathlessly from what is news today to what may be news tomorrow. The policy world might be remade afresh at any moment by the impact of images beamed through space by the global media. It could happen. Very rarely, it should happen. But, a country that enjoys a mature, historically grounded vision of its proper place in world affairs, and of the duties thereto pertaining, should not be a candidate for violent swings in policy or in scale or character of military provision. All of which presumes, of course, that the country's vision of its international role is fundamentally appropriate, which is to say desirable and feasible.

NINE THEMES

So, what are the strands that comprise *The Argument*?

THE ARGUMENT

1. World order is neither self-enforcing nor is it comprehensively enforceable. Nonetheless, every such "order" requires a sheriff, or some other agent of discipline.

2. The United States is the, indeed the only, essential protecting power for the current world order.

3. The United States serves itself by serving the world selectively.

4. September 11 was an accelerator to a United States that already was (slowly) coming to terms with its role as sheriff.

5. Conditions of preponderance must erode over time, but they can be prolonged, or shortened, by wise or foolish policy and strategy.

6. Sheriff is a role, not a strategy or doctrine.

7. Strategy is difficult. Military effectiveness need not mean strategic effectiveness, while strategic effectiveness may not translate into enduring political advantage.

8. Technology is vital, but does not determine military or policy success.

9. History is our best guide to the future.

1. World order is neither self-enforcing nor is it comprehensively enforceable. Nonetheless, every such "order" requires a sheriff, or some other agent of discipline.

In the modern European, then world, system, which is to say since the late eighteenth century, the ordering mechanism was the balance of power, with occasional corrections imposed by war. Order is the prime virtue; it is the essential prerequisite for security, peace, and possibly justice.[2] Disorder is the worst condition. Because this study is not deterministic, it is possible that the necessary rule-keeping job might be abandoned and not resumed for a while. Even in that un-happy event, my argument does not sink. Rather does the world cope as best it can in the absence of a superior, and by and large legiti-mate, force, until such a force reappears. Periods of anarchy, or at best of only very weak international governance, are far from un-known historically. Invariably they invite ambitious opportunists to try their luck. That development may, or may not, suffice to awake the sleeping benign giant, should such be conveniently available to be stirred from slumber.

Every condition of international order works for the particular benefit of some countries and interests more than others, and needs defending. The alternatives to an American-led international order are just possibly eventual leadership by some other polity or coalition (probably Chinese, though possibly European, led), or, more likely, a lengthy period with no one wearing the sheriff's badge. In that unwelcome event, every predatory regional and local power, and many a dissatisfied ethnic or religious minority, most probably would chance its arm and seek its own destiny, by violence if need be. Violent struggle is all but essential to the success of the process of nation building.[3] No doubt there are many ways in which order for security, hopefully promoting peace and justice, might be established and maintained. In the life of the modern states' system, which is to say from the Treaty of Westphalia in 1648 to the present day (though many now proclaim the demise of this system), in practice only one ordering mechanism has been available: the balance of power. The dying embers of that hoary approach limped on even until 1991, when many of its American aficionados could still be found mutter-ing about "the strategic balance,"[4] while through the 1990s many a serious reference still was made to that abominable consequence of Cold War military competition, a condition of stability keyed to the mutuality of assured destruction (MAD). But, today there is no stra-tegic balance, central or otherwise, and there is no political context of hostility to provide meaning to military rivalry between the United States and the new Russian Federation. There is no balance of power serving as the mainstay, the organizing architecture, of the current world order.[5] What we have instead was flagged in 1995 as a strong desideratum by the classical historian, Donald Kagan.

What seems to work best, even though imperfectly, is the possession by those states who wish to preserve the peace of the preponderant power and of the will to accept the burdens and responsibilities required to achieve that purpose.[6]

As written, Kagan's words could just about fit the folly of the theory of collective security. Of course, he has no such noble nonsense in mind. What he is saying is that peace has to be kept, actively, and that it is best kept by a preponderance, not by an ever contestable balance, of power.[7] Kagan's historical judgment will serve as the text for this sermon on security. In principle there is both good and bad news in Kagan's claim. It is good news that his lifetime's ruminations on peace and war have yielded definite advice. Many academics would be uncomfortable writing as boldly as does Kagan. The bad news is that to the best of our knowledge, there is no hidden hand of history commanded to ensure that only commercially minded popular democracies shall inherit the mantle of preponderant power. It was never probable, but that power at century's close might have been Nazi Germany or the USSR. Fortunately, chance favored civilizational merit for once, and the only candidate for sheriff today is the United States, a fact which is our second theme.

2. *The United States is the, indeed is the only, essential protecting power for the current world order.*

Again, this is not to be deterministic. Although there are no other bidders for this crown at present, it does not follow that the United States is condemned to play this role. After all, American world leadership in Paris in 1919 was succeeded post haste by a scuttle from many potential international obligations. Americans today could elect to withdraw from the outside world, insofar as they could in political-military ways.[8] They would hope that the civilizational offense given by the soft power of their now globally beamed culture would not be found unduly provocative abroad.[9] Whether The Great Satan, as Iranian spokespeople have delighted in calling the United States, would be allowed to hunker down in peaceful sanctuary in North America, we should doubt. Still, it could be tried. After September 11, 2001, isolationist sentiment temporarily has lost much of its appeal. We may not be much interested in terrorism, but it would appear that terrorism is interested in us. For good or ill, we are what we are. Exactly what this is has been explained in no uncertain terms by Henry Kissinger in the opening lines of his book, *Does America Need a Foreign Policy?* No prizes are awarded for guessing that his question is strictly rhetorical. Kissinger proclaims that

> At the dawn of the new millennium, the United States is enjoying a preeminence unrivalled by even the greatest empires of the past. From weaponry to entrepreneurship, from science to technology, from higher education to popular culture, America exercises an unparalleled ascendancy around the globe. During the last decade of the twentieth century, *America's preponderant position rendered it the indispensable component of international stability.*[10]

The condition of unchallenged, indeed unchallengeable, primacy will not endure—it is not strategic history's "last move"—but while it does the United States is the only candidate for sheriff. If Americans should decline the honor, they are at least uniquely well equipped to ensure that no one else could possibly succeed in that informal office. As Donald Kagan provided our basic text, quoted under the first point above, so it is only fitting that he should also be allowed to sound the warning bell. Kagan advises that

> Unexpected changes and shifts in power are the warp and woof of international history. The current condition of the world, therefore, where war among major powers is hard to conceive because one of them has overwhelming military superiority and no wish to expand, will not last.[11]

Quite so. However, historians, perhaps especially ancient historians, should be expected to take the long view. And in the long view everything crumbles. But a suitable vision for the inspiration of policy, judicious choice of policy goals, and competence in strategy, should allow Americans to prolong their current strategic moment, as a later point makes explicit.

To be the sheriff of the current world order is a thankless role. American power may be necessary to restore such order as may be restorable, but Americans will not be loved, or even much appreciated, as a consequence. The rest of the world will be envious, fearful, and resentful, all the while seeking to use the leverage of American power for local purposes. There is no term extant that precisely captures the emerging U.S. role as sheriff of world order. For the first time since the mid-1960s, it has begun to be fashionable to refer to American policy and tasks as imperial. Andrew Bacevich, for one thoughtful example, suggests that "the preeminent challenge facing the United States in the twenty-first century is not eradicating terror but managing the informal American empire acquired during the course of the century just past."[12] Empire, imperium even better, and hegemony, for all their popularity and at least partial suitability, carry baggage that can be distracting. Unless we are careful, such concepts themselves become part of the problem in the effort to conduct focused debate on U.S. policy and strategy. Despite the grounds for unease, we cannot deny the reality of common usage. For example, a review essay in *Foreign Affairs* opens with this claim: "The fact of America's empire is hardly debated these days."[13] Allowing for the hyperbole and a certain imprecision of meaning, still it is noteworthy that the author, Thomas Donnelly, feels able to make such a bold statement.

I prefer to think of the United States as the sheriff of the current world order, for reasons both of cultural fit of concept and of tolerable accuracy.[14] Naturally, this American role is largely self-appointed, though it can enjoy added dignity when it is blessed formally by majority votes in multinational institutions. For example, the Security Council of the United Nations licensed the United States to lead military action against Iraq in 1990–91, while the war against Yugoslavia over its "ethnic cleansing" of Kosovo in 1999 was a collective NATO, though not a UN, undertaking. Because world politics comprises a distinctly immature political system, we have to be somewhat relaxed about some of the legal niceties. To call the United States the sheriff of the current world order is both description and prescription. This lawman role derives most essentially from the contemporary distribution of power, which so markedly favors the American superstate. Beyond that derivation, however, the role of sheriff is made easier to sustain by the more or less willing, though variably grudging, acquiescence of most countries.

Sheriff is of course a metaphor. By its use I mean to argue that the United States will act on behalf of others, as well as itself, undertaking some of the tough jobs of international security that no other agent or agency is competent to perform.

3. *The American sheriff serves itself by serving the world selectively. This role requires the clearest of foreign policy explanations, lest it descend into strategic opportunism, or at least appears to do so.*

U.S. material and spiritual resources are great, but not inexhaustible.[15] They should not be expended casually in pursuit of goals of only marginal national interest. Notwithstanding September 11 and its aftermath, the jury is out, and is likely to stay out awhile longer, on whether American society will tolerate the sheriff's role as specified here, except in contexts highly specific to obvious American interests. Those contexts may not include some which the world order will need a prudent sheriff to influence coercively (if not necessarily with force).

The United States is not, and should not and cannot be, the world's policeman *vis à vis* any and every disturbance. The actions of this American sheriff of order are guided frankly by a national interest discriminator. The U.S. President needs to know: what has happened (or plausibly might happen); whether it matters to the United States, and if so, how much; what, if anything, he can do about it; and what costs, of all kinds, are likely to attach to action, or inaction. If the United States does not serve itself through its peacemaking behavior, its career as sheriff will be brief indeed. Altruism has a thin record in strategic history and, we must assume, an unpromising future. That is just the way it is in world politics. However, if the United States seeks to serve only itself, and rides roughshod over the interests of others, again its career as functional sheriff will be brief. The world at large will discern scant reason to cooperate with the United States, if American statecraft is crassly applied strictly on behalf of narrowly American interests. At the level of principle, if not always in attempted application, some of the critics of American so-called unilateralism are correct.[16] The United States often is more powerful when it can act with others. This is not an invariable rule. By extension, when the sheriff departs the town he has cleansed, he wants to leave it in the hands of right-minded and hopefully capable citizens. One of the indispensable keys to success in this emerging era of American guardianship is for the maximum number of countries, and extra-national interests, to believe that the United States is protecting a world order in which they all have a vital, if sometimes differential, stake. People may resent the American sheriff, and naturally be residually suspicious of American motives. But they should be prepared to welcome American ordering activity which benefits all potential victims of disorder. Americans do not need to be loved. It is sufficient to be respected and, perhaps, appreciated for the self-assumed lawman role.

The United States has an imperial history, of a sort, but it has never acquired much of an imperial mindset.[17] Commentators may discover new forms of imperialism to cover current American attitudes and behavior, and perhaps, but only perhaps, there is some small merit in the exercise. Americans are apt to view the world through missionary lenses. America is an idea, a civilization even (to stretch conceptual domain), rather than just another state. Globalization, beneath the hyperbole, is seen in America and elsewhere as equating approximately with Americanization. Whether or not, or to what extent, that is true is not a prime concern here. Instead, our gaze is fixed upon America's role as chief protector, guardian, or sheriff of this new world with its globalizing flows of information, people, and goods. First and foremost, the United States is the agent of its own national interest, an interest that Washington, on a prudent day,[18] judges vitally bound up with a particular idea of world order. The national interest discriminator to which reference has been made, allows a fairly reliable four-way categorization of issues. Issues can be of a survival character; they can be vital; they can be major; or they can be "other." Survival issues must be fought for. Vital interests should be defended forcefully. Major interests might possibly be protected militarily. "Other" interests should not attract the U.S. cavalry—unless, that is, the cost is believed to be extraordinarily low (but beware of the surprises that friction and chance in war may throw your way). The political context, or perhaps the timing, may multiply the significance of matters that otherwise would be of little concern to Washington (e.g., almost anything in the Balkans).

A useful approach to understanding the U.S. role as sheriff is by means of another four-way split. Given the contemporary, and at least short-term predictable, distribution of power (which admittedly is different in its political-military, economic, and cultural dimensions), the objectively desirable U.S. role typically is as plain as it is not yet quite acceptable politically to proclaim out loud. With respect to protecting the world order, my second four-way split, tied inalienably to the four-way national interest discriminator, is the following: There are problems that only the United States can address in hopes of achieving decisive success; there are problems that the United States should stand a reasonable prospect of meeting and at least alleviating; there are problems concerning which the United States should be expected to fare poorly; and finally, there are problems that the United States has absolutely no plausible prospect whatsoever of alleviating, let alone of resolving (e.g., rescuing and restoring certain failed states).[19] It may be needless to add that in most cases the active support of some friends and allies will, on balance, be a significant, though rarely essential, benefit.

The United States could pick up its military ball and go home. It could choose to rely for world order on the hidden hand of universal commercial self-interest somewhat guided by such regional and local balances and imbalances of power as may be extant or might emerge. In effect, frequently this would translate as a green light for regional bullies to mark out their territories (and sea space and air space). Thus far, the contemporary United States is showing no persuasive evidence of an inclination to bring itself home as a political-military influence. The issue is not whether America's skills in statecraft are fully adequate for the sheriff role (whose would be?). Rather, is it whether there is to be a sheriff at all. If the United States declines the honor, or takes early retirement, there is no deputy sheriff waiting, trained and ready for promotion. Furthermore, there is no world-ordering mechanism worthy of the name which could substitute for the authority and strength of the American superpower. At present there is no central axis of a balance of power to keep order, while the regional balances in the Middle East and South and East Asia are as likely to provoke as to cool conflict—and conflict with weapons of mass destruction (WMD) at that.

It is simply a political, military, and even economic fact of the present, that if the current world order is to benefit from the inevitably flawed performance of a sheriff, only the United States is available to play the role. What that means politically and militarily is the subject of much of what follows in this book.

4. *September 11 was an accelerator to a United States that already was (slowly) coming to terms with its role as sheriff.*

In a democracy, public mood is the principal influence on the size, and sometimes the direction, of the national defense effort. September 11 has had an impact on U.S. policy and strategy analogous, in its way, to that achieved by the North Korean invasion of June 25,

1950. In both cases, an unpleasant surprise event dropped the curtain on a lengthy post-war period (respectively, five years in the 1940s and ten in the 1990s). A decade of heated debate over RMA, or military transformation, and the understandably somewhat half-hearted moves to implement radical change, had lacked a compelling strategic purpose.[20] With the Soviet Union *hors de combat*, China more than a generation distant from posing even a potentially serious threat, it has been hard for American policymakers to compose and sustain a rational defense program. So, when political guidance is unhelpful, the troops will tend to go on doing what they know how to do and generally like doing.[21] But, why were they doing it? Which capabilities best fit America's view of its probable strategic demand for military support in the early decades of the twenty-first century? To answer these questions, the country was in need of a new vision of its strategic role. Even a clear statement of an old vision would have been helpful.

The Revolution in Military Affairs, or RMA, refers to an actual, or prospective, radical change in the character or conduct of war. The contemporary American RMA marks a historic shift from the era of wars of industrial mass production, to the era of wars dominated by information-led forces. Armed forces will be smaller, lighter, more mobile, and vastly more deadly in the precision with which they can utilize firepower. Such, at least, is the basic vision.

By focusing on military means rather than political ends, let alone on the strategy bridge between the two, the RMA debate of the 1990s tended to sideline expert discussion into contesting second-order topics. The weakness underlying the debate was revealed all too readily if one stopped to enquire, RMA or transformation for what purpose? A talented analyst on the transformational wing of American defense opinion, Michael Vickers, noted accurately enough that

> For a small but influential core of soldiers, defense analysts, and journalists, one issue above all others has dominated the defense agenda throughout the 1990s: The Revolution in Military Affairs (RMA).[22]

But, what was it all about? Why should the country risk transforming an already apparently excellent military machine, when no very demanding strategic missions loomed on the horizon? Since there was nothing of outstanding interest, let alone seriously menacing, to study on the threat board, the U.S. defense community reverted to its first love and zeroed in on the promise of new technology (provided it did not threaten new or upgraded "legacy systems").

September 11 changed all that. By effecting a sharp nonlinearity in political context, as Korea did in June 1950, it enabled the first truly hard-edged definition of the U.S. global role to be advanced for a decade. Much of the literature on the subject has wise-sounding professors and other commentators advising readers to take counsel of their fears.[23] Objections to the role of sheriff are not exactly in short supply. They are accorded the respect that they deserve at suitable junctures below. Insofar as proves possible, we shall focus on the strategic dimension of the sheriff's assets and duties. Needless to say, such a focus will be eminently contestable. With some good reason, many people believe that uneven economic, social, and political development around the world is the source of much of the disorder that triggers the U.S. policy demand for military action. That argument is partially valid, but it is beside the point for my thesis. Globalization has winners and losers, and the United States lacks the knowledge, the skills, the wealth, and the political will to try to remake the world. It is true that many Americans regard globalization as a codeword for the global diffusion of American culture and values, but that manifestation of hubris will not be allowed to distract us from our strategic focus. The twenty-first may well be another American century, but American society, for all its genuine and potent soft power, is not about to remake the basis of world order by reconstructing the outside world in its own image.

Three elements came together in 2001 to produce the situation that I describe and analyze. First, a new team of generally experienced, conservative realists assumed command of the executive branch of government. Individuals and their personal beliefs matter. The neorealist literature of academic International Relations, which treats states as interchangeable billiard balls, is seriously incomplete, with its deliberate neglect of domestic factors.[24] The policymakers of the second Bush administration comprised a body of people ready to define a new, or redefine the old, policy and strategy.[25]

The central premise of neorealism is that the distribution of power is the most potent factor shaping foreign policy. While the distribution of power certainly is important, it is a mistake of potentially lethal proportions to discount the roles of local culture, the psychology of leaders, and national traditions. Individuals matter, and so do the differences among societies. Theory that ignores the domestic contexts of states may make for an elegant reductionism, but it has little to offer serious scholars of international security.

Second, the new President and his Pentagon team were committed to the transformation of the U.S. military establishment. Just how much transformation was necessary, achievable, desirable, or affordable are interesting issues. But there is no doubt that the RMA debate of the 1990s had educated a cohort of incoming policymakers in 2001 to be more or less cautious revolutionaries (if that is not an oxymoron).[26] By the turn of the century, the downsizing of an essentially unreconstructed Cold War military arsenal had proceeded about as far as prudence, safe operation, and strategic rationales would allow. The Gulf War of 1991 increasingly looks like the last war of the industrial era, rather than the first of the post–Cold War period. Notwithstanding its novel features, that conflict was a clash between rival masses of military material.

Third, September 11 burst upon the new group of policymakers just as they were completing their initial assessment in the congressionally mandated *Quadrennial Defense Review*. The outrage had the effect of the modern version of a mobilization proclamation for American society. It was all but inevitable that the United States would overreact to the event. Whether that proves to be so, there is no doubt that September 11 helped propel the country in a direction that already found favor with a majority of policymakers in the new administration. To the people around President Bush, and to the promise of enhanced and more discriminate military power, September 11 added the all-important element of focus. Now the country had an actual declared enemy. Osama bin Laden and his al Qaeda network was the principal foe, of course, but America was now at war with terrorists, and terrorism, in general. Victory over so diffuse, even inchoate, an enemy, will be exceptionally difficult.

For the first time since the end of the Cold War, the United States could identify a clear mission. Moreover, that mission—to wage war on terrorists—points to a unique national role: as the sheriff of the current world order. This is not exactly new. After all, the United States did lead a large UN-blessed posse against Iraq in 1991 (not to mention North Korea in 1950). However, this time the mission is generalized, the bedrock of justification is the inherent right of self-defense, and the preferred strategy is misleadingly called preemption, but actually is prevention.[27] The United States, legitimized by both the authority of its power and its special status as victim, has staked out the sheriff's role. This will prove habit forming. From standing up for the world order against terrorism, the United States will discover that it has more extensive, and probably more perilous, duties as lawman.

5. *Conditions of preponderance must erode over time, but they can be prolonged, or shortened, by wise or foolish policy and strategy.*

Over the decades immediately ahead, it is unlikely that America's material strength will prove unequal to the task of peacekeeping and, if need be, forceful peacemaking. It is more probable that the United States will undertake missions unwisely, when the situations in question were better left to work themselves out without active intervention by the sheriff. Particular missions may be inappropriate for forceful American attention, either because the political or cultural context is unduly polarized, or because the United States lacks a suitable coercive instrument. In the 1960s, Washington showed that it would not lightly be discouraged by a poor fit between the tasks at hand and the military power that was ready to go.[28] We are not short of awful precedents. However, it is a hallmark of a superior military establishment that it has the flexibility of mind, organization, and equipment to find a way to win, even when confronted with a deeply unwelcome challenge. No one prepares perfectly for the next war. Indeed, the conduct of war always is a race between the belligerents to see who can correct the more serious of peacetime errors most rapidly.[29]

Edward Luttwak and Eliot Cohen might be correct in their insightful, if contestable, claim that the American way of war has been revolutionized over the course of the past ten years.[30] It could follow, on their logic, that the noble and bold role of sheriff of the new world order can be no more robust than is the course and outcome of the latest venture in American peacemaking. If a Beirut bombing, normal "friction" in downtown Mogadishu, or virtually any tragic happening, could produce an American scuttle-and-run, then the United States may have little future as the ultimate guardian of the contemporary order.

I am respectful of Cohen's argument, a point of view that he expressed most cogently with reference to NATO's strange war with Yugoslavia over Kosovo in 1999. But I was never convinced that

Americans demand the conduct of war without pain to themselves. Ways of war change with demography and prevailing values, and all the other domestic influences that oblige a country to fight according to its character, which is constantly evolving. Nonetheless, the proposition that a risk-averse American society demands American casualty-free warfare, though a fair reading of the history of the 1990s, may speak less to the changing mores of Americans than it does to their fundamental disinterest in the tasks their armed forces were assigned in the first post–Cold War decade (after Iraq in 1991).

If I am correct, sufficient popular support can be built for sometimes difficult military and quasi-military tasks. But the U.S. government needs to shape a consensus, building on the near and longer term reaction to September 11, which for the first time since the fall of the USSR would have at least the makings of a coherent and effective doctrine of national and international security. In principle, there is nothing new about this. The United States rode to the rescue of Europe three times in the twentieth century (albeit at German invitation in 1941), while in the 1990s an American military commitment of some description typically was indispensable if incompetent allies or toothless humanitarian interventionists were not to make bad situations in the Balkans worse. But, the American people have to understand their country's role as sheriff, and their armed forces will need to be somewhat transformed so that they can meet the new strategic mail. For the time being, leadership of the global war on terrorism will suffice as accurate enough explanation of the American role. A fairly pro-active, not to say preemptive or even preventive, approach to counterterrorism, in the context of a determination to counter forcefully (if need be) the dissemination of WMD, assuredly will have the consequence of sliding the United States firmly into the role of sheriff. For the next few years the challenge of the era may be al Qaeda and its ilk. But come the 2010s, or at the latest the twenties, the peril of the decade for world order is probably going to be the return of old-fashioned, state-centric great power geopolitics and geostrategy, as China challenges the regional security order of East Asia, or perhaps as "Old Europe" and Russia attempt to clip the American eagle's wings.

America's international dominance in the political-military sphere is not merely extraordinary, it is literally historically unprecedented. Never before has a polity enjoyed such a hegemonic position. This condition of relative advantage will erode with time—certainly as

China continues to improve its military establishment behind its impressive economic modernization. Beyond China it is close to impossible to identify any even semi-plausible great power foes of the U.S. lawman, though certainly one can speculate about a reimperializing Russia, to borrow Henry Kissinger's concept,[31] and a Europe no longer content to lack nearly all political authority in the world. It is no part of my mission to indulge in speculation about candidate enemies over the next several decades. Indeed, the argument developed below is essentially indifferent to their identity. The sheriff of the world order dispenses his form of justice to whoever proves in need of its healing balm.

The duration of America's role as sheriff will be governed by such factors as: the strength of motivation and the ability of potential adversaries to raise significant opposition; American skill in co-opting or isolating those actual or potential adversaries; and the multidimensional costs of the lawman role, as not all exercises play out according to a dream scenario wherein America arms achieve decisive victory promptly and cheaply.[32] Moreover, as America was reminded over Iraq in 2003, a decisive military victory is not necessarily synonymous with a decisive political victory. It should follow, of course, that the better adapted the U.S. military posture is to lawman's tasks, the more likely it is that American interventions will succeed at bearable cost; that should translate into a more durable tolerance of the sheriff role by American society. But, is there a right military posture for the United States in the early decades of the twenty-first century?

6. *Sheriff is a role, not a strategy or doctrine. A single defense design will not suffice for the global security mission. Variety, flexibility, adaptability, and some complexity need not mean confusion.*

The United States, as the guardian power, requires a military posture with global reach. That posture should be capable of defeating any adversary or combination of adversaries. As sheriff of the world order, the United States is not interested in balancing power with regional trouble-makers. Instead, it needs to be able to defeat them decisively.[33] It is a near certainty that this new century will see the United States challenged in warfare of many kinds—regular and irregular, symmetrical and asymmetrical. Large-scale regular warfare between states appears to be in retreat at present, in part, at least, because of the unmatchable prowess of American conventional arms.

It may well be that even the state-centric warfare in America's future will be markedly asymmetrical in character, if not quite irregular. A strong regional polity, perhaps a returning great power like Russia, would seek asymmetrical, or different, ways to employ its regular armed forces from the methods considered orthodox in the mental universe of the American defense establishment.

As the ultimate, though not quite sole, defender of world order for decades to come, the United States must be able to prevail in warfare of all kinds. In particular, the country will have to be able to resist forcefully the neutralization of its policy and strategy by enemies who can pose risks that Americans would judge unacceptable in the context of the modest political stakes at issue. Overall, U.S. defense policy must be geared to defeat efforts to deter American military intervention. Such efforts could take the form of air and missile threats to forward-deployed U.S. forces and to local U.S. friends and allies, or of the posing of a WMD menace to North America itself. That menace could take the highly irregular form of catastrophe terrorism, with terrorists resorting to WMD.

It is virtually self-evident that there is no simple, correct defense posture for a United States that, pro tem, has accepted the somewhat thankless sheriff's role. The Department of Defense tests, or more accurately, justifies, ideas on force structure by means of scenario-based planning, among others. A new capabilities-based approach is discussed later. But history tells us that we are certain to be surprised. The challenge to defense planners is not to avoid surprise, which is impossible; rather, it is to avoid major damage and disadvantage from the effects of surprise.[34] Fortunately, in planning how they should be capable of defending the new world order, Americans do not need to attempt the impossible. They do not have to spot the identities, the dates, and the issues that will define future conflicts. In a sense, happy is the defense planner who confronts a single dominant and relatively stable threat from decade to decade. From the 1680s until 1815, and as a residual anxiety until 1904–05, Britain knew that the first charge on its defense preparation was the necessity of frustrating French ambitions for continental hegemony.[35] More recently, the U.S. armed forces were suitably fixated for forty years on the geostrategic threat posed by Soviet power to the rimlands of Eurasia,[36] and the cover for that threat provided by their long-range nuclear forces. Because this book is about the purpose and structure of the American defense problem, I am not especially interested in providing guesses as to which among the regional villains is likely to prove most troublesome in the near term. Similarly, there is no particular merit in my striving to pick a winner or two from among the potential great powers, as the probable adversary of twenty, thirty, or forty years hence. Fortunately, such an exercise is as unnecessary as it would be futile. To indulge in such guesswork, save for some limited illustrative purposes, would be a repudiation of my fundamental argument, as outlined tersely here.

At present the United States is the only possible sheriff of world order with respect to the more testing of strategic threats to that order from any quarter and of several kinds, both regular and irregular.[37] The three great American interventions in world conflicts in the twentieth century were all highly specific as to adversary. That is not the case today. The American sheriff must be ready to combat and defeat threats from whatever quarter they derive, and in whatever mode they appear. Islamic fundamentalists with transnational networks may be the menace of this decade, but that danger may not long persist as a lethal peril, notwithstanding its WMD dimension.[38] It is too soon to say. Moreover, the contemporary war against terror, and similar linguistic abominations, highlights America's global role, it does not define and drive it. The United States is not the sheriff of the current world order because there are dangerous terrorists out there. Many of the world's terrorists today choose to target Uncle Sam precisely because he is so imperial. As Robert Kagan has written, in words quoted in an epigraph to this book, "outlaws shoot sheriffs, not saloonkeepers."[39]

Because sheriff is a role and not a strategy, it is not self-evident what acceptance of its obligations implies by way of choices for national military strategy.[40] It is commonplace to affirm that the defense effort should be strategy-led, rather than budget-led. This ancient desideratum risks posing a false opposition, since all strategic argument and choices wear a dollar sign.[41] Even a country that is "poised to spend more on defense in 2003 than the next 15–20 biggest spenders combined,"[42] cannot afford simply to add together the wish lists of every military constituency and call it the defense budget. Moreover, no such mindless exercise should be permitted. Strategy is about choice. It requires the selection of some, rather than other, ways of opposing threats and, if need be, applying force, to achieve the strategic effect necessary to secure policy goals.

As usual, there is good and bad news for the American defense planner. The extraordinarily good news is that there are no actual or plausible near-term potential enemies abroad who can pose serious threats to U.S. military operations. The U.S. military lead, particularly—though not exclusively—in the exploitation of new technologies, is long and continues to grow. That said, the bad news is that the undoubted facts of American military superiority threaten to obscure the possibility that some particularly cunning or lucky foes may find geographical and political contexts that work to negate much of the nominal American military advantage. For a leading example of a limiting context, the galloping urbanization of the Third World means that a high, and sharply growing, percentage of the world's population lives in habitat that could approximate a no-go zone for American soldiers.[43] As potential battlespace, the megacities of Asia, the Middle East, and South and Central America would comprise the least permissive of terrain for the application of U.S. military power. As usual, Sun-tzu had a term for it: "fatal terrain."[44]

Although it is blessed with the most permissive political-military context enjoyed by any superstate in all of history, the U.S. defense establishment of today also faces some unusual difficulties. Other imperial powers were able to relate alternative force structures to the general prospects for imperial expansion, or specifically to protection against local opposition or great power rivals. But the contemporary U.S. imperium is not of that nature. The American sheriff must develop military capabilities which, as threats, lack particular addressees. Instead, metaphorically they carry a label that reads, "to whom it may concern." In addition, and despite the radical seeming declaration by George W. Bush in 2002 of a doctrine of preemption, the sheriff usually must exercise a binding self-discipline before lawbreakers cross the line, create disorder, and thereby unambiguously license the sheriff to ride forth and administer justice, Texas-style. Leaving aside, at this juncture, issues of politics, ethics, and law, just from the narrow perspective of defense planning the United States can hardly help but concede the first move to the agents of disorder. Given the variety of disordering behaviors by both symmetrical and asymmetrical means that fertile brains can devise, the American sheriff must find itself severely challenged strategically. For example, a doctrine of preemption has much to recommend it against known terrorists,[45] among other agents of disorder, but as a general rule for U.S.

statecraft it is fraught with difficulties. A little reflection reveals that this new doctrine implies a willingness to shoot on strong suspicion. Preventive self-defense is a sensible idea, but is rarely practicable, not to mention the fact that it would set a precedent inviting emulation which could provoke great disorder.

Recognizing its role as sheriff, the United States needs now to identify the military capabilities which should enable it to deter and, if necessary, defeat at least the majority of potential challengers to the current world order. Those capabilities may not lend themselves to neat packaging as a single dominant national military strategy, given the range of contingencies with which they will have to deal. Suffice it for us simply to point to the kind of military abilities that the American superstate sheriff of world order must sustain, or obtain, if it is to succeed in its mission. The United States needs to be able to:

- exert, protect, and exploit control of the sea, air, space, and cyberspace environments;

- protect its homeland from all manner of threats;

- be able to enforce access to geography of interest, in order to

- project military power in its several forms (as firepower and as boots on the ground) rapidly; this obliges the armed services

- to place a premium on developing agile forces for swift deployment;

- provide logistical support for its global strategy;

- follow-up the rapid insertion of light forces with heavy (armored and mechanized) formations;

- deploy forces forward that can loiter with menace—or at least ambiguously—from sovereign U.S. bases, and this means maritime power;

- rely on having available tolerably accurate intelligence about adversaries, including information that is culturally empathetic;[46]

- have confidence in a nuclear posture that fits the requirements of the new century, and not the standards of the old one;

- have ground forces trained to win the peace as well as the war.

To list these exceedingly demanding requirements is not to suggest a strategy or doctrine. Rather, these are simply the ingredients from which strategy can be fashioned. First, the country must decide on the doctrine that most effectively and prudently matches the role of sheriff of the world order, and the mission that gives meaning to that role. Each item has to be considered holistically, in relation to block-building for a national military strategy worthy of that title. The acquisition and maintenance of military power is, of course, essential. But military power is not synonymous with strategy. Such power is not self-directing in the service of policy, any more than it is inherently automatically effective as a deterrent. In both cases, a critical filter of human intervention is mandatory—in the former instance by us, in the latter by our enemies.

7. *Strategy is difficult. Military effectiveness need not mean strategic effectiveness, while strategic effectiveness may not translate into enduring political advantage.*

The lethality of American arms is not in question today, but that potency is most apparent as military effectiveness, particularly against regular, or reasonably symmetrical, armed forces. Against enemies who are sufficiently unsporting as not to provide concentrated targets for stand-off demolition by U.S. firepower, a heavy preponderance in nominal military effectiveness could prove largely irrelevant. This is the classic challenge for the regular belligerent in conflict with an irregular foe: how to bring that enemy to battle, where he can be destroyed.[47] Understandably, the highly asymmetrical, or irregular, foe must avoid the physical concentration for open combat where he presents ideal targets for American sharpshooting from all altitudes.

The U.S. government sensibly seeks to pursue a measured pace of military modernization, a process fashionably and officially now more modestly termed transformational rather than revolutionary.[48] It is probably important to note that while the U.S. defense community is earnestly working on a military transformation, a small but influential body of scholars is claiming that radical changes in the political, social, and cultural contexts of war are transforming warfare. Historical experience suggests that enhancing the tactical and operational performance of American forces should be relatively straightforward. Much less straightforward is the double translation, first of tactical prowess into strategic leverage, and second of strategic effectiveness into a postwar order with political advantage for all essential parties that can endure. The politically purposeful use or threat of force, which is to say strategy, is not a traditional American strength. The sheer scale of American resources in the twentieth century enabled the country to triumph in most of its conflicts without needing to make truly difficult choices. So long as the enemy could be met in battle, a large superiority in quantity of military effectiveness would deliver eventual victory quite reliably through the process of tactical attrition.[49] Although tactical competence is always desirable, it is not sufficient for strategic success. Tactical superiority could no more deliver decisive victory for the United States in Vietnam than it could for Germany on any front in World War II. The United States played either a significant or a leading role in the military triumphs of 1918, 1945, and 1991 (in the Gulf), but in all three instances it is plausible to argue that the country won the war but proceeded to lose the peace. The jury is still out on whether that pattern will be continued following the apparently decisive defeat of Ba'athist Iraq in 2003. Through poor strategic performance in the conduct of militarily victorious war, the scene is set for political tragedy thereafter. It is usually easier to win a war than it is to win the peace that follows. A United States justly proud of its military prowess is particularly prone to slight the all-important, albeit exceptionally difficult, subjects of strategic and then political effectiveness. Michael Howard probably exaggerates, but still he makes a valid point when he argues that

> Few wars, in fact, are any longer decided on the battlefield (if indeed they ever were). They are decided at the peace table. Military victories do not themselves determine the outcomes of wars; they only provide political opportunities for the victors—and even those opportunities are likely to be limited by circumstances beyond their control.[50]

For good or for ill, the still essentially anarchic nature of world politics, and the unprecedented disparities in power, mean that the American sheriff has to deal with the agents of disorder without much real material assistance from a posse of law-abiding world citizen-polities. Furthermore, so immature and otherwise flawed are international institutions, that from time to time the United States will need to act as judge, jury, and even executioner. Americans have a history of being better at generating military effectiveness than they are at crafting fighting power to produce strategic leverage. Similarly, they are better at winning wars militarily than they are at transmuting the lead of armed conflict into the gold of a peace that can last. The United States needs to learn to apply the wisdom of Carl von Clausewitz, as opposed merely to quoting his words reverentially. War is a political act, waged for political reasons, and at its highest level the realms of policy and military violence merge.[51] Eliot Cohen's masterwork, *Supreme Command*, restates and abundantly illustrates these truths,[52] while in recent years a few writers have attempted, with only uncertain success, to specify the inherent difficulties that perennially harass the strategic practitioner.[53]

So great is the contemporary American defense advantage over any and all friends or foes, that in practice the United States must rely overwhelmingly on its own sources of political and strategic wisdom, as well as on its own material strength for military effectiveness. It is too little appreciated that the waging of war often is conducted with scant strategic intelligence. Furthermore, while the decisive winning of war certainly provides a necessary platform for the construction, or restoration, of a tolerable post-war order, skill in the former has no necessary carryover effect yielding wisdom in the latter. A United States now lonely in the preeminence of its power is in the most urgent need of some rapid education in the arcane art of strategy. The military context is none too promising in that regard. A debate over defense transformation, in the notable absence of a named foe (with China "standing in" and doing nominal duty for a semi-plausible enemy), encourages what amounts to military autism. In other words, the U.S. defense establishment will transform itself selectively, and it will be inclined to focus on the military effectiveness it should be able to ring up against preferred foes. War as a duel, and military effectiveness as the fuel of strategic effectiveness for political results, may well suffer neglect in this autistic context.[54]

8. *Technology is vital, but does not determine military or policy success. U.S. performance in the role of sheriff is hostage to a defense establishment that may be unduly risk-averse, and to a domestic opinion that is not resilient in the face of military setbacks when the mission does not involve obviously vital national interests.*

Discussion of U.S. defense policy often reduces to debate over the merit of particular technologies or weapons. It is close to a truism to maintain that societies wage war according to their nature.[55] Hence it is scarcely surprising that the United States chooses to fight when it can (and sometimes when it should not) with high technology, and that its military operations rest on and feature a material abundance typically provided on so generous a scale as to threaten logistical overload (or the "logistical snowball," as it has been called). My argument endorses the importance of effective new technologies. For example, air and missile defenses, and the ability to control space (Earth orbit), are literally essential if the world order is to be defended. The issue is not one of attitude toward technology, but rather of technology's importance relative to other factors. The factor that tends to receive short shrift in the close and expert analysis of budgets and weapons systems, is the central matter of human beings. Scholars and other commentators can neglect the people who must "person" the weapons and work the logistics chain, not to mention the people back home in whose name and on whose behalf the military instrument is forged, threatened, and employed. Such neglect, when it occurs, is unfortunate because America could have vulnerabilities on the human dimension that might prove fatal to the prospects for success in its global ordering mission. Erudite, not to say grandiose, expositions on geopolitics and strategy, and ambitious, forward-looking visions of military transformation could all be frustrated by unanticipated human behavior.

It is time to augment the first thread to the argument, which claimed that world order is not self-enforcing. We must add the parallel proposition that military (for strategic and for political) effectiveness is not inherent in particular technologies, organizations, and doctrines. Instead, that effectiveness has to be achieved by *our* people against *their* people, and the price that we pay in the currencies of war, especially blood, has to be acceptable to our society. The human dimension to military and strategic effectiveness probably is ignored, taken for granted perhaps, because it can seem so obvious as not to warrant specific treatment.[56] That is a generous view. Rather less generous is the judgment that so much of the American defense literature slights the human element because it fails to recognize its truly vital nature, except, of course, in a fairly dutiful and pro forma way. For a revealing example, consider the case of a major 2002 publication of the National Defense University, fashionably titled *Transforming America's Military*.[57] The book has excellent chapters on almost everything except the two classes of human issues that loom as threats to American military, strategic, and hence political performance. It examines new missions, new technologies, strategy, the army's "objective force," the Navy's idea of "network-centric warfare," and so on. Space, cyberspace, technology, and logistics, are all treated with proper respect. But the U.S. military establishment, with some reservations having to do with long traditional interservice antagonisms, can be trusted in those areas. Real problems lie elsewhere. Two of those problems are potentially serious enough to require exposure here.

First, there are some grounds for the suspicion that America's transforming military is led at all levels by too many risk-averse careerists, who understand, apparently correctly, that with respect to the promotion game the costs of error far outweigh the rewards of success.[58] In the Balkans and in Afghanistan, when Americans deploy on the ground they promptly fortify (build "Fort Apache" or "Fort Bondsteel"), with force security apparently holding sway as "job one." In and of itself, prudent attention to force security is not merely commendable, it is essential. But, if that task is pursued at high opportunity cost to other tasks, including those which explain the deployment, priorities are clearly skewed. If bold warrior-leaders are not the type of soldiers regularly rewarded with promotion—after all, they tend to be disruptive and they make mistakes—prudent careerists will shape their behavior to fit the profile of those who are reliably preferred for advancement. Historically, armed forces have been undone far more often by deficiencies in human performance than they have by poor equipment. It is distinctly possible that the United States, with its somewhat transforming military, is constructing and encouraging a rather blunt instrument at all levels of war. That instrument should be tactically first-rate, courtesy of its superb training and its generally excellent equipment. But it may not be an instrument of bold decision against a competent foe. Sometime in this new century, the country will fight an enemy who betrays neither the folly nor the kind of weakness that privileges a safe-siding American way of war. Then we will discover whether the ocean of ink spilt in the debate over RMA and military transformation, and the tens of billions of dollars committed to selective innovation, took adequate account of the country's military need for war leaders, indeed for warriors, at all levels. Iraq in 2003 illustrates nothing very much about U.S. military prowess, because of the rank incompetence of the enemy. It has been noticeable, however, that American forces in Iraq hastened to provide for force security by means of extraordinary fortification of a kind almost calculated to isolate them from the people they came to liberate.

Second, if America is to play the sheriff role, as it ought, certainly as the world order requires, the American people will need to understand that the country cannot limit its military initiatives strictly to cases of clear and present danger. The sheriff cannot always prudently delay taking action until crimes against world order are actually committed. Even President Bush's new-sounding doctrine of preemption is inadequate, because to shoot first at the last possible moment— the strict meaning of preemption—could be far too hazardous when adversaries are armed with WMD. What the United States will have to develop is a grand strategy of preventive action, designed to arrest a slide into a condition that could be described as one of clear and present danger. As many commentators have hastened to point out, a strategy of preemption or prevention will either be on, or more often over, the line of what passes for legality in the jungle of international politics. State sovereignty, though frequently breached under pressure of claimed necessity in times both recent and distant, nonetheless is the basis of modern international law and is the principle on which the United Nations organization was founded.

The American people are probably highly resilient to the multidimensional costs of war when they can relate the stakes in conflict to their vital interests.[59] But if, acting on behalf of the world community (to employ the somewhat optimistic concept), the United States judges itself obliged to behave in places and for reasons remote and obscure to most American voters, domestic support for the role of sheriff would likely prove fragile. If success is achieved swiftly and cheaply, all may be well. However, it would only take one or two military setbacks, such as that suffered in Mogadishu in October 1993, for public and congressional acquiescence to evaporate with embarrassing speed. This would prove not merely inhibiting for performance of the policing mission, it would also be potentially fatal. A U.S. government committed to the guardianship role will need to explain the necessity for occasional strategic preventive behavior, both to its electorate and to an outside world that is uneasy about, or even hostile to, the American mission.

At present it is an open question whether the human dimension of America's defense of world order is adequate to handle the military and political traffic that must come its way. While most of the professional defense community focuses today on transformation, it is appropriate to worry about the attitude toward risk that dominates the armed services. Also, there are grounds for wondering whether armed forces admittedly so preeminent in the conduct of regular warfare, are appropriately trained to oppose irregular combatants. In addition there are grounds for uneasiness over the country's willingness to support a policy of selective intervention when there is no gun, smoking or otherwise, pointing directly at the United States.

9. *History is our best guide to the future. There is no modern world, or modern strategy.*[60]

Times, players, fashionable political theories, and technologies, *inter alia*, all change. But those are second-order matters. To journalists writing copy hot from a leak, or to officials who serve the nation memo by memo and meeting by meeting, it can seem that immediate issues are all that there is; the long run is a series of short runs. Neither enjoys, indeed usually can afford, historical perspective. The burning topics of national defense are right now. Often it will seem as if the country's fate hangs in the balance, as crisis inexorably succeeds crisis in that elaborate political dance which long has been dignified by description as the policymaking process. That process entails extensive negotiation within the executive and legislative branches, as well as between the two. The process of defense planning, defense budget preparation, and then submission, is nearly continuous.[61] The making of defense policy should be understood as a permanent burden, or discipline, upon the defense community, broadly understood. Much of this quite regular activity unquestionably is important. This is not to deny that most of it would appear to have been designed to produce dead souls and to burn up person-hours at a wanton rate. There are competent defense analysts who keep adequate track of the fortunes of individual weapon programs, as well as of shifts among categories in the defense budget, and the like. I rejoice in their expertise and laud their devotion to detail, but have no intention of emulating their endeavors.[62] The last of my nine themes of argument claims that the more important aspects to the defense of world order usually are not in daily dispute, and do not attract conference committees or hot news stories. As theme number nine affirms, history's continuities far outweigh the discontinuities, usually both in number and significance.

Such a conservative creed is not a little un-American. After all, as an optimistic people are we not supposed to believe in progress, in benign transformation? This creed also may appear to flout the spirit behind the new official orthodoxy, which is to push hard, though not unduly so, for military transformation. Contrary to appearances, perhaps, at least in principle this book is not at all opposed to the idea that the military establishment should be transformed, provided it is effected selectively at a prudently deliberate pace. However, I am unmoved by the unhistorical belief that technological superiority is the key to decisive victory. Friction, uncertainty, the fog of war and crisis, and particularly all manner of surprises and complications triggered by the unpredictable behavior of enemies, will long continue to ensure that the conduct of war is more art than science. Whether or not the United States on balance succeeds or fails in its historic role as guardian of world order for a lengthy period, will depend on the health of a variant on what Joseph Stalin called "the permanently operating factors," not on the modernization of its firepower or even of its information technologies. The United States needs to perform well with its behavior in answering the questions, and respecting the caveats, that command attention in the pages of Thucydides, Sun-tzu, and Clausewitz, in particular.

To cite just one famous example, Sun-tzu advises: "Thus it is said one who knows the enemy and knows himself will not be endangered in a hundred engagements."[63] In the eighth theme advanced above, with reference to the human dimension (as soldier and as citizen), anxiety was expressed that Americans may prove incapable of playing the quasi-imperial role of sheriff. Details of the defense program matter, as to both quality and quantity. But they are topics of concern strictly secondary to some social issues, to matters of high policy, and to strategy. The twenty-first century is witnessing the inevitably confused birth of a new world order, and some competing ideas on how it can best be protected. So much is indeed new. What is not at all new is the emergence after a great conflict of a different order. Nor is it at all novel for efforts to be expended on behalf of the role and function of guardian, here termed sheriff for obvious reasons of political identity and popular culture. As with each of these themes or threads which, when interwoven, create the total argument, the claim that history's continuities contain the most vital of clues to the demands for performance in the future, is visited in the text below.

THE PLAN

The nine themes that comprise the general argument are applied and examined in detail in the chapters that follow. Chapter 2, Protecting World Order, exposes and employs the first three points outlined above. That chapter explains the idea of a world order, pursues the historically grounded belief that all such orders require guarding and therefore need a guardian, and reveals the less than startling insight that only the United States can attempt to fulfil that role at the present time. Threads of argument four and five inspire chapter 3, Staying Number One. That discussion focuses on the significance of September 11 in accelerating the pace of American adjustment out of the "strategic pause" of the post–Cold War decade. It addresses the potential threats to American performance as sheriff, and it explores the extent to which the current extraordinary American political-military preponderance might be prolonged, or shortened, either by design or by accident.

Themes of argument six, seven, and eight inspire the exploration in chapter 4, The Strategic Dimension. Although the role of sheriff expresses a clear vision, it does not specify a strategy. This chapter exposes the chasms that can yawn, first, between American military effectiveness and strategic effectiveness, and second, between strategic effectiveness and political results. We note that today, as always, the strategy store in Washington is not generously peopled—when one can even locate it, that is. The analysis is particularly interested both in the relative significance of technology, and in some possibly overlooked weaknesses in the emerging new American way of war. Is military transformation key to the sheriff being able to perform for world order at acceptable human cost, or is that long process of innovation being oversold? Finally, chapter 5 sets the American role as sheriff of the current world order in its historical context. This last chapter, The Familiar Twenty-First Century, emphasizes the continuities in political and strategic history. In so doing, the discussion provides the historical context for argument about America's role in the world that so often is all but wholly absent from public debate. To those who know little history, any and every policy initiative can appear as a dangerous break with settled patterns of behavior.

Much of my subject has attracted, or will attract, sharply critical commentary. Careful scholars advise against "America's Imperial Ambition," and so forth.[64] Good points have been raised, and many more will surely follow. They are treated with the respect they deserve at the appropriate juncture. There can be a fine line between taking counsel of one's fears and exercising a prudent caution. And now we must begin by examining the world order that requires the duties of an American sheriff.

CHAPTER 2

Protecting World Order

It is important not to be confused about matters that are fundamental to national and international security. World order, for a leading example, though in theory an eminently contestable concept, in practice is sufficiently clear in its implications as to provide adequate guidance for high policy. It should be understood, without much need for elaboration, that the notion of order the United States is stepping up to protect and advance is one that reflects and privileges American values and interests. No apology should accompany this less than startling revelation. The United States must serve itself if it is to serve the world at large. However, it is a challenge to American statecraft to ensure that it does not approach its duty to the national interest in so narrow and self-regarding a way that great, especially gratuitous, damage is wrought on the interests of others. In both this chapter and the next, the point is made that although the role of sheriff is uncontested, indeed is incontestable for many years to come, whether performance of that duty is relatively painless, or quite the opposite, is very much an open question. Here in chapter two, we explore the necessary historical background to the current situation that has witnessed the United States pin the sheriff's badge on its own chest. The discussion proceeds to explain just what we mean, or should mean, by sheriff of world order. It is unfortunate but true that some of our more useful concepts are as crystal clear in their essential meaning and principal implications as they are opaque and debatable when we venture away from the core of their meaning. The concepts of sheriff and world order are both of that nature. Their meaning, speaking to us in our political culture, could hardly be plainer. Indeed, it is only because their meaning is so unambiguous that they warrant the prominence accorded them in this book. In fact, the coherent analysis provided in these chapters is possible precisely *because* the core notions are so clear—to us in our culture, at least. Consideration of second-order strategic matters, for example, will not threaten the basic integrity of the argument.

ANOTHER AMERICAN CENTURY

A country can have greatness thrust upon it by historical circumstance, whether or not it is entirely ready for such high honor. So it may prove for the United States at the beginning of the twenty-first century. This is far from being America's first "strategic moment" worthy of the name, but it is by far the most elevated and the loneliest. Previous "moments," when the United States played a starring role in the course of world strategic history, were of course coterminous with its leading participation in the three world wars of the twentieth century (two hot, one cold).[1]

It is my purpose to help clarify that which politicians and officials either are obliged to obscure for reason of political sensitivities at home and abroad, or perhaps have yet to think through to its logical and practical conclusions. Busy public officials typically must deal with problems as they arrive, most frequently in the terms in which they are raised, no matter how inappropriate those terms may be. Hence, if officials sometimes appear to have lost the plot of why they are behaving as they are, the mundane truth may well be nothing more sinister than the working of Gresham's Law. The law holds that bad money drives out good. So, also, many important ideas and issues that bear upon national security are driven from widespread circulation by faddishly fashionable concepts. The immediate, even the apparently urgent, is all too easily confused with the important. Furthermore, since strategy is inherently difficult to design and perform well—for reasons we shall explain in detail as this narrative unfolds[2]—there is an almost magnetic pull to debate those tangible military items that the country buys through its budgetary process. Few people think strategically or, indeed, are obliged to do so. It is much easier to focus on personnel and equipment, rather than on the effect that forces should achieve upon the course and outcome of conflicts. Strategy, properly understood, is the bridge between policy and its military instrument.[3]

Many people, Americans and others, will find both parts of my title controversial and pointing to an undesirable American preeminence. Certainly there are grounds for concern lest the role I assert should prove beyond the country's resources to pursue. American society might decline to serve, to cite but the most obvious of potential difficulties. It is no less likely that America may succumb to hubris and slide into the kind of triumphalism that has come to be known as the victory disease.[4] When a very great power is mesmerized by its own greatness, it is wont to deem all tasks doable. National will and probable national achievement are confused in an orgy of pride that confounds truly strategic thought and action. It is precisely the importance and feasibility of the guardianship role, in the context of the array of dangers, that makes this book so necessary. At this stage let us assert the historical claim that, including current endeavors, the United States has already played the guardianship role four times in a century.

The facts of war should not be permitted to obscure the world-ordering function of U.S. policy in 1917–18, 1941–45, and 1947–89. It is usual to focus not so much upon the periods of combat, but rather more upon the periods immediately following hostilities, when new world orders of variable merit were established, encouraged to evolve, or simply allowed to drift into a semblance of existence. Those three broad options correspond tolerably well with the events of 1919, 1947–50, and 1990–2001, respectively.[5] The American strategic guardianship, which is our principal theme, differs today from its previous historical appearances in the international context for its performance, not the purpose it is designed to serve. On the three earlier occasions the United States was contending with an enemy, or enemies, who was a worthy and significantly symmetrical foe. American policy sought victory in the wars of the twentieth century, not merely a judicious balancing stalemate. The guardian role is the reality today, but can be controversial because it appears discretionary in a way that the previous episodes were not.[6] The absence of a symmetrical adversary tends to obscure the need for a guardian of world order. Also, without the discipline and guidance that major competition provides, the United States is all but foredoomed to overreach or underreach in its strategy. It can be difficult enough to behave prudently when there is a powerful enemy actively in the field. How much more challenging must it be when the country is so preeminent, at least in political-military terms, that little beyond its own volition can restrain it from military action.

Because history offers a continuum of experience for our education, we should be grateful for the strategic enlightenment it can provide. Naturally, we need to be sufficiently wise as to avoid confusion by the mainly superficial differences that distinguish one historical period from another. As I acknowledged in the previous chapter, as the author of a book with the title *Modern Strategy*, I am guilty of surrendering to popular usage. In fact, I am exceptionally guilty because I chose that title in full knowledge of the redundancy in the adjective. It is probably the case that most people who talk about modern strategy have no notion that strategy is strategy regardless of period, adversaries, or technology. Furthermore, they may well harbor the attractive and characteristically American belief that tomorrow will be better than today. American optimists, whether conservative or liberal, would be appalled to be told that international politics in general, statecraft and strategic behavior, have not changed in their essentials over the course of two and a half millennia. Proof of this extravagant sounding claim is easily supplied. Two of the three greatest books of all time on statecraft and war were written in late-fifth-century (B.C.) Greece and China, respectively by the disgraced Athenian general Thucydides and by the imperial court advisor Sun-tzu (who may not have been an actual person).[7] The third classic author was, of course, the nineteenth-century Prussian, Carl von Clausewitz. Attitudes toward progress, indeed toward the feasibility of, and what may be accomplished through, a process of transformation, are important to our story. The dominant stream in American culture sees history as arrow-like rather than cyclical; it rests on a notion of national exceptionalism which feeds a self-flattering missionary worldview; and it looks to technology as the cutting edge of progress. At best, these broad characteristics are a mixed blessing, given the extraordinary role of guardian of the current world order that has fallen to the country's lot.

In the mid- to late 1980s, ironically just as the Soviet adversary slid irreversibly toward political oblivion, it was briefly popular to make fun of Henry Luce's 1941 claim for "the American Century." Wits of the period referred to the American half-century. They could cite Paul Kennedy's popular book, *The Rise and Fall of the Great Powers,* by way of heavyweight scholarly support for a pessimistic view of America's future. Whether that was an entirely fair reading of Kennedy's warning of the perils to the United States of "imperial overstretch," a distinctly un-American expectation of a diminished national future certainly was fashionable for a few years.[8] Whatever the explanations preferred for that phenomenon—and we should mention in particular the long shadow of failure in Vietnam and the no less enervating burden of apparent incompetence in central economic governance—the force of fashionable belief should not be despised.

Ignoring for the moment the point that probably there are no truly new ideas in the security realm, while allowing for the fairly steady evolution in the "toys,"[9] genuinely original thinkers are rare in any generation. Moreover, the scarce individuals who have the priceless potential to be market leaders with powerful new (or new sounding) ideas, do not cogitate about national security in a void. French philosopher Raymond Aron hit the target when he wrote that "strategic thought draws its inspiration each century, or rather at each moment of history, from the problems which events themselves pose."[10] To which wise judgment one should add Bernard Brodie's observation that strategy "is nothing if not pragmatic. . . . Above all, strategic theory is a theory for action."[11] Taken together, these two contemporaries advise that the big ideas of the day about security and strategy are most likely to be both fabricated in response to some unmistakeable challenge and shaped for their pragmatic utility to help guide behavior. The sheer size of the American extended defense community, with its thousands of players and dozens, perhaps hundreds, of organizations, yet with its paucity of original minds, means that policy debate tends to be a mob scene of "me-tooism." The American community of theorists, analysts and commentators is so uniquely extensive that its inevitable tendency to rally around the concept *du jour* can easily obscure the distinction between passing fad and important idea. For example, if a hundred articles, books, studies, and speeches all appear discussing America's decline, or Revolutions in Military Affairs (RMAs), or military transformation, surely the concept in question must have much to recommend it. Could so many expert thinkers be fundamentally wrong? Could this be a case of the emperor's new clothes?

The point of this caveat about fashion and its appeal is to recognize the damage it can wreak upon the national security. By repetition and absence of direct evidence in refutation, unsound variants, typically Bowdlerized versions, of interesting and even valid ideas, can capture the high ground of policy. Whether they capture policy action as well as policy declaration is, of course, another matter. The history of American defense policy shows that this has happened even with respect to the "jewels in the crown" of the modern strategic enlightenment. Many years ago Stephen Peter Rosen revealed the fragility in the American theory of limited war; much more recently, Keith Payne has committed near heresy by mounting a merciless assault upon the orthodox theory of deterrence (and the purported requirements of its most glittering product, strategic stability); while, some years ago, I endeavoured to demonstrate logically and empirically that the standard theory of arms control was notably flawed.[12] Mere iteration and volume lend an authority that can propel shaky propositions to the halls of high policy for serious consideration for adoption as official strategy. So it was, for example, with the action-reaction hypothesis of arms race dynamics. In the 1960s and 1970s, the idea was promoted from its proper sphere of contestable theory to service as the intellectual underpinning of U.S. policy on strategic arms and arms control. The ABM treaty of 1972 was justified, *inter alia*, by the apparently conclusive, though actually speculative, logic of action-reaction theory.[13] Whatever the merit in that treaty, it did not encompass a prohibition decisively fatal to the incentive presumed to reside in defensive options as a license to offensive weapons acquisition.[14]

The Soviet-American arms competition was not an elementary spiral of anticipatory offensive and defensive deployments. The popular, indeed official, American theory was certainly oversimplified, and probably was thoroughly misconceived. Albert Wohlstetter, the dean of American defense analysts, exposed the "legends of the arms race" in 1975, but he found that often it is more difficult to expel or demote a demonstrably weak idea than it is to introduce a promising new one.[15]

The primary focus of this analysis is upon contexts, purposes, and strategy. Policy, strategy, and military means can be considered intelligently only if the relevant national and international contexts are appreciated, and if the reasons behind broad policy choice are exposed and interrogated. For easily understandable economic and military reasons, it is a matter of great significance that the United States has plans to acquire 3,000 or more of a new generation of combat aircraft: the F-22s, F/A-18E/Fs, and Joint Strike Fighters (JSF). But a matter of still greater significance is the general purpose behind the decision to recapitalize and modernize America's seriously aging fleet of strike aircraft. It is my contention that the new American security role in the world is not well understood at home or abroad. Much of the discussion and argument over issues of procurement and force structure are in danger of functioning in what amounts to a political and strategic context-free zone.[16] Some of us who have debated the concept of RMA (now known as transformation) for the better part of a decade have wondered about the answer to the basic question, "transformation for what purpose?" It is possible that that is not a sensible question to ask, though I resist such potential correction. Perhaps the United States simply needs its military establishment to be all that it can be. U.S. defense may be pulled by a vision of military-technical excellence, rather than be pushed by some pressing need to solve problems critical for the defeat of particular enemies. As we explain in chapter 4, the country is striving to solve the military problems that are, or could be, posed by particular foreign capabilities, in what is claimed to be a new approach to defense planning. Presumably, if we can cope with their military capabilities, their political owners will be thereby defanged.

The opening subheading of this chapter claims that the twenty-first is another American century. While allowing for an element of aspiration in the statement, we intend to convey much more than merely a sense of material preponderance. It is important to know that U.S. defense expenditures currently are greater than those of the next eight countries combined, and are nearly double the level of all the countries of NATO-Europe combined; and that America's 31-percent share of the world product is equal to the share of the next four countries combined.[17] As a strategic analyst, though, this author seeks an answer to the quintessential strategist's question, "so what?" What purposes should American military power serve? And, scarcely less important, how should it serve them? All too often, those questions are either missing from the political action, or they attract only innocuous, if worthy, pabulum in exploration. We will strive to do better, albeit at the risk of exposing much that diplomatic discretion would prefer to conceal or understate.

History shows not only that people matter more than machines, but also that individuals can make a vital difference. There is a school of academic International Relations scholarship that would have us believe that calculations bearing on the distribution of power (however that mysterious condition is assayed) move policy, regardless of cultures, persons, or other local particulars.[18] My analysis rejects such a worldview, while still holding to the principal tenets of a classical realist perspective.[19] There is something to be said for the proposition, or hope, that the circumstance brings forth the person. But, still I believe that individuals and their relationships can make history. Studies such as this, which tend to be long on strategic ideas and geopolitical concepts, are apt to fail to accord people the significance they deserve. Keith Payne's recent deconstruction of deterrence theory provides a fearsome object lesson in just why decisions for peace or war can hang on all too human factors.[20] Those careful calculations leading to rational choice of strategic gain and loss, which neorealist scholarship asserts transcend personality and culture, often prove to be nothing of the sort. Rational calculation may be a universal activity (provided the people in question are in command of their senses, which is not always a safe assumption), but the rationality at issue is not immune in its reasoning to the influence of personality or culture. To be rational is not necessarily to be reasonable in the view of other, no less rational people.

The United States begins what should be its second eponymous century with quite extraordinary, but still vulnerable, advantages. A number of commentators, including this one, have offered dubious analogies with the Rome of the late Republic and early Empire.[21] The analogy has some merit, in that not for two thousand years has a state so dominated its external environment militarily, as does the United States today. However, American soldiers, if not all of their triumphalist domestic cheerleaders, do not usually need reminding of what Carl von Clausewitz wrote about war:

> Only one more element is needed to make war a gamble—chance: the very last thing that war lacks. No other human activity is so continuously or universally bound up with chance. And through the element of chance, guesswork and luck come to play a great part in war.[22]

To which we must add the further Clausewitzian concepts of the fog of war and friction:

> Everything in war is very simple, but the simplest thing is difficult. The difficulties accumulate and end by producing a kind of friction that is inconceivable unless one has experienced war.[23]

As if chance, fog, and friction were not sufficient to render the conduct of war a high-risk enterprise, we cannot exclude from recognition the large basket of limitations that conflates conveniently as human error. The Roman analogy is compelling. A study of the Roman army argues that, "If a balanced [Roman] army kept together and made no mistakes, even moving in battle formation, then a Parthian force could not hope to beat it even in the open."[24] The noble Publius Crassus demonstrated at Carrhae in 53 B.C. just how wrong things could go when an unbalanced Roman army (one deficient in "high-quality cavalry and missile armed troops") was poorly led. America's military power may be uniquely formidable by most measures, as was Rome's at the time of the Principate, but it needs to be available when and where required, and it has to be employed skillfully. American generals are certainly better trained than were their Roman counterparts, who were not trained at all in generalship, but the worthy goal of error-free warfare is as remote as is the immortal soldier. Mistakes are made in war and soldiers die. America's military experience over the past decade does not provide thoroughly convincing proof that domestic opinion really understands that errors and casualties are entirely normal in war. This is a cultural theme to which we will return. If Americans require their military instrument to perform immaculately, and without suffering more than nominal casualties, then the second American century is unlikely to persist for long.

The first requirement, if American arms are to stand a fair chance of success, is for the policy and strategy that give them purpose and provide guidance to be wisely chosen. U.S. strategy cannot succeed without reference to an organizing vision. Many countries are so placed geostrategically that a grand organizing vision for their military forces, let alone for their national security, is either glaringly obvious or would be an absurdly pretentious redundancy. Be that as it may, in good part for reasons of geography the United States appears to be both blessed and cursed with a historically exceptional measure of discretion, at least in its range of choice, over policy and strategy.

STRATEGIC PAUSE: THE "LONG WEEKEND" OF THE 1990s[25]

The international political context that gives meaning to U.S. defense policy is one wherein the United States is itself the balance of power. The Clinton administration was uneasy with the condition of political-military preeminence. It never succeeded in defining or articulating a national security policy that matched the facts of America's contemporary dominance, or that recognized explicitly the global role that that dominance implied. Probably it is just, as well as humane, to be generous to the American policymakers of the 1990s, because the Cold War had ended with so little prior notice. After 1991, arguably after 1989, the country's national security policy was adrift without reliable navigation aids. Although, as just suggested, it is sensible to risk erring on the side of generosity, it is difficult to resist the suspicion that a unique historic opportunity to reshape the structure and the terms and conditions of functioning of world order, was permitted to slip by underexploited.

On August 2, 1990, speaking in Aspen, the first President Bush ventured uncharacteristically into the high conceptual zone when he referred to a "New World Order." That speech was so overshadowed by Saddam Hussein's seizure of Kuwait, also on August 2, that the Bush White House could promptly drop "the vision thing" and, with relief, get down to the practical business of dealing with the challenge of the hour.[26] The American policy process was struck at its weakest spot by the geopolitical, and hence geostrategic, revolution wrought by the collapse of the Soviet Union and its imperium: It suffered a well-nigh paralyzing blow to its conceptual and imaginative faculties. As it was, those faculties had long been underused, given the apparently settled character of the bipolar contest with the USSR.

For more than forty years, or two generations, Americans had not needed to review and reconsider first-order matters of national security. The "what" question had been answered in the late 1940s with bipartisan adoption of the policy commitment to contain Soviet power and influence. That commitment lent itself to quite precise geopolitical and geostrategic expression. Following the geopolitical ideas of Halford Mackinder and Nicholas Spykman, it was American policy, and strategy, from the time of the Truman administration to that of Bush senior, to oppose the domination of the Eurasian landmass by a single (i.e., Soviet) power or coalition.[27] With varying degrees of credibility and with variable enthusiasm, the United States underwrote the security of countries and quasi-countries (e.g., Taiwan, South Korea, South Vietnam) all around the "rimlands" of the great dual-continent. These barrier allies, from Norway to Japan, functioned geostrategically to keep the USSR effectively landlocked. As the leader of a global maritime alliance, the United States, obeying the same logic that had educated British statecraft and strategy for centuries, was able to control the chokepoints that Soviet seapower must transit if it was to reach the open ocean and hence the world.[28]

There was much scope for argument over how and where containment should be best effected. But at the all-important master level of an organizing vision, containment proved entirely adequate for forty years. Containment, though initially controversial because of its apparently defensive, or passive, implications, came to serve as the Pole Star for the guidance of U.S. policy for those forty years. Awesome and challenging innovations in military technology occurred under its general guidance, while political and economic conditions around the rimlands of Europe and Asia altered almost beyond recognition. No matter. What the United States had discovered and adopted, in large part courtesy of the analytical and conceptual genius of George F. Kennan,[29] was a grand organizing vision in containment that sufficed to make sense of the country's national security policy in general, and its military preparations in particular.

This is not a study in praise of the theory or the practice of containment. There is much that can be criticized about the theory, and even more about the practice. Nonetheless, the official American adoption of the idea of containment merits praise for its obedience to a single golden rule of statecraft. The American consensus on containment meant that the country had gotten the biggest of big things right, or right enough. To the golden rule of the necessity of getting the big things right with respect to the object of policy, American leaders and executives added the paying of careful attention to prudence, which, it may be recalled from chapter 1, Raymond Aron identified as "the statesman's supreme virtue." In an ever more nuclear age, it was almost as important for U.S. policy to proceed prudently as it was for it not to lose focus on the big picture.

Whatever can be said in praise or criticism of containment, that concept served adequately as the organizing vision informing American policy and grand strategy for forty years. It provided the necessary context for foreign and defense policy. If anything, it probably provided too much meaningful context, in that it functioned with a seductive imperialism. As with any potent idea, containment lent itself to abuse by the unscrupulous and the ignorant. Still, it was uniquely valuable in expressing clearly the central instrumental purpose of American statecraft, and it did so in terms that made geostrategic sense.

With the formal demise of the USSR in 1991, following the collapse of its imperium in 1989, the United States apparently was suddenly, even shockingly, deprived of the authoritative organizing vision that had yielded the context for high policy and strategy for forty years. We must say apparently, because the policy logic of containment for American statecraft was not negated by the fall of the USSR. It is as sound today as it was during the Cold War for American policy to oppose the domination of Eurasia by a single power or coalition. On grounds of the potential for global mischief that enjoyment of a unified sway over Eurasia's many assets might encourage, the principle behind containment retains an enduring authority. What has altered is not the validity of containment's logic for policy, but rather the novel absence of any plausibly worthy foe in Eurasia who appears in urgent need of being contained. Such, at least, is the relatively benign contemporary international situation in which American policymakers find themselves today. It may seem somewhat churlish, perhaps insensitive, to describe the contemporary condition as benign. After all, the global struggle that has been proclaimed against terrorists, and especially against terrorists increasingly likely to be armed with weapons of mass destruction (WMD), hardly invites description in relaxed terms.[30] However, the principal risks today, and for many years to come, are orders of magnitude less catastrophic than was the case only a decade and a half ago. The pull of the immediate must not cause us to lose our sense of proportion. Al Qaeda and its ilk might cause nuclear or some other form of mayhem.[31] But, on the scale of potential catastrophe, any disaster they may trigger would barely register when compared with the possibilities latent in the great engines of strategic nuclear destruction developed and maintained by the superpowers in the Cold War. Moreover, we must hasten to add, the danger of truly large-scale nuclear catastrophe has not been banished, as by some benign hand of an antistrategic History. That danger still lurks in particular regional conflicts—in South Asia, for example—and it is a powerful menace residual in the essentially anarchic character of international politics. All that we can affirm with some confidence is that extreme threats to American society are currently neither extant nor plausibly on the horizon. Whether, or for how long, that fact endures is, of course, an important subject.

The high ideological content of U.S. policy in the Cold War, as well as its novel nuclear dimension, tended to obscure for Americans the fact that their strategic behavior was quite standard, prudent power-balancing activity. Similarly, the rhetorical enthusiasm shown by the Clinton White House for the spread of democracy, and by the second Bush White House for "the benefits of freedom," though no doubt sincere, did not provide much by way of useful guidance for policy or strategy. At least during the Cold War there was no confusion about the main event. Americans understood that the first charge on their resources, both material and spiritual, was the need to balance the power and influence of the USSR. The primary U.S. role in international politics was plain beyond scope for significant, let alone intelligent, domestic challenge by 1949 at the latest. The first-order question concerning America's role in the world was settled by the close of the 1940s. That role, as balancer of Soviet power, was not really debated thereafter for the entire duration of the Cold War. The national soul searching over Vietnam after 1968 scarcely affected the popular consensus which supported the country's role as principal opponent of the Soviet empire. If anything, the Vietnam commitment came to be viewed as a threat to the effective containment of an expansive USSR. Naturally enough, the war did trigger some revisionist writings on Cold War history, but they fell far short of provoking an American debate about first-order matters of foreign policy.[32]

In the 1980s, Mikhail Gorbachev predicted that he would cause a crisis for U.S. national security policy by depriving the United States of its enemy. He was correct. American political and strategic culture is not duly appreciative of those lessons of history, and rules for the prudent conduct of statecraft, that theorists of a realist persuasion deem fundamental. Many Americans, including some in high places, had difficulty separating the U.S. role in the world from its role as container of the late Soviet imperium. With the USSR almost instantly defunct, what was the U.S. role to be?

It can be difficult to distinguish agent from opportunity. For example, the French Revolution wrought such havoc, domestically and abroad, and in particular it destroyed established hierarchies so thoroughly, that it created a context ripe for exploitation by ruthless, ambitious, and competent generals. Napoleon won that contest, but the competition for power occurred only because of political events of which he was the principal beneficiary but not the prime mover. Americans recognized the unexpected and successful conclusion of the Cold War as a moment of opportunity—but an opportunity for what? American pragmatism temporarily was baffled. The dominant threat of forty years was no more; at least it was no more in terms of identifiable political motivation. Much of the menacing military capability of the erstwhile Soviet imperium not only remained intact, but regrettably would degrade only at a graceful, if uncertain, pace. In decades to come, the 1990s may be judged a period of lost opportunity. There could be some merit in such a call, but political and strategic history always provides a rich vein of inspiration for those attracted to the fundamentally unproductive and self-indulgent exercise known as virtual history.[33] In the wonderful realm of "what if," we can conjure up alternative 1990s. But there were reasons additional to the effect of lack of imagination and skill in statecraft, which suffice to explain what did and did not happen in that decade.

New world orders typically have emerged, either rapidly or over a protracted period, in response to a pressing need. Usually they have been constructed by a collective act of will, through hard bargaining, in the immediate wake of a great conflict. The gathering of statesmen after victory was for the salutary purpose of remaking the map of Europe—and, consequently, the world—while distributing rewards and punishments and settling on the rules that should govern interstate conduct. Facsimiles of that agreeable duty were performed in 1648, 1713, 1763, 1815, and 1919, and—in minor key—at many dates following lesser conflicts in between.[34] The experiences of 1945 and 1989–91 yield intriguing parallels, despite their obvious differences. The former registered a decisive victory on such a scale as virtually to define the character and meaning of the term, whereas the latter was contestable as constituting a Western victory at all. There was no doubt over the totality of the political defeat of the USSR, but the Russian Federation, the rump successor state to the USSR (to ignore the shadowy half-life of the Commonwealth of Independent States, established in December 1991), retained the undefeated military muscle of its predecessor. Neither the mid-1940s nor the early 1990s witnessed a grand conclave after the fashion of Vienna 1815, or Paris 1919, determined to remake the world and legitimize some new order. One might argue that the creation and subsequent existence of the United Nations (UN) organization in effect served that purpose, but the argument cannot withstand close scrutiny. The UN reflects its membership and the state of their relations; it does not have a potent independent authority.

Strange to note, the 1940s and the 1990s had much in common, despite their obvious and monumental differences. In neither case was there a formal peace conference, though the summit meetings at Yalta and Potsdam in 1945 certainly handled much of what would have been on the agenda of such a conference. In retrospect, the Gulf War of 1991, while arguably the first war on behalf of a new world order, was a huge distraction for American statecraft at a moment of historically rare opportunity for creative policymaking.[35] Furthermore, it was a distraction that had a high potential to mislead. Although U.S. diplomatic and military behavior to coerce Saddam Hussein can be seen as a precedent of sorts, it was a precedent that proved to have little authoritative legacy value for the grand design of policy for the next ten years.

To avoid needless misunderstanding, it is probably important to state with the utmost clarity that this book is not designed to point a finger of blame at particular policymakers or administrations. The argument is forward looking, not historical. However, it does matter that past errors, or perceived errors, should be recognized, so that the odds against their repetition should be increased. The nine points marshalled in chapter 1 as the argument of the book comprise more or less close variants on what amount to some eternal truths about international politics and strategy. It is never wise or just to target policymakers with powerful criticisms of their failing either to know what they could not possibly have known at the time, or to select a controversial policy course that the author happens to favor. I may not evade those sins completely, but to the best of my ability I will avoid the error of hindsight-foresight. With respect to the more contentious ground of policy choice, the U.S. role in the world outlined in these pages, and the national security policy and military strategy thereto pertaining, are less controversial than they may appear at first sight.

There is some truth in the claim that the 1990s were both a postwar and an interwar period.[36] The world shook down from the bipolar organization that had dominated the previous four decades, and tentatively explored what new security environment—a popular verbal formula in the early 1990s—was in the process of emerging. Because the Cold War ended with a fairly protracted and mercifully anticlimactic whimper, rather than a bang, American statecraft was not much challenged at the levels of guiding vision and high policy. This is not to deny the superior diplomatic skills of President George H. W. Bush and Secretary of State James A. Baker. But it is to remark on the fact that those skills were predominantly focused on pragmatic, tactical tasks. When we consider the potential for explosive error inherent in the diplomatic management tasks of the period

1989–91, it may seem ungenerous to be critical at all. Successful oversight of the peaceful unification of Germany; the conduct of constructive relations with a USSR that was both adjusting to the loss of imperium and empire, and conducting a most painful fundamental domestic political transition; and the assembly and leadership of a global coalition to eject Iraqi forces from Kuwait: these were practical tasks of formidable difficulty. One might say, however, that they were tasks given by history to the United States. One could argue plausibly that for two generations the U.S. policy of containment had so shaped the security environment, that the Soviet meltdown of 1989–91 was in a vital sense a triumph for American statecraft and strategy. We can be confident that historians will never agree on the answer to the question, "to what extent did the USSR fall, and to what extent was it pushed?"[37]

When the diplomatic business of the day included such portentous issues as German reunification, the conclusion of hostile relations with the USSR, and the conduct of what might have been a bloody struggle in the Gulf, it is easy to see how tactics, strategy, policy, and vision all tended to conflate in practice and reduce to the essential mission of succeeding well enough now. In the 1990s, circumstances and personalities conspired to delay full recognition, and hence expeditious emergence, of a new organizing vision to replace the anti-Soviet theme of the Cold War decades. Inevitably, the Clinton administration devised what it called "a national security strategy for a new century." The key ideas, in what passed for an organizing vision, were the feel-good, heavily multilateralist concepts of global engagement, enlargement, and American leadership.[38] These ideas did not have much merit as framed and articulated, appealing though they were to traditional liberal sentiments. In the 1990s, the United States toyed with a policy of highly selective engagement primarily for what, one may conclude fairly, were more missionary than strategic purposes. In practice, America's humanitarian interventions comprised an ugly mixture of the ill-conceived and poorly conducted (Somalia and Haiti), the unduly belated and then somewhat ill-conceived and often counterproductive (the former Yugoslavia), or the hugely incompetent and fundamentally non-serious (Iraq, and the so-called "war on drugs"). As for the potentially momentous project of NATO expansion, the rationales offered in explanation were so various and inconsistent that American officials seemed determined to repeat the policy style of the Johnson administration. Whenever an administration feels obliged to offer a list of reasons to explain a controversial decision, particularly when it is an ongoing list, it is a reasonable bet that the policy lacks coherence. This is not to say that NATO enlargement was a poor idea. Not at all. But it is to claim that those in charge of the United States in the 1990s gave every appearance of being out of their depth in global statecraft.

The difference between verbiage and vision is not always as clear to the authors of the former as it ought to be. Henry Kissinger calls it correctly when he writes, censoriously of course, that

> At the apogee of its power, the United States finds itself in an ironic position. In the face of perhaps the most profound and widespread upheavals the world has ever seen, it has failed to develop concepts relevant to the emerging realities.[39]

Which one might translate as, "if only I were still Secretary of State." Nonetheless, he is correct. To be more precise, he was correct. Hopefully, the concepts for which he called are now emerging and being pressed urgently into service. He offers more valuable wisdom when he warns that "at the beginning of a new century and of a new millennium, the United States will not discover any panacea." He continues by advising that "less in need of a specific policy than of a long-range concept, America is obliged for the first time to devise a global strategy stretching into the indefinite future."[40] For a final dip into the Kissinger wisdom-nugget barrel, he observes, with words lethal to much of the Clinton record in foreign affairs, that "despite the mantra of globalization, there are geopolitical realities that overwhelm fashionable reveries about universality."[41] The tragedy was not that the Clinton administration did not care about doing good in the world; rather, it did not really understand how the world works, has always worked, and will continue to work in the future. The distinguished Australian theorist of International Relations, Hedley Bull, made a comment for the ages in 1972 when he stated that "the sources of facile optimism and narrow moralism never dry up, and the lessons of the 'realists' have to be learnt afresh by every new generation."[42] Bull was not writing in general praise of the academic theory of realism in the study of International Relations, by the way. U.S. policy in the no-name era of the 1990s (the post–Cold War era is almost an anti-name) yielded ample testimony to the aptness of Bull's comment. In Mogadishu, in Bosnia, in the Taiwan

Straits, over Kosovo, and—time after time—over Iraq, to cite but a few, the rougher realities of international life continued to spoil the picnic for those who wished to spend a post–Cold War "peace dividend" from a declining defense budget and celebrate "the end of history."

Francis Fukuyama provided one of the most influential ideas of the 1990s, with his thesis that the age of great political and ideological struggles had ended.[43] With culturally characteristic directness, President George W. Bush repeated at least a part of that message ten years later, on September 17, 2002:

> The great struggles of the twentieth century between liberty and totalitarianisms ended with a decisive victory for the forces of freedom – and a single sustainable model for national success: freedom, democracy, and free enterprise.[44]

Prudently, however, the President did not proclaim an end to history. Moreover, those American theorists and wordsmiths who gloried in the triumph of the American way over the evil empire of the Soviets have been shown by recent events to have selected too narrow an ideological focus. Adam Smith may have triumphed over Karl Marx, but rogue variants of Islam in the impressionable minds of some of the losers in the contemporary process of globalization, are demonstrating a potency that challenges some of the liberal nostrums of the 1990s.[45]

Unusually for the end of a great conflict, the Cold War concluded so gracefully that events did not appear to demand inspired statecraft of the United States. That probably was fortunate, because the victorious Western Alliance in the 1990s appeared as bereft of statesmen with vision, or indeed even of statesmen who could boast a secure intellectual grip on the workings of international politics, as had been the European democracies in the 1930s. Individuals do count, even in the politics of security at the highest level. It is often said that the United States can be relied upon to do the right thing eventually, after it has first tried all the alternatives. For the nameless post–Cold war decade, the United States gave every appearance of knowing neither the right thing to do, nor how to go about finding it. This was not simply a reflection of the uncertainty natural in geopolitical and geostrategic circumstances so suddenly transformed. It was more a case of a cohort of American and other political leaders who were out of their depth on the world stage. An important reason why the country seemed to lurch behind events, and then to react erratically, was that the official American worldview of the 1990s was fundamentally flawed.

The only purpose worth serving by pointing to the amateurism of American statecraft in the 1990s is to alert those who will listen to the perennial danger of wishful thinking that lurks in a society whose culture is characterized by an optimistic ideology that believes profoundly in progress. American and British policy toward the world is always the product of a competition between the urges of a noble liberal idealism, and the disciplinary effect of the persisting rough realities of quasi-anarchic international life. The Western democracies are ever apt to indulge their ideological preferences when the times grow more permissive, rather than what they should know from historical experience. So it was for the first post–Cold War decade. This is not a case of being wise long after the incompetently handled event. It was obvious in the 1990s that the United States lacked an organizing vision for its national security policy. Washington talked about leadership, just as it talked about enlargement, engagement, cooperative and common security, globalization, and the spread of democracy. The words were generally admirable, as were the values they expressed, but they were fundamentally not serious. They did not amount to a coherent, historically founded worldview suitably focused on genuine international problems, and on what the United States, uniquely, needed to be ready to do. Some commentators, thinking primarily about the apparent drift in the defense effort, talked of a "strategic pause." Indeed, the American national security debate of the 1990s was more than casually reminiscent of the British Treasury's "Ten-Year Rule." From 1919 until 1931, policy guidance for the British defense effort had as its centerpiece the assumption that "the British empire will not be engaged in any great war in the next ten years, and that no Expeditionary Force is required for this purpose."[46]

For ten years the United States was adrift in world affairs. That fact was somewhat obscured by the fortunate absence of any obvious great challenge in need of an immediate creative response; by the obvious intelligence and articulateness of the President of the day; and by the appearance and, to be fair, the reality, of some successes overseas. In 1995, for example, the abominable Bosnian Serbs were taught an unduly belated lesson in the cost of beastliness.[47] In 1999, the United States, again very belatedly, succeeded in coercing an end to ethnic cleansing in Kosovo and, ultimately, set the stage in Yugoslavia for the fall of Slobodan Milosevic and his appalling family.[48] My point is not that the United States failed in all its endeavors for a decade; it did not. Rather, my claim is that much of what was done should have been done earlier, or more rigorously, or not at all. What was lacking was evidence of an appropriate guiding light for high policy. There was no organizing vision that could be properly so called.[49] There was no clear sense of what needed to be done and no adequate understanding of what the United States could and should contribute to that mission. The fundamental problem was the absence of a clear-eyed, historically rooted grasp of how and why international history moves as it does. The British and French statesmen in the 1930s who took counsel of their fears and therefore elected to indulge their hopes, were rewarded with the emergence of a war-bound Third Reich. At least they had the potent excuse of the recent trauma of the Great War and the shocking and unanswerable emergence of the triple threat posed by Germany, Italy, and Japan.[50] The American policymakers of the 1990s did not have the experience of the Somme or Verdun as a plausible excuse for being gun shy. If the Anglo-French "long weekend" of the 1920s and 1930s concluded with a rampant Adolf Hitler, the American strategic pause of the 1990s was brutally terminated by Osama bin Laden and the terrorists of al Qaeda. Whatever else September 11 may be held to mean or imply, it demands that serious people develop and act on a serious organizing vision for the U.S. role in the world, and for the national security policy and strategy to implement it.

THE ORGANIZING VISION: SHERIFF OF WORLD ORDER

It is important to avoid confusion between first- and second- order matters. Too much of the public debate about America's world role remains blissfully oblivious to this distinction. There are second-order matters of importance, especially those bearing on ways and means, but they are topics of subordinate significance. Let us revisit some core items of our argument.

- World order requires keeping by some agent, agents, or agency. Every such order meriting the ascription needs guarding, and hence needs a guardian.

- In the absence of a super agent or agency keeping order on behalf of the international system, disorder prevails, to be partially overtaken by such order as the stronger players are able to impose and enforce.

- At present, and hopefully for many years to come, the United States is the only possible super agent of world order.

- The guardian of world order, here termed sheriff, must please itself in the process of serving the general good. Policy will be sustainable only if Americans can identify their national interest in the actions undertaken in their name. U.S. national security policy, and particularly any active military behavior, is not governed by a philanthropic impulse, at least it should not be. As ends in themselves, a praiseworthy desire to improve conditions here or there must prove too shallow a motive to bear the traffic when unexpected costs are suffered. (Witness the disaster that was the American humanitarian intervention in Somalia in 1993–94).

My argument is inherently neutral with respect to an issue that has excited many commentators: the question of unilateral or multilateral action. That is a second-order matter. The organizing concern for U.S. national security policy, that which was missing from the American playbook in the 1990s, is the thesis that the United States is and should be the sheriff of world order. If the role thus indicated lends itself to multilateral support and endorsement, and if it can be given some added dignity through institutional endorsement by the Security Council of the UN, so much the better. What matters most is that we keep our eyes on the ball, and do not allow ourselves to be diverted by inherently second-order considerations. The "ball" at issue here is the protection of world order; it is not giving minimum offense abroad.

Self-evidently, diplomatic style and policy substance interpenetrate. National style matters greatly, because clumsy behavior that is indifferent to or ignorant of the interests and sensitivities of others, must heighten the risks of policy failure. Nonetheless, it is not intelligent to try to hold a great debate over the second-order matter of style in policy execution. What we need, first and foremost, is the utmost clarity in our minds concerning the American role in the world. Furthermore, we have to recognize that the master idea that should guide us must be suitable to serve as our organizing concept, the "containment" for this century. Recall that containment, though a powerful idea, was subject to rival interpretations and, inevitably, to a highly variable quality of actual performance when executed by real people coping with uncertainty.

It is my contention that the United States must try to serve as the sheriff of the contemporary world order. This argument is both open-ended in its future historical domain, and not specific to particular issues. Most probably, the war against terrorists that is the issue of the hour, perhaps even the decade, will be superseded by challenges and perils with different characters, as the century advances. We noted earlier that the United States already has played what amounted to the sheriff's role three times in the twentieth century, albeit repeatedly in the geopolitical context of the conduct of war. The difference now, and for some decades to come, is that there is no actual or putatively hostile superpower to be balanced through war or deterrence. It should be needless to add that that context of unchallenged, even currently unchallengeable, American preponderance must prove temporally finite.

To be useful, an organizing vision for national security policy must be both crystal clear in its driving idea, yet sufficiently adaptable to accommodate the full range of future surprises. What matters most is a lack of ambiguity about the central notion. A problem with such worthy ideas from the 1990s as global engagement and enlargement, and even cooperative security, was that they lacked focus and provided no usable criteria for the operational guidance of policy behavior. They were meritorious intentions, but really only words. However, because the choice of words does matter profoundly, it is time for this text to explain as tersely as possible just what its organizing concept does and does not imply.

A careful scholar has remarked all too persuasively "that the term 'world order' is a notoriously slippery one."[51] He continues by noting that "most discussions around world order refer to a stable pattern of relations among sovereign states." However, there is far more to international politics than the relations among states. The theorist in question, Torbjorn L. Knutsen, argues that "'order' exists when a relatively stable pattern of human relations characterizes the international scene." Further, he insists usefully that "such stability . . . is upheld by rules of international conduct."[52] In his *magnum opus*, Hedley Bull insisted that "in this study world order entails something different from international order. Order among mankind as a whole is something wider than order among states; something more fundamental and primordial than it; and also, I should argue, something morally prior to it."[53] In a compelling analysis, Bull maintains that

> World order is more fundamental and primordial than international order because the ultimate units of the great society of all mankind are not states (or nations, tribes, empires, classes or parties) but individual human beings, which are permanent and indestructible in a sense in which groupings of them of this or that sort are not. This is the moment for international relations, but the question of world order arises whatever the political or social structure of the globe.[54]

In recent years, scholarly theorists of International Relations have developed a somewhat belated, but nonetheless generally welcome, interest in world order, as they have shifted focus from the causes of war and wars to the causes of, and conditions for, peace. I have no interest in adding to that theoretical literature, at least not in these pages.[55] What we need is simply clarity concerning key terms. Although the concept of world order invites all manner of qualification and caveat, it is plain enough in its meaning to serve our purpose. Similarly, the proposition that the United States should serve as the sheriff of the current world order is not an especially demanding one to corral, lasso, and break in as a source of broad guidance for national security policy.

This book is about the need for America to defend world order, with particular focus on the strategic dimension of the mission. Such a perspective can be only partial. I do not deny that world order can be menaced, and supported, by elements other than the strategic.[56] Similarly, as noted above, I recognize the difficult terrain into which one can stray when a concept as inherently contestable as world order is employed. But in the spirit of strategic pragmatism, this analysis needs only workable definitions of key, albeit slippery, concepts.

World order is a somewhat ambiguous concept that is descriptive, normative, and prescriptive. In line with Knutsen's formula, I understand the concept to refer to a reasonably stable pattern of relations among the political entities of all kinds that comprise the players in world politics. We can note the contested issue of the proper level of analysis, whether it should be individuals, states, or other kinds of security communities, but we should not permit that matter to detain us for long, given the intention of this text. World order, especially if dignified by addition of the definite article, so it becomes *the* world order, thus refers to: the contemporary patterns in relations among political entities; a fairly stable—meaning predictable—pattern in those relations; and a tolerably steady pattern in relations characterized by features that we deem desirable. Because of its normative content, it is not adequate for the concept of world order, even *the* world order, to refer simply to the current state of play in international politics, regardless of the degree of anarchy and general mayhem. But, since world order is always a project in motion, its contemporary realization cannot help but leave work to be done by the sheriff of the era.

No prizes will be awarded for the design of a condition of world order more attractive than is the current one. But because this is a book written principally in the tradition of strategic analysis, we are more concerned with defending world order than we are with defining it, let alone reinventing it. It is very much what it is. Although the American superstate can play a dominant role, and in our view should do so on occasion, the contemporary world order is neither *the* American, nor even *an* American, order. The political context at the beginning of the twenty-first century is quite precisely as suggested by the title of this book. The role of sheriff may be self-appointed or sometimes licensed by a multilateral international body. It points to a class of duties that needs to be performed on behalf of the world, or, more exactly, on behalf of orderly relations among the world's political entities.

Some commentators favor reference to an American empire, and find it appropriate to approach the challenges facing American defense policy by means of an explicitly imperial strategy. In my view, the definite merit in the imperial idea tends to be offset by the pejorative baggage that is inseparable from this value-charged concept. It may seem unwise and even perverse for this discussion to proceed very far in the absence of detailed deconstruction of such vital concepts as world order and empire. I offer a trinitarian self-defense, in which I appeal to strategic pragmatism; to the necessity not to lose focus on my theme; and, for a culture-laden principle of which scholars are often rightly suspicious, to the notion of common sense. Were this book a venture into the theory of International Relations, many no-doubt scintillating pages would be occupied with the various meanings of empire and a lengthy discussion of both international and world order. As it is, and obedient to the worldview outlined by Bernard Brodie earlier in this chapter, our need for powerful, if somewhat ambiguous, political ideas is limited and pragmatic, though certainly of the most serious kind. What we require is ideas that work well enough; just as we need to identify an organizing vision for U.S. national security sufficiently definite in its meaning that it inspires and enlightens, rather than confuses. The vision we choose must not be so rigorously defined that it could deny us the flexibility we will need to adjust to changing international and domestic contexts.

As a matter of elementary political prudence, it will be advisable for American policymakers to be modest in their public articulation of the sheriff's role, and the policy and strategy that makes it a reality. Such calculated understatement, however, must not hinder appreciation of contemporary actualities. A large majority of world opinion will not only tolerate, but probably assist a United States in a role that certainly would not be approved formally by the UN Security Council or any other body (were there any rivals, for some healthy competition). It is something of a polite fiction to see the United States as the occasionally authorized agent of a world order defined by, and expressed through, the United Nations organization. For my purposes here, U.S. relations with the UN are of only minor interest. This is not because we are disdainful of the UN or sickened by the hypocrisy that flourishes there. After all, we classical realists expect nothing better. Practical statespersons must use whatever tools are available, and that includes the UN. More to the point, we are in no important sense hostile to the UN, or inclined to deny it a useful role in support of world order. It is our contention that the United States is, and should long remain, the principal sheriff of world order—not that the United States is alone in wishing to promote and protect that order. Neither is it our position that the United States is condemned to act alone. The sheriff should often succeed in raising a posse, duly blessed by multilateral bodies. A significant reason why the United States is able to function as sheriff is precisely because it usually behaves in a manner that serves the general good as well as its own interests.[57]

What does it mean to be sheriff of world order? As a candidate organizing vision, what kind of guidance can it offer? Provided we do not allow ourselves to be sidetracked by second-order issues, the sheriff's role should serve us well enough for decades to come. Second-order issues do matter, sometimes to the point where if they are mishandled they will thwart achievement of first-order goals. This point is the same as is often asserted as existing among strategy, operations, and tactics. Although the hierarchical superiority of strategy cannot sensibly be contested, if the troops cannot perform tactically, operational and strategic grand designs must remain as monuments to impractical ambitions. In practice, warfare is horizontal in structure as well as, or even instead of, hierarchical.[58]

It is essential that the political context for the argument be stated here with the utmost clarity. Six explicit assumptions, or claims, provide the bedrock of all that follows through the remainder of the text.

First, by any plausible definition the United States today is the sheriff of world order. Uncle Sam's is the number you call when truly "greater than expected threats" menace your neighborhood, and possibly all our neighborhoods. The world still does not have a police force. In a world of supposedly sovereign political actors, the members of the well-nigh universal UN, and particularly its great-power dominated Security Council, can license action on their collective behalf. But, as the saying goes, "someone actually has to go and do it." The UN is both a blessing and a curse for world order and its American sheriff. Fortunately, my argument is not vulnerable to the range of readers' attitudes toward the UN. The organizing vision of American guardianship is inherently relaxed about UN, or other institutions', involvement in U.S. performance of the lawman's role. To coin a phrase, whatever works and is helpful should be used. Moreover, the United States may be obliged to have to resort to some multilateral diplomacy which, although it is likely to be more of a hindrance than a help in a technical sense, may still be politically valuable.

Second, and to extend the first claim, for the better part of a hundred years the United States has already acted as the sheriff on occasions both great and small. The facts of ongoing war, certainly of a distinctly live balance of power, may obscure the historical reality. Ever since 1917, and notwithstanding its appalling military unreadiness, the United States has behaved more as a *deus ex machina*, a savior from across the sea, than as just another country, albeit a powerful one. In the three world wars of the last century, the United States functioned in effect as sheriff. Because of its resources, both material and moral, America played the lawman role. Since the end of the Cold War, particularly in Bosnia in 1995 and Kosovo in 1999, it was once again U.S. intervention that was decisive. A sheriff has to make a vital difference (if he does not, it is time to step down). He should not merely complicate an already bloody contest. Radical changes in political context have contributed to confusion over how the American role today compares with its role in times past. Of course, the contexts for American policy could hardly appear more different: in 1917, to choose to join in a great war as an Associated Power (rather than an ally); in 1941, to be summoned to a two-ocean conflict and really to wage two distinct wars, one against the super-power of the moment (a moment which U.S. strength notably helped render relatively brief)[59]; in 1947, to balance the influence of Stalin's expanding empire (a term employed here in its precise technical meaning of rule over foreigners); and then, half a century later, occasionally to exercise muscle and exert leadership when alternatives were signally lacking.[60]

Third, the role of sheriff carries the obligation to do the heaviest of heavy military lifting on behalf of the international quasi community. Perhaps more precisely expressed, the sheriff's role obliges the United States at least to consider doing that heavy lifting. The United States is not locked into a competitive struggle with another self-appointed would-be law officer. As a general rule, though there will be exceptions, Washington is not bidding for world approval, or looking for superpower-worthy wrongs to right. By and large, it will be the case that if the United States declines to act, or neglects or fails to deter, then an alternative brand of justice will most likely be administered by a deeply partial regional polity in pursuit of its own interests. Because the United States is master of its own cause and endeavors, acceptance of the informal sheriff's role carries general, not usually specific, implications for policy. The United States must and will consult its own national interests and weigh the risks as well as the possible benefits of action. As more and more security communities acquire WMD and their means of delivery, so the American sheriff, realistically any guardian power, is going to have to pursue strategies that re-balance risks with gains. A so-called preemptive strategy would be one approach; deployment of robust missile and air defenses must be another.

Recognition of the role of sheriff probably fuels healthy expectation on everyone's part more than it suggests particular occasions for action, let alone a particular character to such action. It is important for the world at large to know that there is an exceedingly powerful state committed to the maintenance of stability and predictability in the flow of international relations. In many cases of possible regional adventure, American military intervention could not by any means be taken for granted. It is not the sheriff's role to dash from conflagration to conflagration around the world, responding mindlessly to strategic fire alarms. Rather, it is the American role to undertake, or enable others to undertake, the occasional mission to deter or, if need be, coerce, that is as important as it is feasible only with American participation. To put the matter plain beyond possibility of misunderstanding: In its role as sheriff, the United States voluntarily accepts the duty, in principle at least, to occasionally "take the trash out" for the world community, see off the well-armed intruder, and generally be willing and able to function as the strong arm for us all.

As the global political context evolved, the sheriff's role had the United States intervening three times in the twentieth century to help prevent the domination of Eurasia by a hostile power, not to mention the *de facto* and *de jure* invitations to fight that were received in 1917 and 1941, respectively. In the new century the sheriff's role bids fair to lead Americans on a long and somewhat frustrating campaign against terrorists, while ambitious but medium-sized regional powers, rising regional great powers, and perhaps a returning great power, could all warrant some focus of the American lawman's attention. What matters most, since one cannot foresee the future, is to be absolutely clear about the meaning of the American sheriff's role. It carries a beneficially menacing message "to those whom it may concern." The message is to the effect both that their activities are being monitored closely, and that there exists a political agent of world order, with a suitable military instrument, possibly prepared to take coercive action on a scale and of a kind that would brook no effective opposition.

Fourth, the United States requires the means and methods to deter, coerce and, if need be, defeat whoever is judged to pose an intolerable threat of disorder. Those means and methods will evolve with social mores, technology, doctrine, and experience. Also they will have to be sufficiently adaptable to give pause to a great regional power, as well as to be suitable for hunting terrorist cells through some of the roughest country on earth, both natural and man-made. The sheriff's role thus comes with the nonnegotiable requirement that the United States and its friends and allies maintain "the preponderant power," to quote again the telling and uncompromising proposition of Donald Kagan.[61] It is scarcely less important that the American sheriff is known to be willing to use that preponderant power. The United States could learn a lesson from Rome's style in world ordering, or imperial policing. Rome could be so deliberate in the pace at which it set about restoring order, or inflicting punishment to discourage others, that one might almost have believed that the offense at issue had been forgotten, if not forgiven. Not so. Rome could be slow and deliberate because generally it was under no great compulsion to move swiftly. Roman punitive justice tended to be as inexorable in its inevitability of arrival as it was final in its bloody consequences for the disturbers of the Roman peace.[62] Duly amended for some modern sensitivities, the principle just illustrated, that the Roman, or American, sheriff "always gets his man," no matter how long it may take, has much to recommend it. This is particularly true as we enter an era wherein the leading strategic challenges appear to stem more from asymmetrical and irregular threats than from the regular armed forces of states. However, America's duty as sheriff is likely to extend beyond a period wherein al Qaeda and its collaborators comprise the truly heavy-duty traffic menacing world order. The United States does not have the luxury of being able to settle comfortably on a single dominant kind of threat. The country cannot prudently transform all of its military establishment so as to optimize likely performance in the chasing of elusive terrorists. There could be dangers out there in the future compared with which even the sick dreams of al Qaeda would pale.

Fifth, we must insist that the United States is nominated, indeed is the only possible contemporary nominee, for the role of sheriff, because it is *the* superpower, not because of September 11, 2001, and its consequences. Chapter 3 explains how the country already, if perhaps slowly, was accommodating the idea of the guardianship role, when 9/11 lent wings to its feet by providing the acceleration that a clear political purpose has a way of providing. It is probable, though, that many people confuse the national response to September 11 with America's role in the world. Should further clarification be required, we assert here that the United States is the only possible sheriff of world order because now it is the only superpower or even great power left standing after the repeated struggles of the last century. After three hundred fifty years of typically European-centered balance-of-power warfare, the United States temporarily stands alone. And that solitude implies, though cannot mandate, an awesome responsibility for the protection of world order. It was ever thus. September 11 occurred precisely because of America's preeminence on several dimensions. The current global campaign against terrorists, with a particular eye to those who might secure access to WMD, has to be seen as only one front in the permanent struggle to protect world order against whomever or whatever might emerge to pose dangers that may be barely imagined today. Strategic history has a nasty habit of ambushing those complacent policymakers who have settled on comforting assumptions. As the only plausible sheriff of the world order of the next several decades, the United States needs a national security policy that can ride some inevitable unpleasant surprises, allowing the country, and world order, to tolerate the surprise effects.

Sixth and finally, although this book focuses largely on the strategic aspects of national security policy, it is not blind to the high importance of the less "hard" aspects of American power. An important reason why the United States may succeed somewhat against the odds, and in the face of much grim historical precedent, is because America is a civilization as well as a superstate. Joseph Nye and others are, of course, right.[63] "Soft power" matters, though it is not all that matters. In the world today the United States is uniquely attractive as a civilization. But it is also true that many people are repulsed by American civilization, or profess to be so for reasons that psychologists, sociologists, and historians have little difficulty understanding. The preponderant state of an era needs to offer the beacon of its civilization to the world. The United States in the twenty-first century, the second American century, is proceeding where the Roman and British Empires went before. Each was more than just a powerful country. Each was an idea, was uniquely attractive to foreigners in its period of preeminence, and exerted much of its influence, in part on behalf of the contemporary understanding of world order, through the attractiveness of its culture. So it is now for the American sheriff. But if the sheriff neglects to keep his powder dry, no amount of cultural sparkle will be of much help to the world order project.

CHAPTER 3

Staying Number One

The United States should wish to remain Number One for as long as proves feasible. Naturally and necessarily, U.S. determination to remain preponderant, especially militarily preponderant, is self-serving. The United States is serving its own national interest. This is nothing to be ashamed of; indeed, it could not be concealed even if desired. Critics of U.S. statecraft often seem to inhabit a fictitious world wherein foreign policy is, or should be, a form of missionary activity, undertaken simply because it is virtuous. Those critics, domestic and foreign, need to step up to the reality that the sheriff role is frequently going to be unpopular, is always going to be more or less costly, and is occasionally going to be painfully unsuccessful. Given these grim certainties, the American people will require the largest possible stake in the role. It is well for Americans to derive some pleasure, some pride, in being Number One. It is also essential for them to appreciate that in serving world order, they are serving their own best interests. Without these domestic sources of psychological and political support for its global role, it is unlikely that the United States would be able to weather the bad times that most certainly lie ahead, interspersed with the good. This chapter explains: the more serious threats that may ambush the United States as it steps up to perform as principal protector of world order; how the global policing role emerged explicitly after September 11, 2001, and provided the immediate grand purpose that national security policy had lacked previously;[1] and how the long American international lead in the assay of power that is essential for the sheriff's role might be prolonged.

THREATS TO AMERICA'S MISSION

The U.S. role of sheriff, generally unblessed by UN clergy, is likely to endure beyond its prudent sell-by date. The reasons why Americans will find the lawman's burden unduly heavy should similarly weigh negatively in the policy calculations of others. If and when there should emerge a plausible superstate or coalition rival to the United States, that strategically functional peer will discover that the joys of preeminence are amply balanced by the dangers inseparable from its security obligations. To be the principal guardian of world order will be no light policy or strategic undertaking, as this new century proceeds to record a continuing proliferation of weapons of mass destruction. That undesirable but inevitable trend comprises a major source of menace additional to, and indeed often intertwined with, familiar geopolitical tensions and conflicts in a world that will remain primarily state-centric.

This is all rather discouraging. Nonetheless, it happens to be realistic. In this book thus far, the argument has focused far more upon the necessity for performance of the sheriff's role, and the unique fitness of the United States to play the muscular lawman, than upon the risks and burdens of that job. This chapter should foreclose on any criticism that I underestimate the difficulty and understate the risks that attend the role of sheriff. Four distinctive but interacting sets of problems will challenge and harass, and eventually may diminish markedly, the U.S. guardianship role that is the binding theme of this analysis. It is convenient to label the four sets of problems geopolitics, proliferation (of WMD), military-technical competition, and domestic (economic and cultural, hence political). These are not listed in order of importance, and there is absolutely no intention here to suggest that these comprise discreet sets of possible difficulties. Challenges rarely appear singly, conveniently seriatim.

Accepting the risk of trying the reader's patience with repetition, the point of this discussion may be clearer if we cite again the golden thought of Donald Kagan, who wrote that "what seems to work best, even though imperfectly is the possession by those states who wish to preserve the peace of the preponderant power and of the will to accept the burdens and responsibilities required to achieve that purpose."[2] Americans' motives may well be mixed, but the historical record is tolerably clear in support of Kagan's claim. U.S. hegemony, meaning only preeminence and leadership, not detailed direction of most aspects of political, economic, and social behavior, is by far the best prospect for world order in the twenty-first century. It cannot guarantee peace, because the U.S. superstate will, from time to time, need to wage war or at least apply coercion on behalf of order. Nonetheless, with global security the interest of peace will be advanced prodigiously for so long as the United States is willing and able to sustain its current position of preponderance. A good part of the contemporary difficulty into which American statecraft has stumbled derives from a lack of understanding at home and abroad of the truth in Kagan's dictum. In addition, of course, there are critics who understand the theory of the benign hegemon and reject it. They may dispute its authority in historical experience,[3] as well as in logic and common sense, or they may find it all too credible, plausible, and distasteful.

It is important to be crystal clear on the meaning for world order, which really translates as peace with security in several dimensions (military, economic, cultural, and so forth), of the United States staying "Number One," as we put the matter here. Many critics of American hegemonism, especially when that hegemonism is expressed in a Texan accent, would seem to believe in a theory of international security and world order that is quite at variance with that which guides this text and, indeed, is at variance with accessible historical experience. From the perspective of world order, there is no superior option for the twenty-first century to a preponderant United States acting as sheriff. Since there is no rival polity or coalition in the near term, the alternative to American hegemony is disorder on a haircurling scale. The American sheriff will not, and indeed cannot, prevent all disorder. But it can dissuade, deter, bribe, coerce, and sometimes physically defeat those who threaten to create conflagration in their neighborhood and beyond. As we shall see, the joys of hegemony are easily exaggerated until they are contrasted with the costs and risks.

At present the alternative to American hegemony is not hegemony by some other polity, though that will be a significant probability in the longer term. Modern history shows us what the world is like when there is no dominant state extant. World politics from 1900 until 1945 provide a fair example of a leaderless condition. Between the demise of Great Britain as the vital power balancer in the nineteenth century and the emergence of the United States as the superpower in a class of its own in mid-century, the course of world history demonstrated what can happen when international security is contested by rival teams of state. All too few of America's more systemic (i.e., first-order) critics have felt obliged to suggest an alternative theory of global security governance, let alone to subject any theory that they might present to interrogation by the possible, and admittedly ever arguable, lessons of historical experience. Such experience is, of course, the only evidence available to us.

The four sets of menaces to American preponderance, and hence to the feasibility of the sheriff's role, have yet to be accorded the weight that they merit in debate over U.S. national security policy. American defense analysts are inclined to focus on military questions, with scant regard to political purposes or context. American foreign policy analysts, in contrast, serve up a rich diet of political context, but are apt to be fatally weak on military issues. Coherent, holistic, and plausible analyses of the threats to the U.S. role in the world are all but nonexistent, despite the ocean of ink spilled on the subject of American policy today and tomorrow. Hopefully, the four threat sets identified here and discussed immediately below will serve well enough to capture all that is truly essential in an inclusive effort to grasp the perils that probably lie ahead for the United States as sheriff of world order.

The first source of prospective challenge to American preponderance is the geopolitical. Geopolitics is a compound concept that is as useful and important as it is frightening to many commentators who still see in it shades of Nazi doctrine and, almost as heinous, a suggestion of geographical determinism. It is no part of my purpose here to promote the long overdue rehabilitation of geopolitical ideas, but if some small advance in that direction were to be achieved serendipitously, I would not be displeased.[4] Geopolitics refers to international politics in their geographical context. Variant definitions include "the relation of international political power to the geographical setting" and "the spatial study and practice of international relations."[5] Basically, geopolitics points to the nastier aspects of international politics—aspects which necessarily must occur in particular physical geography, while not infrequently they are also about that geography (though sometimes the geography is imagined rather than physical reality). In the minds and word processors of many people today, geography, particularly of the physical kind, is a dimension of international politics and strategy that is being reduced drastically in importance by modern technology.[6] Liberal optimistic theories of world affairs are wont to argue that international politics and strategy per se, let alone the geographical setting for their misdeeds and schemings, have little future of note as we humans leave behind much of our sadly conflict-dominated past.

The geopolitical view, or at least most geopolitical views, have no truck with what are regarded as liberal fantasies. Geopolitics can serve as a portmanteau term for the traditionally (and mainly classic) realist understanding of why international politics both is what it is and works as it does. American political culture is always attracted to visions of a much brighter tomorrow, notwithstanding the clear message from 2,500 years of accessible human history which suggests powerfully that that glittering future will likely be a long time coming.[7] Notwithstanding the fact that, understandably though perhaps prematurely,[8] a primarily transnational terrorism has been allowed to become the defining threat in the worldview of Washington, the geopolitical view still has some authority in the U.S. government. The capstone public document on national security strategy issued in September 2002 contained the following partially reassuring message:

> We are attentive to the possible renewal of old patterns of great power competition. Several potential great powers are now in the midst of internal transition—most importantly Russia, India, and China. In all three cases, recent developments have encouraged our hope that a truly global consensus about basic principles is slowly taking shape.[9]

The first sentence quoted is prudent, if flawed; the second and third, alas, compound to nonsense. The flaw in the first sentence is the reference to "the possible renewal of old patterns." The pattern of great power competition will almost certainly be renewed in due course. Powerful states will not be comfortable with the United States in the sheriff's role, even though they will derive benefit from the order which that role protects. A superstate American sheriff is a standing affront to the self-respect, as well as a limitation upon the influence—and hence potentially a menace to the interests—of the world's greater polities, those both extant and those that are lapsed.[10] China is only the most obvious of predictable challengers to the American-policed world order. We should not forget that Japan's economy is still four times the size of China's.[11] This new century could well see some geopolitical realignments, diplomatic revolutions even, as world politics shakes off the residue of old patterns from what historians now label "the age of total war." Neither the U.S.-Japanese Alliance, the anchor of the U.S. position and posture in East Asia, nor NATO, similarly the anchor in Europe, can be assumed to be cast in adamantine rock. Both are vulnerable to the pressures of changing times. It is a reasonable prediction, for example, that NATO in its currently diluted extended form could not survive the emergence of a European Union that had a truly unified foreign and security policy. President Bush's second and third quoted sentences are nonsense because the greater states he specified—Russia, India, and China—will never acquiesce to an American-led world order, save insofar as they lack access to prudent alternatives. The implication that these somewhat great powers are being educated into proper appreciation of the merit in America-favored principles of good global citizenship is frankly ridiculous.[12] If history, as well as current indicators, is any guide, there is endless geopolitical trouble ahead for the global sheriff from the top of the table of UN members.

But geopolitics is not only a game for super and great powers. As sheriff of the new world order the United States will find that this very status, albeit informal, automatically involves it in regional quarrels. The United States will be the only extra-regional power able to intervene in those quarrels. The details of future conflicts are as unpredictable as their incidence is certain. The "old wars" of an allegedly now defunct Clausewitzian world remain a deadly and diverse source of geopolitical threat to America's ability—and willingness—to function as benign hegemon.[13] Globalization is not in the process of cancelling geopolitics.

Exactly what globalization means, let alone implies for the future, is very much an open question. The term refers simply to the contemporary fact of the dramatic increase in traffic of all kinds between societies, a traffic spearheaded by the exploitation of information technologies. Some theorists see in the process of globalization the eventual demise of the modern state, as governments are less and less able to exercise sovereign authority over concerns vital to the wellbeing of their societies. Undoubtedly it is the case that there is a much enhanced flow of communications among societies, and it is a reality that many public policy issue areas of first importance (e.g., health, crime, environment, economics) can no longer be addressed satisfactorily on a national basis. However, international security politics remains a long way from being fundamentally reshaped by the pressures of globalization.

The second threat to the policing duty inseparable from America's hegemonic status lies in the proliferation of WMD and their all too diverse means of variably reliable delivery. The problem, though possibly not its full ramifications, is already well appreciated in Washington. A national strategy document issued in December 2002 could hardly have been more explicit in identifying the threat to U.S. statecraft.

> Some states, including several that have supported and continue to support terrorism, already possess WMD and are seeking even greater capabilities, as tools of coercion and intimidation. For them these are not weapons of last resort, but militarily useful weapons of choice intended to overcome our nation's advantages in conventional forces and to deter us from responding to aggression against our friends and allies in regions of vital interest.[14]

As Joseph Joffe pointedly notes, "the United States is not strong because it has nuclear weapons; it is mighty because it can do without them."[15] It is the very mightiness of America's conventional military prowess which all but mandates nuclear acquisition by those regional states determined to discourage superpower intervention. Motives for acquisition of WMD are generally mixed, and the fearsome weapons at issue are intended to make an impression on several audiences, not excluding the domestic one.[16] The American sheriff must anticipate a twenty-first century wherein not only a roguish state here and there will in effect laugh at the idea of a global anti-nuclear taboo. The regional geopolitical rivals of those rogues will be strongly motivated to follow suit and acquire nuclear weapons of their own. Nuclear proliferation is not likely to become commonplace, as was predicted in some of the more nightmarish visions of the 1950s, but neither will it be a problem for world order that the American sheriff, or any other agent or agency, is going to be able to control rigorously.

It is not defeatist—rather, it is simply realistic—to claim that counterproliferation policy is vitally important, can register some successes, but ultimately must fail. It is sensible to be distinctly modest when defining success in this field. We will need to be satisfied with the imposition of as much delay and the terminal discouragement of as many would-be nuclear proliferants as possible. Again, Washington is admirably clearheaded on this matter. Although President Bush declaims boldly that "we will not permit the world's most dangerous regimes and terrorists to threaten us with the world's most destructive weapons," he does not encourage excessive optimism.[17] He notes that "we know from experience that we cannot always be successful in preventing and containing the proliferation of WMD to hostile states and to terrorists."[18] The policy solution to this problem is as obvious as it is certain to prove only partially successful. By utilizing a wide range of counterproliferation and non-proliferation measures, and through making serious preparation to mitigate the effects of actual use of WMD, the United States should be able to alleviate the potential for disorder that lurks in this problem area. Alleviation does not mean reversal of the trend favoring the proliferation of WMD and their means of delivery; rather does it refer to some imposition of delay and possibly some reduction in the scale of the potential problem. After all, a number of countries already have stepped back from commitment to nuclear acquisition, and at least one, South Africa, has passed from nuclear-weapon status to the virtuous condition of being a former nuclear-weapon holding state.

So, all is not lost by any means. Much can and should be done to slow the pace of proliferation, to address particularly menacing examples very directly, and to reduce the political and physical damage that the agents of this problem could wreak upon world order. However, a most uncomfortable question remains in need of answer. Looking to the longer term, will the role of sheriff be sustainable in the context of further WMD proliferation? This first-order question has yet to receive the attention that it merits. Generic arguments praising or criticizing militarily preemptive counterproliferation are important, but in the long view really are secondary. There will be occasions when preemptive action is feasible and desirable. What Americans will have to consider with the utmost seriousness is whether the probable risks and the putative rewards can be kept in a condition of tolerable balance as pivotal regional powers acquire WMD, both for the purpose of local geopolitics and as capabilities to discourage U.S. intervention in their neighborhoods. Even if the United States can provide a persuasively multifaceted military answer to a particularly threatening case, would the American public be prepared to back an active counterproliferation policy, given the risks and the stakes? In the words of the great Prussian, "war is the realm of chance."[19] If things go badly on the WMD front for the American sheriff of world order in the twenty-first century, September 11 might seem almost trivial in comparison.

Obviously my argument is not, and indeed cannot be, that the proliferation of WMD is fatal for the American policy role that is recognized and advocated here. But this text suggests that the true dimension of this threat to world order, and to those who would endeavor to protect it, has yet to be assessed properly. It is one thing to commit to being ready to go into harm's way in the face of dangerous enemies who can conceive and execute cunning asymmetric strategies.[20] It may be quite something else to knowingly take action which carries an incalculable, but possibly high, risk of America or its deployed forces suffering damage from WMD.

Military-technical competition comprises the third class of threat to American preeminence, or, more exactly, to America's ability to translate preeminence into strategic effectiveness. U.S. military preponderance over all comers, singly or in any combination, is simply a fact of strategic life in the early twenty-first century. Moreover, the U.S. lead over potential rivals in military reach and striking power is going to lengthen much further before it begins to shrink. Unfortunately for world order, these robust claims are not the last noteworthy words on the subject. This class of threat—military-technical competition—will probably not come in the form of enemies aspiring to defeat the United States in all-out war. Rather, the threat will be to the United States' ability to perform its self-appointed, and sometimes UN-blessed, mission as principal guardian of world order. Strategic history is replete with examples of great powers losing small wars.[21] It is true that both absolutely and relatively the United States is very much greater than were any of the great states of modern times, but only limited comfort should be taken from that impressive fact. The character of American military power in the twenty-first century, especially in its still growing dependence on information technologies, offers potential opportunities for exploitation by both state and transnational competitors. Such competitors will not be rivals for the sheriff's badge; by and large what they will seek is freedom of action to pursue their interests, forcefully if need be, in the neighborhoods in which they are most interested.

This class of menace to the American role has attracted attention under the general rubric of the asymmetric threat. The concept is almost painfully non-specific. An asymmetric threat is one that is different from that expected. Asymmetry is innocent of specific content.[22] But for all its vagueness and tautology, the idea of asymmetry does point usefully to the dominant terms and conditions which will characterize military-technical competition for the United States for decades to come. President Bush may well be right when he asserts determinedly that "our forces will be strong enough to dissuade potential adversaries from pursuing a military build-up in hopes of surpassing, or equalling, the power of the United States."[23] That phrasing, however, suggests a possibly anachronistic grip on the character of challenges most likely to trouble American statecraft and strategy in this new century.

It is prudent to assume that America's foes, indeed the foes of the contemporary world order, will not all be Iraqis or Talibans, or even Somalis or Serbs. We should recall that the elusive "General" Mohammed Aideed outperformed United States military leaders as a strategist. For another example, even the abominable Slobodan Milosevic, along with his military and para-military agents, was quite effective in embarrassing the might of NATO; against the European Union and the UN it had been no contest at all. The point urgently in need of recognition is that the American-protected world order will be challenged by foes great and small, employing forces both regular and highly irregular. Some conflicts will be "old-fashioned" state-centric in kind, while others will not. The United States will need to remain preponderant not only in the classic sense specified by the President in the words already quoted, truly vital though that must be. In addition, and of more near-term relevance, the United States must be able to thwart enemies of all kinds who will not aspire to surpass, or equal, American power with a competitive military build-up. America's existing and predicted military advantages over all competitors are and will be highly dependent upon the country's ability to perform strategically in permissive contexts. But it is improbable, to say the least, that U.S. military power will be able to select only those conditions for use most likely to flatter its effectiveness. Little of the recent public discussion of, and official pronouncements about, military transformation seems appropriately sensitive to the variety of prospective contextual challenges to the sheriff going about his duty. Similarly, there has been almost no focus on the distinctive challenge of winning the peace—politically, of course—once America's somewhat transformed forces have won the war. Events in Afghanistan and Iraq in 2002 and 2003 provide testimony to this fact and have illustrated its consequences.

The United States needs to stay Number One *vis à vis* a wide range of challengers whose niche effectiveness may be no less troubling just because their political ambitions will be distinctly limited. In some ways, a competitor genuinely plausible as a peer would be less stressful to the American way of defense preparation and war. Certainly the emergence of such a competitor would present the kind of military problems for which U.S. defense professionals have been waiting since at least Christmas Day, 1991, when the USSR went "chapter 11." But, as things are today, and as they are most likely to remain for some decades to come, the U.S. sheriff must achieve military, strategic, and political effectiveness against a dauntingly diverse crew of actual and potential foes.

If the United States is unbeatable in regular, symmetrical warfare, its enemies have no practicable choice other than to seek and exploit chinks in the hegemon's armor. Washington aspires to be so dominant as to terminally discourage would-be competitors. But history advises that local and regional motives to resist American pressure will be too strong, and that even the awesome and shocking prowess of a somewhat transformed U.S. military machine inadvertently will leave room for enterprising foreign strategists to penetrate.[24] In the future, when the United States finds itself in a state-centric conflict conducted by regular armed forces (what some scholars now are labeling an "old war") it will need to be prepared for unusual and unexpected enemy initiatives that may well flout the international laws of war. Truth be told, any state or group that believes itself obliged to resist the American sheriff, be it for geopolitical, cultural, or religious reasons, will have to proceed asymmetrically and be capable of acting in ways far removed from the classically military. They may not succeed. Some of the American strategic literature on asymmetric threats has been suitably paranoid concerning the possible machinations of cunning foes, but has tended to be unduly modest in neglecting to recognize adequately America's asymmetric advantages over any and all who wish it ill.

It is necessary to emphasize the problems that military-technical threats can pose when they are conceived, directed, and executed by genuinely unconventional minds, or at least by minds which follow "thoughtways" alien to the dominant American worldview.[25] The U.S. armed forces do not have an outstanding record in encouraging, nurturing, and employing unconventional talent. The checkered history of the country's special forces establishment attests to this.[26] Large, materially well-supported military establishments that pride themselves on the quality of their average units are apt to be less than enthusiastic about elite, maverick outfits. Such units tend to operate outside the regular chain of command and can have some troubling aspects of the small private army about them. Unfortunately, it is the mindset of the unconventional warrior that U.S. defense planners must seek to replicate, in order to forestall the country's enemies. America's regular military hegemony allows its foes few, save asymmetrical, options if they are to score any points beyond those accorded for brave, if hopeless, sacrifice.

These thoughts carry some troubling implications for U.S. defense policy, and for the direction that its careful and necessarily selective transformation of capabilities needs to take. The United States and the world order it strives to protect will not be menaced only by eccentrically roguish polities or transnational bodies of conspiratorial warriors for Islam. Recall that the first tranche of threat outlined above was the traditional one collectively termed the geopolitical. For decades to come, we hope, strong regional states will be in a league or two beneath that occupied solely by the sheriff of the era, the United States. From time to time, American statecraft will fall short of the Bismarckian standard and will cease to be the essential hub for the more important spokes in world politics, as Joseph Joffe explains the matter.[27] When the American sheriff becomes on balance more problem than solution, then, in the military realm, at least, regional powers will confront a choice. They must choose either to be deterred from competing—the condition that U.S. policy seeks to establish and sustain—or to seek to be able to wage war in ways different from, which is to say asymmetrical to, American expectations. The hope, if not the confident expectation, would be that cunning plans, surprising initiatives, and in general the exploitation of particular American vulnerabilities might offset many U.S. advantages, especially those of a technological kind.

At this juncture I must risk criticism for appearing to rediscover the wheel when I note that America's transforming armed forces are becoming ever more vulnerable to disruption, and one day possibly to actual defeat, by enemies able to compete all too symmetrically in cyberspace.[28] Military modernization led by information technology is the cutting edge of American transformation. The exploitation of information technology to permit network-centric operations is the center of gravity for the still expanding U.S. lead over all comers.[29] An experienced military trainer may be worrying unduly, but his claim that "our advantages in information technology are ephemeral given the cycle of advancements in that field" certainly should encourage some pause for reflection.[30] That critic, Colonel Gregory Fontenot, USA (Ret.), happens to be operating very much on the same page as the Department of Defense. The current shortlist of "transformation goals" places an appropriately heavy focus on the protection of America's information networks and on maintaining unhindered access to space.[31] Of course, aspiration is not synonymous with accomplishment. It may not take a budding Sun-tzu to realize that U.S. forces might be crippled much more effectively, and doubtless vastly more cheaply, by disruption of their information networks (for command, control, communications, and intelligence) than by force-on-force combat.

This third class of threat to America's global security role, the military-technical, therefore encompasses the kind of harassment and disruption that skilful, if irregular, cyberwarriors could inflict. In addition, it embraces the kind of niche military capabilities, including possible excellence in cyberwarfare, that regional states most certainly will develop and deploy for the purpose of discouraging an unwanted American military presence in their neighborhoods. Almost needless to say, perhaps, the WMD options cited earlier will continue to carry wide appeal as the ultimate deterrent to potential American interference. If we are fortunate, strong regional states will be providing expression to Michael Quinlan's potent thought that "a nuclear state is a state that no-one can afford to make desperate."[32] If we are not so fortunate, President Bush may prove to have been nearer the mark when he wrote that "for them [some states that have supported terrorism, already possess WMD, and are seeking even greater capabilities as tools of coercion and intimidation], these are not weapons of last resort, but militarily useful weapons of choice."[33]

If the age of mass warfare is now well behind us, it follows that most traditional measures of relative military strength are worse than useless.[34] Military effectiveness for strategic effectiveness can no longer be calculated from comparisons of armored fighting vehicles, *inter alia*, let alone of soldiers under arms. Nonetheless, before we stride off too far and too speedily toward the endorsement of post-modern notions of warfare, it would be well for the sheriff's defense experts to consider the full range of possible occasions for, and forms of, combat. The much ridiculed "principles of war" may yet have wisdom to suggest.[35] When atmospheric conditions, enemy cyberwarriors, friction, and perhaps a nuclear explosion or two to disadvantage those most dependent on electronics render the American way in war less of a transformed enterprise than we had assumed, the virtues of mass could stage a revival of effectiveness and hence a resurgence in popularity.

Predictions of relative military strength have always been complicated inconveniently by the fact that the enemy's power of resistance is "the product of two inseparable factors, viz. *the total means at his disposal and the strength of his will.*"[36] As Clausewitz proceeded to observe, "the strength of his will is much less easy to determine [than the extent of his means] and can only be gauged approximately by the strength of the motive animating it." Given that the principal strategic challenges to the American defense of world order must take the form of asymmetric threats, the new difficulties of net assessment become readily apparent.

The final of our four classes of threat to the American world-ordering role, the domestic and economic, easily merits separate book-length treatment. Many of my fellow "realist" theorists of International Relations will not be much interested in the domestic context for American statecraft and strategy. In his book outlining a bold theory of "offensive realism," John Mearsheimer admits that "the theory pays little attention to individuals or domestic political considerations such as ideology. It tends to treat states like black boxes or billiard balls."[37] He is honest enough to concede that "these omitted factors [domestic circumstances], however, occasionally dominate a state's decision-making process; under these circumstances, offensive realism is not going to perform as well."[38] Quite so. The problem is that we do not know at present just how permissive American society will prove to be of a grand policy of occasional global peacemaking. What we can assume safely, however, is that neo-realist theory of the Mearsheimer kind has some notable potential to mislead the unwary. While the global distribution of power in America's favor explains much, probably most, of what needs explaining about the U.S. role as sheriff, world politics is not by any means akin to a simple game that operates on the principle of rational choice in pursuit of maximum power and influence.

Three times in the twentieth century the United States either stepped back from, or at least obviously hesitated before accepting, international duties that were pending. This history seems not to impress neo-realist theorists overmuch. First, the country declined to participate in the new world order of the League of Nations that it had primarily helped to establish. Second, from the surrender of Japan on September 2, 1945, until the signing of the Washington Treaty (establishing NATO) on April 4, 1949, and perhaps not really until the decision was made to oppose the North Korean invasion of the South on June 25, 1950, it appeared less than certain that the United States would grasp the baton of Western leadership that non-Soviet-controlled Europe extended. Third, as suggested earlier, U.S. international policy in the 1990s was fundamentally non-serious, notwithstanding all the ink and hot air expended on the subject of America's "unipolar moment."[39] The country was more than content to leave the exceptionally ugly wars of Yugoslavian succession for its European allies, albeit mainly in European Union (EU) guise. Unfortunately, the abysmal incapacity of the Europeans all but obliged U.S. intervention, initially in 1995 and then to lead NATO's belated air campaign over Kosovo in 1999.[40] It was not plausible in the 1990s that the United States would tire of cutting a significant figure in world affairs. Indeed, the country was extraordinarily active, busying itself here, there, and nearly everywhere, as it sought to be engaged in doing good, and as it strove to enlarge the community of democracies. If generally praiseworthy intentions and a great deal of activity were guarantees of prudent statecraft and strategy, then the United States might score high for its international behavior in the first post–Cold War decade. But, alas, that is not the case. It may be a harsh judgment, but it seems accurate to claim that in the 1990s U.S. national security policy gave every appearance of being thoroughly reactive, and certainly of lacking inspiration and guidance by an organizing concept worthy of the title. Global engagement and endeavors to enlarge the column of freer-trading democracies were perfectly reasonable activities to pursue. They did not, however, begin to serve adequately as the principal source of inspiration for the lone superpower's policy guidance. Where was the needed geopolitical grasp of America's role?

Fairly active American guardianship of world order is mandated by the powerful motive of self-interest. Obedient to the strategic logic of anticipatory self-defense, the United States will not retreat into a latter-day variant of isolationism. However, U.S. national security policy could be shaped and executed to protect quite specifically American interests, where those are distinguishable amidst the traffic flows of globalized commerce. Critics of alleged American unilateralism, imperialism, hegemonism, and the rest of the evil

"-isms," might find their wishes fulfilled. The United States could decide that the role of global sheriff carried burdens that exceeded those strictly necessary to bear in self-defense. Global anti-American sentiment might have a political result we can read into the popular warning, "beware of your wishes for they may come true!" The United States is behaving as if it were the sheriff of world order for the excellent reason that it was the sole superpower left standing at the beginning of the twenty-first century. But that role is not strictly mandated by the international distribution of power, as some realist theories might have us believe. Americans could decide that the multifaceted costs of global policing, including the pain of global vilification, far exceed the probable rewards. Americans, like many other peoples, can have difficulty registering their unpopularity.[41] Even if one can proceed beyond the initial barrier of denial, it is a much greater challenge to lead Americans into a calm discussion intended to improve understanding of, though perhaps not empathy with, their quite widespread national unpopularity.

Good intentions, the authority of power, and the legitimacy conferred by popular democracy and a dynamic, if exceptionally ruthless, economic system are supposed to speak for themselves. It is generally difficult to see one's state, society, and culture as they are viewed by others. How the United States is regarded around the world matters hugely if the sheriff's role frequently requires active cooperation from abroad. It matters even if the United States asks no more than tacit acquiescence of most states and other bodies. If they do not help, it is at least strongly desirable that they not hinder. Most especially, the United States has to be alert to the possibility that errors in its statecraft could motivate several or more regional powers, including lapsed and rising great powers, to found an anti-American league. These troubling thoughts are cited here in order to suggest that the willingness of American society to endorse, and stay the course for, the sheriff's role could be vulnerable to an unfriendly international political context. The future may hold protracted difficulties for the U.S. economy, in the sharpest of contrasts with the long boom of the 1990s; some military setbacks, though hopefully not a nuclear Little Big Horn; and intense political criticism from abroad. In such conditions, Americans may decide that while it is wise to remain Number One, they will remain Number One solely to protect Number One. It would not be sensible, but domestic politics are not ruled by strategic reason. Our point is simply that American society cannot just be taken for granted as a source of compliant support for the role of sheriff, virtually regardless of the discouragement that is met in fulfilment of the duties of that informal office.

So much for the bad news, at least for a while. Now that we have recognized some of the leading threats to America's ability to perform as guardian for world order, it is time to move out smartly in a more positive vein.

SEPTEMBER 11 AND PREPONDERANCE FOR A PURPOSE

There are good grounds for optimism about the probable longevity and effectiveness of the United States' performance of the sheriff's role. The threats to that role discussed in the previous section were not knowingly exaggerated, but their presentation did provide only one side of the picture. The United States is far from helpless in the face of any of my four categories of threats: geopolitics, proliferation, military-technical competition, and domestic. This is not to express a blind confidence that Uncle Sam will muddle through regardless. But it is to say that this author is convinced that the threats that are at least generically predictable should be manageable for some, perhaps many, decades to come. There will be occasional setbacks, even defeats, but that is par for the course in global statecraft and strategy. The more ambitious the American role, the more opportunities the country is going to give its enemies to score a point or two. Hollywood will not be scripting the strategic history of future American statecraft. From time to time, poor U.S. leadership, clever enemies, and plain bad luck will produce an American humiliation, or worse. That will matter. Few of the more well-meaning critics of U.S. statecraft today give persuasive evidence of understanding the place assigned to "honor" by Thucydides. The honor, or reputation, of the American sheriff is a priceless asset. With its honor bright, the United States will not need to flex its military muscles often. Naturally, that judgment applies only to those enemies of world order who might be deterred. Some foes will be entirely beyond deterrence. Such enemies of our civilization as the members of al Qaeda, who have signed up to commit expressive, post-modern, catastrophe terrorism, need to be shot or otherwise denied the possibility of wreaking harm.

Paradoxically, perhaps, the very severity of the potential threats to American statecraft cited earlier in this chapter offers a source of reassurance. While the flaccidity, even vapidity, of U.S. policy in the

1990s must be attributed in good part to the synergistic effects of a confusing historical context and uninspired leadership, the absence of a dominant challenge must also bear some responsibility. The U.S. superpower tends to be a big game player. The no-name era that was the post–Cold War decade failed to gift American policymakers with a ready-made major challenge that might have elicited an extraordinary and creative response from Washington. For good or ill, American policymakers from both parties lacked the historical education and the imagination to know what needed doing. The fallacious but attractive beliefs corralled by scholars under the title of liberal institutionalism were endorsed by a White House that gave every appearance of not knowing what it was about in the world, or why.[42]

As Michael Howard insists, "new world orders . . . need to be policed."[43] But the post–Cold War period, which as a brief epoch terminated explosively on September 11, 2001, was interpreted and guided by no master concept for American statecraft, unless simply being a good global neighbor qualifies. There were some politicians in power in the 1990s who could boast a sound grasp of the whys and wherefores of strategic history, but they were not Americans. Alas, it is not sufficient just to have a secure grip on historically well-attested ideas; in addition one needs an authoritative base from which to speak. In the 1990s, when there was only one superstate extant, there was, ipso facto, only one practicable source of ideas for the organization and policing of world order: the United States. Today, as then, if Americans fail to step up to the challenge of defining the principal terms and conditions of international security, there is no one competent to fill the gap. As we have had occasion to comment before, for many years to come the alternatives to a world order defined, shaped, and policed principally by the United States is a general condition of disorder. Geopolitically, fairly autonomous pockets of regional order would be imposed by the strongest, or most ruthless, state in the neighborhood. Alternatively, several regions would be likely to enjoy the quality of order that would be imposed by a nuclear balance.

The ten years less three months from the formal fall of the Soviet Union to September 11, 2001, should have yielded a thoroughly persuasive education in the rougher realities of international history. The 1990s differed from the immediately preceding decades primarily in the geopolitical dimension of the distribution of power among the state players. The game of national and international security was, of course, unchanged in all essentials, as the better texts of realist scholarship maintained had to be so.[44] Thucydides, Sun-tzu, Machiavelli, and Clausewitz remained as relevant a source of cautionary wisdom as ever they had. The decade should have revealed, at least to those who believe that human security affairs can show marked progress, that the aspirations of the UN organization to play an independent, or quasi-independent, role for international security were doomed to lead to disappointment. In fact, it was worse than that because an ambitious, self-promoting UN leadership may well have misled some desperate communities, and not a few Western idealists, into the false belief that real security was on offer. For reasons many of which transcend the scope of this enquiry, the first post–Cold War decade underlined the strategic impotence of both the UN and the European Union when either sought to act for international security without benefit of U.S. participation. Indeed, from the former Yugoslavia, through Somalia, back to Bosnia, and then eventually to Kosovo, the critical nature of a U.S. military contribution was demonstrated time and again. Talismanic though an American presence was often seen to be, it most certainly offered no guarantee of success for the mission at hand: Ask those who strove against culturally impossible odds in Somalia! Flawed but nonetheless essential, having the United States on the team, which usually had to mean leading the team, hugely improved the prospect for success. Without a more than token American military contribution, the ventures in peacekeeping, let alone peacemaking, of the UN, the European Union, and even NATO, were shown to be mere adventures.

For ten years the United States played at international security, and sometimes it played hard. The President inserted himself time and again quite courageously into the murderous politics of the so-called peace processes in Northern Ireland and between Israelis and Palestinians. But there, as with the enlargement of NATO to the East, the ambivalent policy toward China (to contain or to co-opt and conciliate, or both?), and the manifest weakness of attitude toward the unmistakeable, and unmistakeably illegal, Iraqi WMD programs, American statecraft lacked a solid center. It was innocent of a steady navigational beacon to provide the guidance that policy needed from issue to issue. September 11 changed all of that.

September 11 was of course a shock to the body politic. It was also, however, an event that galvanized beneficial mobilization both of public opinion and of official attention, energy, and imagination.

September 11 created an American public mood that enabled the policy leaders of the new Bush administration to explain much more persuasively than they could before the event what the country's role, policy, and strategy in world affairs should be for the indefinite future. This book has emphasized already the essential continuities between the American role necessary if world order is to be protected in the twenty-first century and the role performed through much of the last century. The most obvious difference lies in the geopolitical context. Whether or not it was the experience of September 11, and the popular reaction to it, that spurred a new boldness of American official expression, the fact remains that the explicitly hegemonic message of *The National Security Strategy* document of September 2002 had been foreshadowed in considerable detail a decade earlier. This should occasion no surprise, since, after all, by and large the same team of strategic theorists were responsible for the key ideas common to the principal documents on both occasions.

Specifically, in 1992 Dr. Paul D. Wolfowitz, then under secretary for policy in the Pentagon, was the official most responsible for articulating and explaining an all too clear vision of American hegemony in the draft document, *Defense Planning Guidance for Fiscal Years 1994-1999*. But the first Bush administration, let alone its immediate successor, was not at all ready to step up publicly to such a policy. The draft *Guidance* document, which in the best or worst American tradition had inevitably been leaked to the *New York Times*, was abandoned, repudiated, and criticized in its more exciting aspects with almost indecent haste by the more collectivist diplomatic worldviews that held sway in those days in the White House and the State Department. Nonetheless, the idea of a preponderant America acting as the protector of world order, which official documents began presenting after September 11, reflected geopolitical reality and was a replay of an idea first articulated ten years earlier.

An outraged writer for the *New York Times* interpreted the Pentagon's 1992 vision as "a rejection of collective internationalism," whatever that obviously virtuous agency might be.[45] In addition, the newspaper was less than approving of what it interpreted, not unfairly, as "this concept of benevolent domination by one power."[46] If, as the *New York Times* revealed on March 8, 1992, the "U.S. strategy plan calls for insuring no rivals develop,"[47] what did the United States intend to do with its preponderance? In words for which the country, and even official Washington, would not be ready until

September 11, 2001, the 1992 document made a bold and sensible proclamation. It denied the practicability of the United States becoming the "world's 'policeman,' by assuming responsibility for righting every wrong," but asserted rather that "we will retain the preeminent responsibility for addressing selectively those wrongs which threaten not only our interests, but those of our allies or friends, or which could seriously unsettle international relations."[48] Theorists in the office of the Secretary of Defense in early 1992 certainly had a clear vision of America's protective role on behalf of a new world order, and they were not at all confused about the strategy that should be pursued to advance the performance of that duty. In 2002, the second Bush administration spoke, publicly at least, only about the need to "dissuade future military competition" and to "build and maintain our defenses beyond challenge."[49] But in 1992 the leaked *Defense Planning Guidance* draft had laid bare the essential geopolitical logic.

> Our first objective is to prevent the re-emergence of a new rival, either on the territory of the former Soviet Union or elsewhere, that poses a threat on the order of that posed formerly by the Soviet Union. This is a dominant consideration underlying the new regional defense strategy and requires that we endeavor to prevent any hostile power from dominating a region whose resources would, under consolidated control, be sufficient to generate global power. These regions include Western Europe, East Asia, the territory of the former Soviet Union, and South-West Asia.[50]

September 11 meant, or at least was widely interpreted to mean, that time had run out on the post–Cold War era. For ten years the United States had progressively downshifted its level of military effort, as was only to be expected following the successful conclusion of a mighty conflict. In those years the country was drawn, more than a little reluctantly, into the conduct of a range of military operations other than war, as well as into actual warfare of a character which affronted most, if not all, of the six iconic Weinberger principles. If the Gulf War of 1991 showcased the preferred American way of war, nearly everything that followed until Afghanistan 2001 was a greater or lesser affront to that "way." There were successes, to be sure. In 1995, for example, the Bosnian Serbs learned that one defies a superpower at one's own peril. In 1999, the regime in Belgrade endured the same painful instruction when it chose to cleanse Kosovo of its Albanian majority in defiance of international opinion. In this case, the opinion that mattered most was that within NATO and, most especially, within the United States. The story of the higher direction of NATO's air campaign against the former Yugoslavia in 1999 was a salutary reminder of the trials and tribulations of coalition war making to anyone in need of a refresher course on that often frustrating enterprise.[51]

Much was happening in the 1990s. The American military was busy, even as it was being reduced by a third and more, and as its equipment was aging because of the procurement holiday that celebrated the widespread belief that the era was blessedly one of strategic pause. The defense community debated the hypothesis that an information-led Revolution in Military Affairs (RMA) was underway, or should be.[52] But what was it all for? Strategy never dies, but in the United States it is apt to take a vacation from time to time.[53] From the Gulf War of 1991 to the September 11 atrocity of 2001, the U.S. defense effort was essentially bereft of the kind of hard-edged political guidance that facilitates strategic choice. The favorite concept of the decade among American defense professionals, RMA, was largely astrategic. Why was an RMA—or was it several RMAs?—being pursued? President Bush's new *National Security Strategy* document of September 2002 declared that "traditional concepts of deterrence will not work against a terrorist enemy," that "we must adapt the concept of imminent threat to the capabilities and objectives of today's adversaries," and that "the United States will, if necessary, act preemptively."[54] This was the United States adjusting its strategic thought to meet the needs presented by real world events.

September 11 provided the political context abroad and, primarily, at home that had been lacking if there was to be a major redefinition of the American role in the world, and of the policy and strategy to match. Like Pearl Harbor in December 1941, and Korea in June 1950, September 11, 2001, literally was a defining moment for American statecraft. Events not only enabled and encouraged American policymakers to face the rougher realities of world politics, they required it by their brutal challenge. The change of dramatis personae in Washington early in 2001 carried the promise of a more determined thrust in favor of defense transformation, just as it did of a more vigorous pursuit of distinctly American interests.[55] But prior to

September 11, 2001, policymakers lacked a mobilizing event, a happening that, by presenting a clear and current danger, could move the nation to step up to an expansive vision of, and strategy for, its global role and duties. September 11 was the tragic catalyst that might have been ordered from strategic history to chastise the purveyors of optimistic fantasies, yet again, and to provide at least the near-term purpose that policy and strategy so obviously needed.

It is possible, perhaps even probable, that the sheriff's role and its implied requirement for an enduring competitive advantage over any and all comers would have been articulated by the second Bush administration even without September 11. After all, the country had functioned in that role repeatedly in the 1990s. There can be no doubt, however, that September 11 made a uniquely potent contribution to the politics of national security policy and strategy. History reveals that strategic ideas and concepts for policy attain popularity when they speak to events and problems in the real world that demand urgent attention. Moreover, a September 11, like a June 25, 1950, can so change the domestic political context that a focused response to the shocking event is only a small part of the shift in policy and strategy that is ultimately effected. Before September 11, the United States leaned toward being an existential, rather than a purposefully functioning, superpower. The country was indeed preponderant in both hard power and soft power, but to what purpose was this advantage committed? America's small army of defense analysts and theorists created a library of studies on RMA, or transformation, but to what end should the country's military be transformed? Without clarity and consistency about the national role in the world, defense planning must lack intelligent guidance. Until the United States decided on its global role and faced the inherent implications of that role, it could not have grand or military strategies worthy of the title. As the bridge that relates military power to political purpose, strategy requires the bank to be firm at both ends.[56]

September 11 may have triggered what some Western commentators interpret as the first war of the twenty-first century, even the Third World War.[57] The atrocity only highlighted the need for the United States to come to terms with its role as principal global guardian; it neither created that need nor in any real sense did it define the role. The great issue of the moment, and perhaps the decade or even longer, is the transnational terrorism which stems from the accelerating crisis within Islamic societies. The sheriff for world order, which currently can only be the United States, must give high priority in its grand strategy to opposing terrorists, both for reasons of self-defense and because that happens to be the major menace of the hour. September 11 made the case to Americans that the world is a dangerous place far more persuasively than could have been achieved by any argument unaccompanied by illustrative deeds. Events themselves demonstrated that there is a danger to Americans at home. But those events also showed that the danger was born and bred far abroad, and that it was only prudent for the country to adopt a strategy that was distinctly proactive, rather than passively defensive or strictly re-active.

Quite inadvertently, Osama bin Laden provided U.S. policy and strategy with the energizing purpose that was so obviously lacking during the 1990s. Great debates about unipolarity and RMA were distinctly hollow and undisciplined because they lacked a compelling political context. That lack would not have much mattered, had the American debaters been close and admiring students of Thucydides, Machiavelli, Mahan, and Aron, to name but a few members of the realist hall of fame. But after a famous victory—in this instance a bloodless one over the USSR—liberal institutional optimism tends to reappear. The U.S. government knew that it favored a process of globalization that generally functioned to the advantage of American business. It was also convinced that the spread of democracy was in the American interest. But prior to September 11, 2001, American material preponderance and cultural influence were not related tightly and systematically to a global role that would serve as the guiding light for national security policy. That role is, of course, the one that I elect to identify as sheriff of world order.

The country has stepped up to the sheriff's role under the obvious goad of terroristic misdeeds and menace. But it is really the possibility of a WMD dimension that elevates such agents of disorder as terrorists and so-called rogue states to the level of organizing threat of the hour for American statecraft and strategy. The truth of the matter is that our ever troubled, dysfunctional global community needs policing, but the role is likely to be performed successfully only by an agent with assets of many kinds clearly superior to those of the potential disturbers of regional and world order. Material assets are not everything. Ideological and political authority, strategic inspiration, cultural influence, *inter alia*, may confound the metrics of material balance and imbalance. Nonetheless, in the last resort the polity that seeks to preserve a particular system of order and values needs to be able to stare down, or actually defeat, any challenger. The more secure the reputation as a reliable and militarily successful ordering power, the less often the threat or use of force should have to be employed.

It is greatly to the credit of American policymakers that after September 11 they placed the commitment to conduct the long-term struggle—against terrorists, against rogue states, and against either class of enemy acquiring WMD—firmly in the context of a policy of preponderance intended to support world order. The United States may have overreacted to September 11, and possibly was unwise to declare itself "at war" with terror, terrorism, and terrorists, as Michael Howard and others have argued cogently, though this author is not persuaded.[58] However, the public policy documents of the George W. Bush administration, for all their essential continuity with past endeavors, outlined a clear picture of America's role and strategy. The country was committed to remaining preponderant—hegemonic, if one prefers—or, more crudely, to staying Number One in the global geopolitical league table. The immediate driving purpose behind American preponderance, and the principal source of guidance to grand and military strategy, is unquestionably the determination to make progress against terrorists and the states that cooperate with or enable them. But the U.S. role as sheriff is neither licensed nor bounded by that particular struggle. For all its recognition of the challenge posed by post-modern and significantly transnational terrorism, American policy and strategy remains firmly anchored in a worldview that is traditional and geopolitical. Terrorism is the problem of the moment, probably of the decade, but the role of guardian of world order carries the duty to oppose and thwart potent threats of disorder from any source, be they state-centric or transnational. The United States has clearly grasped that its ability to see off the leading menaces of the period, whatever their source and character, depends vitally upon the maintenance of a useable margin of superior power and influence. Stated in the most direct way possible, America recognizes that it needs to stay Number One for as long as is feasible, including affordable. But how is that highly desirable, indeed necessary, condition to be sustained and prolonged?

KEEPING THE LEAD

The first part of this chapter provided an extensive discussion of the principal threats to America's successful performance of the role of sheriff. The threats were clustered into four columns: geopolitics, the proliferation of WMD, military-technical competition, and domestic. Not without some reservations, we resisted specifying, as a fifth class of threat, actual or potentially hostile political attitudes on the part of a significant fraction of the rest of the world toward American policy. The question is whether or not the sheriff's role is viable if it does not rest upon, at a minimum, the acquiescence of many others. That acquiescence, and in some cases enthusiastic endorsement, can be expressed quite effectively through UN procedures, especially in the voting of the Security Council. Such political approval or tolerance is denied first division status here principally because its discussion at length could distort the analysis and even imperil an argument that needs to be kept uncluttered. Because the United States is a hegemon that must lead rather than rely upon command, and lacks the power and influence to act as sheriff wherever and whenever it chooses, it will seek the cooperation of others. That cooperation may take the minimalist form of an implied grant of legitimacy, or perhaps just of an absence of obstruction, or it may appear as active assistance as a member of the American sheriff's posse, in an ad hoc coalition of the willing.

On balance, we believe it would be misleading to identify the need for international acquiescence or cooperation as a major class of threat to U.S. performance in the role of sheriff. That said, it is inevitable that a hegemon, even a benign American hegemon, is not likely to be popular for long. If it is to protect world order, the United States has to be prepared to take the lead in teaching wrongdoers the errors of their ways. As was demonstrated in 2002–03, there will usually be a majority of states' votes for peace, virtually regardless of the crimes at issue, and most of those votes will scarcely relate to the merit of proposed U.S.-led action. The superpower sheriff likes to be popular, but can settle for respect. Ultimately, the guardian power—the sheriff—in principle at least has to appear to be willing and able to do what it judges necessary for order, regardless of the extent and weight of foreign criticism. In practice, though, this should not be true. The United States will not take military action against those it deems a menace if all significant international opinion is entirely opposed—unless, that is, the action is intended to anticipate or meet a direct threat to vital American interests. International opinion is probably as much of a threat to U.S. policy as Americans choose to allow. The U.S. sheriff can, should, and assuredly will, strive to lead rather than command, but ultimately, in apt if impolitic words borrowed from a thought-provoking novel, "we are here to preserve democracy . . . not to practice it."[59]

What does the United States need to do, or at least attempt, if it is to keep that Number One billing in the hierarchy of states which is close to an absolute requirement for the sheriff's role? The scholarly and popular literatures are awash with wisdom on the crucial matter. Patent solutions, alleged keys to success, and panaceas of all kinds are truly abundant. Many of the confidently touted items of advice on policy and strategy have much to recommend them. Unfortunately, they tend toward the obvious, and hence the somewhat banal, or they express the mood and fashionable opinion of the moment. For an example of the latter phenomenon, the U.S. defense community is prone to generalize from its most recent triumph. Some officials and theorists discern an effective imperial military strategy for the United States in what, inevitably, has come to be called "the Afghan model," following the successful campaign waged against the Taliban late in 2001.[60] It calls for joint and combined forces, mixing local allies with U.S. special operations forces and distant, but on-call U.S. firepower from altitude. To those who believe that one size can fit all cases of strategic need, this model of warfare has appeared to offer a magical solution to the conduct of expeditionary warfare in the twenty-first century. They may be right, but both historical experience and common sense give us substantial grounds for skepticism. The American sheriff needs to be able to conduct operations on more than a single model, which is one reason it needs a highly adaptable military establishment. Because war is a duel, and a duel riven with friction and the play of chance, it is a hallmark of good armies that they will find ways to win; they will adapt in real time as course corrections become necessary.[61]

For now, risking a charge of banality, but not of reductionism or determinism, I will close this part of the discussion by identifying eight broad requirements for the United States to remain geopolitically Number One, a status necessary for prudent performance of the sheriff's role. The identity of these strong desiderata should be more than somewhat obvious.

First, by skilful statecraft and moderation in the practice of hegemony, the United States should be able to markedly reduce the strength of political motivation on the part of other states to form an anti-American coalition. It will not be possible to entirely discourage states from wishing to compete, but it should prove feasible to so conduct American foreign policy that the residual motive to compete in potentially hostile polities fails to achieve critical values.[62] Whether a grand global coalition dedicated to the humbling of U.S. pretensions could succeed ought never to be a question of any live policy relevance. It is all but inconceivable that the United States would so abuse its role as principal guardian of world order that, in the reasonable judgment of a great coalition of states, the need to discipline U.S. power and shrink its influence would be the overriding challenge facing international security. It is difficult even to imagine the United States reprising the hubris of, say, imperial Athens.[63] However, given the sensible current U.S. intention to discourage the rise of rival powers or coalitions, there is everything to be said in praise of a policy that would isolate potential foes, be they regional or supra-regional. Following ancient wisdom—and Bismarckian practice—which advises that potential enemies should be kept divided, the United States should seek to reduce the scale of the competitive burden that accompanies the sheriff's role. By showing a decent respect for the interests of others while remaining consistent with its world order duties, the United States should be an essential, positive contributor to security in many regions. The American sheriff should generally be regarded by local states and communities as a vital part of the solution to regional security difficulties, rather than as a significant part of the problem. However, it cannot be denied that over the issue of Iraq in 2002–03, world politics witnessed the opening moves toward the possible creation of an anti-American, which is to say an anti-hegemonic, coalition.

Second, the American hegemony—the role of sheriff—should be institutionalized as far as proves practicable, even though this is unlikely to be extensive. After all, it is as offensive to the self-regard of some states as it is necessary, and indeed comforting, to many other polities and communities. Even the most sophisticated of liberal institutional theorists fail to grasp some of the realities of the problem. Ikenberry, for example, is persuasive when he claims that "American power is made more acceptable to other states because it is institutionalized. NATO and the other security treaties establish some limits on the autonomy of American military power, although these limits are only partial."[64] He proceeds to argue "that the more that [American] power peeks out from behind these institutions, the more that power will provoke reaction and resistance."[65] Ikenberry advances a misleading half-truth, or perhaps a historical truth unsoundly generalized as a precedent, when he concludes his analysis as follows:

> Institutions can both project and restrain state power. If the United States had not endeavored to build the array of regional and global institutions that it did in the 1940s, it is difficult to imagine that American power would have had the scope, depth, or longevity that it in fact has had. International institutions can make the exercise of power more restrained and routinized, but they can also make that power more durable, systematic, and legitimate.[66]

That is true, but nowhere near as relevant and helpful for the present and future as the scholarly author imagines. What limits the practical force of Ikenberry's apparently reasonable and historically well founded argument is its sensitivity to geopolitical context. Granted, the United States would be well advised to seek such institutional cover and support as can be extracted from other states via the collective security framework of the UN, or the regional collective defense arrangements of NATO. But the price that the sheriff might have to pay for that cover and support could be so heavy as to thwart performance. If the international institutionalization of American power is promoted from its proper sphere—that of a good idea in principle—to the status of a requirement before action can be taken, the result must be the gratuitous strategic enfeeblement of the sheriff. Theorists such as Ikenberry fail to appreciate how inappropriate the analogy is between U.S. power institutionalized and allegedly somewhat tamed by Cold War NATO and that power disciplined by international institutions in the absence of a dominant geopolitical rivalry. In the former case, the United States could be strategically effective because the geopolitical context was so structured as to lend focus and, periodically, urgency to a clear, principal security duty— the containment of the Soviet imperium. But in the geopolitical context of the early twenty-first century, most states discern no real urgency about, or truly agree on, the sheriff's principal security duty. In this new geopolitical context, the international institutionalization of U.S. power is more apt to produce paralysis than the strength of which Ikenberry writes. This is not to praise, and still less is it to urge, unilateralism. However, it is to claim that the price demanded for the additional legitimacy and durability which the institutionalization of multilateralism may well convey is one which frequently would condemn the American sheriff to ineffectiveness. Manifest strategic failure as sheriff of world order would do more damage to the legitimacy and durability of U.S. power and influence than would the occasional showing of some prudent disdain for the opinions of Upper Volta, or even of France and other permanent members of the UN Security Council.

Third, the United States needs to protect the economic, technical, and cultural bases of its contemporary hegemony. In truth these three dimensions of national power and influence should be regarded holistically as one. American military preponderance is not matched at all closely by dominance in the economic and cultural spheres. But American culture is extraordinarily friendly to innovation and encouraging to risk-takers. The necessary economic basis for a U.S. grand strategy of global guardianship appears secure because the country's economic edge is so rooted in conducive attitudes and institutions as to warrant description as cultural. However, although American social mores, institutions, and laws are powerful enablers for the wealth creation that must underpin performance as sheriff, less-favored polities will certainly be able to compete. They may not be able to compete overall, but they probably will not believe that they need to do so. Foes with clever strategists will be motivated to seek out and exploit niche vulnerabilities in the whole architecture of U.S. power and influence.[67] The country may be wise to advance and protect its multi-dimensional strength by pursuing a strategy of "global openness," to quote Bacevich.[68] However, in some key areas, especially the technical and managerial, a more globalized context is one wherein enemies might find ways to compete effectively, if possibly asymmetrically. Bacevich offers a very explicit argument for the "American empire." But even if one perceives less consistency of purpose behind U.S. policy than he does, he still underlines my third requirement for a United States that needs to keep its international lead in order to function as sheriff. He argues that

> those who chart America's course do so with a clearly defined purpose in mind. . . .

That purpose is to preserve and, where both feasible and conducive to U.S. interests to expand an American imperium. Central to this strategy is a commitment to global
openness—removing barriers that inhibit the movement of
goods, capital, ideas and people. Its ultimate objective is the
creation of an open and integrated international order based on
the principle of democratic capitalism, with the United States as
the ultimate guarantor of order and enforcer of norms.[69]

This is not wrong, but it may be overstated. To the no doubt
substantial degree to which Bacevich is correct, it behooves us to
remember that the vision of global openness which is central to his
reading of recent U.S. policy is a potent source of those liberal fantasies that continue to harass efforts at prudent statecraft. One problem in particular merits emphasis. The information technologies that
are purportedly critical to future wealth creation, and are both indi-
rectly and directly essential to the quality and quantity of America's
military prowess, are probably relatively easy to offset and disrupt.
Exactly what strategic benefits might flow from successful competition in the conduct of information warfare is quite another matter.
The point in need of emphasis is simply the nonexclusive nature of
this most central, indeed most characteristic, feature contributing to
the contemporary American preponderance.[70]
   Fourth, it should go without saying that America's performance
in the role of sheriff of world order can endure no longer than its
military preeminence. This is not to deny that military power rests
upon economic strength, social attitudes, and political culture. However, wealth and sensible attitudes are of little use if they are not
mobilized and organized into usable military capabilities. In the political context outlined above under points one and two, a judicious
combination of sustained, unmatched financial allocations to defense
functions, along with an intelligent commitment to modernization,
should preserve the U.S. military lead for as long as is feasible. It is
important to recognize that the character of a meaningful military
lead must be distinctly enemy and scenario specific. The United States
requires military power both so formidable that would-be enemies
are greatly discouraged from attempting to compete, as well as so
flexible, adaptable, and decisively useable as to carry the highly plausible promise of being able to impose prompt defeat upon any enemy. So much for aspirations. In practice, the enemies of America's

world order will assuredly seek to compete militarily in practicable ways. It is to be hoped that American military prowess will be so broad and flexible that neither rogues nor traditional foes will find military paths for effective competition, symmetrical or asymmetrical. The military power of the American sheriff must imply reassurance to many and contingent menace to a few. For some years to come, at least pending the emergence of a serious geopolitical rival, the threats inherent in the U.S. military establishment carry no specific address label: They are simply addressed to those whom this military power must concern. Although mass is always important in military affairs, how best to maintain, and preferably, to extend, a long military lead is not so easily calculated as once seemed possible. Net assessment was rarely as straightforward an exercise as was implied by journalists' lists, comprising, say, soldiers under arms, divisions, and equipment holdings. With the age of mass warfare probably defunct, for the United States at least, the military lead in need of protection and enhancement is the lead that translates into desired strategic outcomes. For many people, this requires a traumatic shift of analytical focus from military inputs to military outputs and their probable political consequences. At the time of this writing, the military profession in the United States and Britain has discovered what it terms "effects-based warfare."

Fifth, it will be vital for the American defender of world order to protect its reputation for militarily effective and politically well judged performance. This can be expressed as the necessity for the United States to guard its honor. What do we mean by honor? Historian Donald Kagan advises that "arguments about morality and ideology involve what Thucydides called honor, and nations from antiquity to our own world cannot ignore it. To exclude such considerations is to engage in the opposite of 'realism.'"[71] Because of friction, sheer bad luck, cunning and competent enemies, and occasional sub-par U.S. policy and strategic performance, from time to time America will fail and be seen to fail. Such experiences will probably have a salutary effect upon a national security community at risk of infection by that sometimes fatal malady of greatness—victory disease. However, the sheriff of world order, the last—and sometimes the first—line of protection for the desperately beleaguered worldwide, cannot afford to make a habit of defeat and humiliation. A reputation for probity and wealth ensures the kind of credit rating that precludes the necessity to pay cash. Similarly, a national reputation for political consistency and strategic effectiveness minimizes the number of occasions when military power actually has to be applied. Since the United States acts on behalf of the entire world order, every polity, international security institution, and political interest, except possibly one dedicated to some brand of disorder, has a significant stake in the protection of America's honor as lawman. Even criminals have interests that may need protection against raids by other criminals. The more reluctant America is to take action against regional bullies, transnational terrorists, and those who tolerate them, and the more forgiving it appears to be of aggressive behavior by a rising China or a returning Russia, the more encouragement will be taken by those who find the contemporary rules of the international road unacceptably constraining. The U.S. sheriff requires a reputation for not shirking the tougher duties involved in policing world order. It needs to be trusted to perform them, either to a decisively victorious conclusion or at least to the point where major strategic advantage is gained.[72] The enjoyment of such a high reputation for effectiveness will not, in itself, keep the peace. But it will be mightily discouraging to those many potential agents of disorder who might be influenced by deterrence, other forms of discouragement, or even perhaps a well-crafted strategy for positive inducement.[73] Bribery is usually cheaper than war, provided it is seen as integral to a policy of strength and not of weakness.

Sixth, America's benign hegemony and performance in the role of sheriff will be prolonged if its political leaders select strategies that work well in practicable missions. This advice is much easier to give than it is to apply. Officials, theorists, journalists, and voters are all apt to forget Clausewitz's potent words of caution: "No other human activity [than war] is so continuously or universally bound up with chance. And through the element of chance, guesswork and luck come to play a great part in war."[74] As we shall develop in the next chapter, truly strategic thinking, planning, and performance are certain to be at a premium if America's aspirations to protect world order are to endure long into this new century. There will be conflicts in the future which will share with those against Iraq in 1991, Taliban-Afghanistan in 2001, and Iraq again in 2003, the attractive feature that they would have been extremely difficult to lose. However, U.S. strategic performance in those famous victories was less than totally convincing. Clausewitz's advice is more quoted than followed by Washington. He advised, of course, that "war is simply the continuation of political intercourse, with the addition of other means."[75] Although much good work was done for regional order in 1991, 2001, and 2003, victory in 1991 failed to resolve the problems posed by the beast of Baghdad; victory in 2001 was secured over the hapless Taliban rather than the sterner stuff that was the true foe of order, al Qaeda; while the military victory of 2003 was but the precursor to the strategic challenge of winning the peace. A country as abundantly resourced as the United States, unused to waging closely contested conflicts against worthy, if smaller, enemies, is not in the habit of devoting much effort to strategic thought. This can prove expensive. Strategic effect is the consequence of military threat and actual use. Whether or not a particular world-ordering duty is prudent must depend critically both on American leaders' performance as strategists and on how lethal American arms prove to be in combat against an enemy that may deserve respect as a strategic actor.

Seventh, the American sheriff cannot police world order if domestic opinion is not permissive. The longevity of U.S. guardianship depends vitally upon the skill, determination, and luck with which the country protects and burnishes its reputation for taking strategically effective action. But it also depends upon the willingness of American society to accept the costs that comprise the multi-faceted price of this particular form of glory. The American public is probably nowhere near as casualty-shy as popular mythology insists, though the same cannot be said with equal confidence of the professional American military. Such, at least, are the conclusions of the major recent study on this much debated subject.[76] It is the opinion of this author that popular American attitudes toward casualties stem fairly directly from the sense of involvement, or lack of the same, in the matters at issue. If valid, this judgment is good news for the feasibility of U.S. performance in the sheriff's role, but a dire systemic problem may still remain. Specifically, as principal global guardian, the United States risks being thwarted on the domestic front by the central and inalienable weakness that mars attempts to practice the theory of collective security. Bacevich and others advance powerful arguments connecting American strategic behavior to the promotion of what they see, not wholly implausibly, as an informal American empire. But many, if not most, American voters will be hard to convince that U.S. military action is warranted save in those mercifully rare instances when it is directed to thwart some clear and present danger. A doctrine of military preemption, typically meaning prevention, no matter how strategically prudent, will be as difficult to justify domestically as abroad. There is an obvious way to diminish the amount, intensity, and duration of domestic political opposition to military operations conducted for purposes that do not resonate loudly on Main Street. That solution is to adopt a style of warfare that imposes few costs on American society, especially in the most human of dimensions—casualties. But since war is a duel, the United States' ability to perform all but painlessly as sheriff can never lie totally within its own control. Nonetheless, the potential problem of a reluctant domestic public should be eased if care is taken in selecting policing duties and if the troops who must execute the strategy are tactically competent. All of this would be more reassuring were we not respectful students of Clausewitz's teaching that "war is the realm of chance," an aphorism that we have had occasion to quote before.

Eighth and finally, the point made immediately above concerning the necessity for, and possible fragility of, domestic support requires us to state that the American sheriff will be able to sustain the role only if it is willing and able to bear the pain of casualties. We must anticipate that pain to include occasionally suffering casualties on a relatively heavy scale. Much earlier in this chapter, we outlined the menace posed by WMD to American performance on behalf of world order. It is virtually axiomatic that the sheriff's role is feasible only against the backdrop of a serious commitment to provide for homeland security. That security needs to be measured against both threats stemming from traditional geopolitical sources, though probably manifested in somewhat asymmetric form, and the menace posed by highly irregular enemies who do not operate consistently from a fixed address. A geographically forward national security policy, which lends itself to explanation either as a global guardianship for world order or as a prudently expansive approach to self-defense, should arrest most growing menaces before they mature. However, no U.S. policy can be 100 percent successful in nipping burgeoning dangers in the bud. Bear in mind that there is no time limit on U.S. performance as sheriff for world order. The country seeks to remain Number One, and to be ready to act against the agents of disorder, for as long as should prove practicable. Offensive and defensive counterforce options will certainly help reduce the risks to American forces abroad and to the American homeland. However, they will not eliminate those risks. Moreover, in the future those risks must include a strong likelihood of enemy action with WMD. There is no all-purpose "silver bullet" panacea to remove this peril. Our final point is that the United States needs to think in a much more sophisticated and differentiated way than it has in the past about what might be achieved by dissuasion, deterrence, coercion, and—as an essential addition—positive inducement or bribery. Ultimately, though, there is no evading the fact that Robert Kagan points out so effectively in one of the epigraphs to this book: "outlaws shoot sheriffs, not saloon keepers."[77] If the United States cannot bear the pain that forceful police work for world order will surely bring, then it had better effect a prompt change in its international role, policy, and strategy. Whether, or to what degree, defense policy and strategy might control the risks that attend global policing is the subject to which this analysis now turns.

CHAPTER 4
The Strategic Dimension

U nfortunately, Plato spoke for all time when he declaimed pessimistically that "only the dead have seen the end of war." That familiar aphorism bears frequent quotation because we classical realist theorists, with our somewhat unfashionable positivist approach to world politics and security, are always trying to dodge the slings and arrows of a legion of optimistic liberals.[1] Many liberals believe, as an attractive article of faith, that "this time" things will be better—which is to say they will be different from the 2,400-year-long course of history from Plato's time until today. Liberals of various stripes are not entirely wrong in believing that we humans can improve the way we make provision for peace. They are just mistaken when they confuse occasional eras of relative stability and good order with a progressive and generally linear trend. This author knows of no plausible reason why the twenty-first century might lack a strategic history. That is to say, our future will be influenced, perhaps even shaped, by the threat or use of force. The force will not always be applied in regular and familiar ways by states, but it will be warfare nonetheless. It is time, perhaps even more than time, for this book to deal explicitly with the vital military dimension of its argument. The narrative trajectory below proceeds first from policy to strategy, to connect the extensive earlier discussion of America's role in the world with the realization of that role in practice, especially in the vital military regard. Next, the analysis considers the all-important subject of strategic performance. In particular, the discussion reviews actual and potential impediments to success. Finally, the chapter focuses on the promise, and on some of the possible consequences, of the current U.S. commitment to a long-term process of military transformation. The discussion explores the limitations of an even somewhat transformed military establishment in the contexts both of war as a whole and of strategy in particular. Some problems characteristic of the American superpower are treated with particular attention. The role of technology in relation to human agency is one such problem area. Other areas include the possibilities that American society and its armed forces may be risk-averse to a strategically inhibiting degree and that a country so evidently militarily mighty may become perilously disdainful of asymmetric enemies.

FROM POLICY TO STRATEGY

Lest there be any misunderstanding, I must emphasize the primary, first-order importance of the strategic dimension to America's role in the world. This all but invites misunderstanding. To reduce, though probably not eliminate, that possibility, everything that follows in this chapter about military matters is written in the context of appreciation of the merit in some extra- and even anti-military arguments. War should be threatened or waged only for political purposes. Military power is not self-validating. "Strategic nihilists," as Eliot Cohen perceptively calls root-and-branch skeptics of strategy,[2] challenge the Clausewitzian dictum that war must be an act of policy, or at least of politics. If politics is master, then the economic and social contexts that provide the surplus wealth to fund the military establishment are, in a sense, fundamental.

To the primacy of politics and the critical value of taxable wealth and public support (willing citizens), we must add the importance both of diplomacy in general and of taking necessary coercive actions with whatever substantive assistance and political protection allies can afford. Furthermore, we grant readily that America is a potent civilization, and is indeed potent as a civilization. Those who stress the importance of the "soft power" that is American culture are right to do so.[3] Therefore, our argument is in no sense dismissive of or indifferent to the political, economic, and cultural dimensions of national and international security. It is precisely because of the obvious priority given the political guidance implicit in America's chosen role in the world that detailed discussion of the strategic dimension is presented this late in our enquiry. But now, at this juncture, it is essential that military matters not be slighted.

Sheriffs are sheriffs because they can shoot, not because they are rich, erudite, or popular. Naturally, life is easier for a state-sheriff if it is extraordinarily wealthy, if it is governed by wise people with a sound grasp of what is required for policing world order, and if it can carry much of global opinion with it due to the skill of its diplomacy.

Ultimately, however, the sheriff of world order can only function as such if it is a military superstate. History records the deeds of very few such. The leading state of an era has typically been primarily continental or maritime in orientation, each with different implications for order, and almost invariably has found its preeminence checked by the collective efforts of fearful rivals.[4] Largely by geopolitical accident, the United States now finds itself the "last polity standing" from the great powers of modern times. Moral force is not to be despised and diplomatic cunning is always useful, but in the final analysis world order needs protecting by a state or coalition that is willing and able to exercise superior coercion. Of course, there is much more to the guarding of world order than the readiness to inflict pain upon those who would disturb the norms of civilized behavior. But if the military dimension of the ordering role is ineffective, it is not usually possible to find adequate compensation elsewhere—at least not for long. Revolutionary powers, would-be hegemons, regional bullies, transnational terrorists, and other troublemakers cannot long be held in check by bribes or imaginative diplomacy, let alone by appeals from decent international opinion or nose counts in the United Nations. The extant world order needs someone willing and able to stand up for it in the face of the ultimate threat—the threat of war. If the United States gets the military dimension seriously wrong in its commitment to international security, nothing else will matter very much. Military humiliation and defeat could cancel the benefits from "soft power" and from a globalized, open world trading system. Crude and old fashioned though it may be, military power in its many forms is an enduring threat to order. It can only be dissuaded from appearing when it is challenged on its own terms.

Sheriff is a role and not a strategy. The principal guardian of world order commits to defend and advance the rules of tolerable international behavior against whoever chooses to challenge them. If we assume that the United States will play the role of sheriff for many decades to come, we must also assume that the identity and character of the dominant contemporary threat to order will likely shift several times during America's watch. The United States may be playing a fundamentally defensive political role, but it does not follow that U.S. military strategy should also be defensive. Not infrequently, the guardian polity is obliged to conduct an offensive military operation because an agent of disorder needs to be turned out of its ill-gotten gains. So it was in 1990–91, for example, over Iraq's seizure of Kuwait. Aggressors are typically delighted to allow diplomacy to legitimize their crimes. In addition to the familiar need to compel aggressors to disgorge their gains, some kinds of threats to regional or world order are better stifled in their infancy when they cannot be prevented altogether. U.S. Secretary of Defense Donald Rumsfeld is characteristically plain-speaking on this matter. He observes that "people are used to a different century. People are used to Pearl Harbor. They are used to being attacked and then responding."[5] In a period when deterrence and even coercive diplomacy have lost much of their shine, the case for military coercion applied preemptively has quite suddenly assumed all but unchallengeable strategic authority.[6] Political and moral authority is, of course, quite another matter. World opinion has yet to come to grips with the grim operational necessities that must govern action against agents of disorder who may be beyond deterrence and who could be armed with WMD. To respond after the dread event would be too late. To eschew timely offensive action to disrupt, and hopefully destroy, the WMD threat before it could be launched would be to place a wholly unreasonable burden of perfect performance on active and passive defenses alone. Historical experience, along with the rules of good military practice—sometimes known as the principles of war—argue strongly against conceding the initiative entirely to enemies whose strategic culture has not been molded in graduate seminars at Harvard or Columbia.

To find the strategy that fits the role of sheriff and the policy of protecting world order is not as simple a matter as one might believe. It is certainly true, as this text has cited already, that U.S. budgetary allocations to defense functions are in a quite extraordinary class of their own. Moreover, this is a fact which is likely to persist for many years, probably several decades, to come. Naturally, it is a source of huge advantage to be able to outspend militarily not only any rival or coalition of rivals, but in effect the rest of the world combined. However, one should not be too easily dazzled by defense inputs, when, after all, it is defense outputs that are the metrics of interest. How much military effectiveness will the United States buy for its tax dollars? Even more important, upon how much strategic effectiveness will the country be able to rely?[7] And, to be truly demanding and determinedly Clausewitzian, how much political effectiveness will the United States be able to achieve and sustain as a consequence of its military and strategic prowess? As the great theorist maintained, *"war is only a branch of political activity."*[8] Global military domination by the American sheriff would seem to be assured by the brutal logic of raw economics. After the fashion of the leading European soccer teams, but in sharp contrast to the practices permitted in America's NFL, the United States should be able to buy itself several decades, and probably longer, of military preponderance.

In practice, though, the kind of military dominance that is necessary for performance of the role of global sheriff should not be assumed to flow automatically from America's awesome lead in defense investment. It matters how the United States spends its defense dollars and it matters even more how the country employs the military power created and sustained by that investment. Context is crucial. As deterrence cannot reliably be purchased directly, regardless of the potency of the military machine acquired, so strategic and political effectiveness do not stand in a linear relationship to defense investment. This is because the strategic context wherein U.S. military power is tested is notably complex. As sheriff for world order, the United States does not inhabit a realm that in its military dimension lends itself to simple attritional modelling. That military dimension cannot always be assured with complete confidence on the basis of comparisons of defense inputs. If military strength was approximately of the same character from country to country and stateless group to stateless group, and if it could be translated into strategic, then political, effect with the assistance of a global conversion chart, then we could speak with more confidence of American military preponderance. Even then, the challenge of accurate net assessment, taking account of the fact that war is a duel, might well prove beyond us. To possess a great deal, even a seemingly overwhelming quantity, of military power is not necessarily to be very powerful in particular contexts. American military strength may be negated, or at least much reduced, by political, legal, and moral constraints; by a character of conflict, including geopolitical and geographical contexts, that hugely privileges the regional foe; and by an enemy who is able to wage a style of war at every level—strategic, operational, and tactical—that reduces the nominal potency of American military power.[9]

Two important questions overhang this discussion, with the answer to the second depending critically on the answer to the first. First, must the U.S. defense effort be substantially reshaped to cope optimally with the dominant threat of the era? At present that threat is defined as the menace of terrorism, and especially of terrorism that might involve WMD. Second, has the United States devised, or is it in the process of devising, a new method of warfare that is well suited to meet any challenge during this period? Rephrased, does the country essentially face one kind of threat, to which a single style of military response is most appropriate? We will argue that although terrorism may well persist indefinitely, it is not likely to effect a definitive replacement of traditional geopolitical difficulties. On that logic, the United States does not have the luxury of being able to conduct its defense planning with virtually sole reference to the irregular class of threat posed by terrorists. Even if counterterrorism is appropriate as the dominant organizing concept of this period, for how long will this period endure? We argued earlier in this book that the United States, though accelerated in its acceptance of the role of sheriff by the events of September 11, 2001, is in that role by virtue of its geopolitical preeminence. The American role did not begin with, is not defined by, and will not be restricted to countering terrorists and their state supporters.

Major items of military equipment, certainly the principal platforms or vehicles, are designed to perform through a service life of thirty years or longer.[10] They need to be adaptable to potentially major changes in the threat environment. Should the United States decide to adopt a particular style of war exclusively, it would be choosing to discount Clausewitz's words of warning about war as "the realm of uncertainty."[11] The problems would be twofold. The preferred American way of war might not provide effective answers to some future threats. In addition, even if America's military style does carry a convincing promise of being able to achieve decisive success, intelligent and capable, which to say adaptive, enemies may find ways to wage war that would negate some of its strengths. To repeat the fundamental Clausewitzian point that "war is nothing but a duel on a larger scale" is not to say anything specific about any particular war.[12] However, it is to remind those who may benefit from the reminder that interaction is basic, indeed literally essential, to the very nature of war. States can grow so arrogant with military success, or so desperate with the need for such success, that they forget that war is a duel and that the enemy may prove to be tactically, operationally, and even strategically adaptive.[13] He may not be able to adapt sufficiently or quickly enough, but it is never prudent to underestimate him. Every war is a learning process for both sides. Today's military solution is apt to be tomorrow's military mistake, because of the paradoxical logic of conflict. What works well today will not work well tomorrow precisely because it works well today.[14] The choice of formulae for military success all but invites enemies to design ways to frustrate their predictable application. The simpler the preferred way of war, the fewer major variants a belligerent can play out and the simpler the task of the adaptive duelling foe.

The argument above is offered only by way of a necessary caveat. It is not a prediction that America's enemies will often be able to succeed through smart adaptive behavior. Nonetheless, since the country first emerged as a military superpower in the 1940s, every enemy of the United States has adapted its style of warfare in an effort to offset U.S. advantages. From the Germans to al Qaeda, with North Koreans, Chinese, North Vietnamese, Somalis, Serbs, and others in between, America's more competent enemies look for the weaknesses that may lurk in and around particular U.S. strengths. The less flexible the American way of war, notwithstanding its undoubted potency under favorable conditions, the more likely are materially much weaker, but perhaps strategically more intelligent, enemies to find workable solutions to the problems posed by American military prowess. Most obviously, for example, if the American way in high-technology warfare promises lethal strikes against identified assets, the obvious answer is to hide those assets. War continues to be a tactical duel between hiders and finders, as it does between defense and offense. Similarly, the conduct of war remains the product of a constant dialogue between fire and movement. These pairings—hiding and finding, defense and offense, fire and movement—are persisting fundamentals in the very structure of warfare. They are not abolished or decided definitively on one side or the other by new technologies or styles in war.[15]

So much for sounding a warning against the perils of unduly reductive, albeit militarily powerful, formulaic approaches to warfare, at least for the moment. Despite the many direct and implied criticisms of, and caveats concerning, American military power that are increasingly prominent in this chapter and the next one, my argument is basically optimistic. I am what might be called a strategic positivist. I believe not only that strategy per se is feasible, in contrast to the strategic nihilism of, say, John Keegan, but that it is possible to identify key elements of a military strategy for the United States which should be good enough to serve as the sword arm of the global sheriff.[16]

The sheriff must have a broad strategy, and the military capabilities to give life to that grand design, if political vision and policy are not to be mere windy rhetoric. Because strategy is an exceptionally difficult function to perform competently, it is quite common to find it seriously neglected.[17] Policymakers, as professional wordsmiths, are wont to paint attractive pictures of their vision of global order, a brighter future, and so forth. They are obliged to descend quite frequently into the more contentious regions of policy controversy, a process that is likely to see them energetically debate policy goals. Meanwhile, down on the farm, as it were, the defense community—quite narrowly understood—is doing the best job it can with the dollars available to be responsive to such policy guidance as comes its way. At the same time, American defense professionals must lead, or at least be well in touch with, the exploitation of developments in military and relevant civilian science.[18] Lest the structural point has been lost somewhere in the course of this tale, strategy is the function, the activity, that should link the military forces that the defense community provides with the much more rarefied and politically superior realm of policy. In practice, the proper relationship between war and policy may often seem to have been reversed, with the latter serving the former rather than vice versa. However, Clausewitz explained the basic chain of authority in words that should serve for all times and occasions: "Subordinating the political point of view to the military would be absurd, for it is policy that creates war. Policy is the guiding intelligence and war only the instrument, not vice versa. No other possibility exists, then, than to subordinate the military point of view to the political."[19] We strategic positivists like our authorities to be as clear as they are uncompromising in the basic architecture of their argument. But in the real world of actual policymakers, defense planners, and warriors, the bridge that is strategy is frequently in poor repair, if it can be located at all.

Strategy will always be at work during a conflict in the form of strategic effect, whether or not we, or the enemy, have purposeful strategies in the sense of plans.[20] Remember the venerable quip, although you may not be interested in strategy, strategy is interested in you? That familiar saying had a particular piquancy during the Cold War in the context of the mutual hostage relationship which bound together the societies of the two superpowers.[21] The binding was probably not as close in strategic terms as it seemed to the American celebrants of a symmetrical condition of vulnerability to assured destruction. Prospective symmetries of societal holocaust might not have translated automatically into strategic and political symmetries. Though admittedly an extreme case, that example of distinctive political and strategic cultures points to a subject of great significance for an American superpower that is required to coerce and influence peoples whose worldviews are different from those familiar along the Potomac.

Crises large and small will come and go, and wars both bloodily messy and seemingly neatly surgical will punctuate the future as they have the past. Those events will need a good enough strategic performance by the guardian of world order. Many people have difficulty understanding the nature and function of strategy. They have little difficulty with the concept of political vision—an open, U.S.-friendly world or an American imperium, for example—or policy, and even less difficulty with the meaning of military power. But what is strategy? And how does it work? Politicians and their advisers are experts at crafting policy, just as soldiers have traditionally been viewed as the professionals in "the management of violence."[22] Who is it, though, that patrols the no-man's land between politics and military force? That is the realm where strategists should roam. Where and how were they trained to be strategists, since excellence in the strategic dimension of life (and death) does not appear to figure prominently in many people's curricula vitae?

STRATEGIC PERFORMANCE

To be effective as global sheriff for as long as possible, the United States will need to perform with a skill in strategy that it has shown all too rarely since it emerged out of the shadows onto the center stage of world politics. It is a useful exaggeration to argue that the modern United States, once mobilized for war, was so powerful that it had scant need of strategy. In other words, only infrequently did it really need to make hard choices among competing means, methods, and objectives. A happy condition of material abundance allowed Americans the luxury of avoiding many of the tougher decisions that faced strategists in less well endowed belligerent nations. The costs of playing sheriff for a typically ungrateful and often resistant world may well encourage more purposefully strategic performance from the U.S. government, though I doubt it. People and organizations tend to continue doing what they have always done and what they believe works well enough for them.[23] Persuading Americans to think intelligently, even frugally, rather than to cover most possibilities with the products of abundance, would be a hard sell. Nonetheless, changes in strategic and military culture can and do occur. Moreover, very rarely, a country may radically change the way it wages war. Such an RMA, or transformation, can occur, but it is always likely to be over-sold, as these developments invariably are and indeed probably need to be. Whether or not the United States is currently undergoing a process of military transformation worthy of the name, and what the implications might be for military, strategic, and political effectiveness, is an important subject to debate. Suffice it for the present to record a brief word of caution, even skepticism, when claims of military revolution are in the air. Changes in American society and technology assuredly might overturn the way of war that was authoritative from the time of Ulysses S. Grant until that of Colin Powell and Norman Schwarzkopf.[24] And the new American way might appear ideally suited to the rougher needs of imperial governance.[25] But still there are points to ponder in Samuel P. Huntington's words from 1986:

> The United States is a big, lumbering, pluralistic, affluent, liberal, democratic, individualistic, materialistic (if not hedonistic), technologically supremely sophisticated society. Our military strategy should and, indeed, must be built upon these facts.[26]

With almost painful candor Huntington argues that "bigness not brains is our advantage, and we should exploit it."[27] The proposition is that, primarily courtesy of an information-led RMA, the armed forces of the United States can transform themselves into an imperial police force able to enforce order with rapier-like precision. The idea is not entirely ridiculous, but it invites challenge on several fronts. To name but a few of the more obvious grounds for concern, Will the somewhat selectively transformed American military perform as well as expected? Will America's foes find ways to thwart, or at least painfully harass, the new American way of war? How will American forces control the former "battlespace" once it has won the war with precision fire and decisive maneuver? After all, success in war is about the character of political context that it creates. Will the much-advertised military transformation prove to be so partial, even so superficial, that the military establishment will rapidly revert when under pressure? One must add that it may not be bad if the prophets of, and executive agents for, American military transformation are somewhat frustrated by resistant institutions, society, and culture. Military revolutions, by their very nature, are likely to imperil what is valuable as well as what is harmful in the forces, institutions, and doctrines they are revising. History suggests that it is no small matter to overturn a long-settled, preferred national way of defense preparation and conduct in war. Of course, social attitudes evolve, but one should still be cautious of welcoming new ways in warfare, almost regardless of how favorable to the performance of the sheriff's role they appear to be. With Clausewitz in mind, we must never forget that the greater the benefits we anticipate from a new approach to the use of force, the greater must be the motivation of our enemies to seek out ways to frustrate it.[28]

Huntington has argued wisely that "American strategy…must be appropriate to our history and institutions, both political and military. It must not only be responsive to national needs but also reflect our national strengths and weaknesses. It is the beginning of wisdom to recognize this."[29] When we consider the military implications, both probable and possible, of the role of global sheriff, we should also consider some of Eliot Cohen's words. Cohen braves the reality that an important truth can appear banal when he claims that "it is a sociological truism that military organizations reflect the societies from which they emerge, and here at least the United States is no exception."[30] Many beliefs about allegedly dominant attitudes in American society—casualty shyness, for a leading example—may well be largely mythical, or at least unsound.[31] But what most emphatically is not mythical is the great and persisting difficulty the American defense establishment finds in performing in a purposefully strategic manner.

By strategic performance I mean purposeful strategic performance for specific intended consequences, not merely the strategic effect that any threat or use of force must have. One need not have a strategy in order to function strategically. The key difference is that if one has a strategy one might perform strategically well, whereas if one does not one is all but certain to perform poorly. As a distinctly unfashionable classical realist positivist, this author believes that the military dimension of America's role as sheriff lends itself to analytical treatment focusing on a shortlist of elements vital to the country's strategic performance. Some of these points have been raised already, others not. These elements, discussed briefly below following an analysis of strategy itself, tell us most of what we need to know about how America can maximize its prospects of succeeding militarily as sheriff, always given a tolerably permissive political context (e.g., assuming that a great coalition is not forged to oppose American influence).

The master characteristic necessary for superior U.S. strategic performance has to be an educated respect for strategic thought, strategic planning, and purposeful strategic behavior. As often as not the absence of purposeful strategy will pass unnoticed, so unfamiliar are its thoughtways to most people. Moreover, because American political culture with reference to national security has decided that strategy is desirable, even essential, it is a potent criticism, if sustainable, to accuse an administration of not having one. it is probably preferable to be accused of pursuing the wrong strategy than it is to appear guilty of lacking a strategy altogether. In truth, strategy is extraordinarily difficult to do well, and errors in its performance have a way of lingering on with a lethal half-life that can persist for generations, even from war to war.

Broadly viewed, there are at least five classes of difficulty likely to impede the quality of purposeful strategic effort. As mentioned above, "strategist" is not a job description that one encounters very often. The strategist is the person who asks and answers the "so what" question. Following Clausewitz, as we should for want of a better guide, we know that strategy is about "*the use of engagements for the object of the war.*"[32] The first class of difficulty lies simply in the shortage of strategic expertise and the near impossibility of training strategists. Strategists seem to be born rather than made. People can of course be trained to think strategically, to translate the threat or use of force into its political consequences, but that they can be well trained is another matter altogether. In order to undertake the daunting task of relating force to political results via predicted strategic effect, the strategist may need to understand the enemy in ways that far transcend the narrowly military. If we approach deterrence and coercive diplomacy as strategy, as we should, the American strategist will need psychological, cultural, and political information about the intended deterree that is not found in the classic texts on deterrence theory.[33] It is helpful to have some understanding of the minds that we seek to influence, and of the cultures that create the mindsets with which we must deal. Ultimately, though, there is no evading the exercise of judgment or, frankly, guesswork. It is quite helpful to be reminded by Clausewitz that "the conduct of war, in its great outlines, is therefore policy itself," but his advice never provides specific formulae or principles that can be applied to resolve our dilemmas.[34] The kind of knowledge necessary for good strategic judgment is not mastery of the abstract logic of American strategic theory, neither is it expertise in the making and exposition of policy, nor skill in the organization and management of violence. The American strategist needs to know how much and what kind of force, as threat or in action, should produce the political results sought by our policy. Men and women blessed with that knowledge, or perhaps with the ability to guess right enough answers, will always be in exceedingly short supply.

The United States has need of few strategists, which is fortunate because they cannot be produced to order. Policymakers and soldiers should be taught to ask the strategist's question ("So what?") while the defense community can generally be encouraged to recognize the vital nature of strategic effect. But the ability to exercise good strategic judgment is a rare talent that can be improved only at the margin by conscious effort on the part of our institutions of higher education, military and civilian. Personal experience and observation of the experience of others, which is found by reading history, is probably the way to gain such expertise in strategy as may be attainable. Napoleon was persuasive when he wrote in his *Maxims* that "tactics, evolutions, the duties and knowledge of an engineer or an artillery officer may be learned in treatises, but the science of strategy is only to be acquired by experience, and by studying the campaigns of all the great captains."[35] Superiority of strategic judgment will be rare, but the U.S. government should at least recognize its importance by doing what it can to keep the strategic flame burning by the Potomac.[36] More often than not, truly strategic thought is hard to find in the regular defense budget cycle.

The other four classes of difficulty that typically undermine and attrit strategic performance may be summarized as the sheer complexity of strategy's nature; the implications of that complexity for the enervating potential of friction; the problems of command, of dialogue, even just of meaningful communication, between politicians and soldiers; and the challenge inherent in needing to prepare for the hypothetical crises and wars of the future. So many distinctive dimensions of strategy are always in play that the potential for some fatal shortfall is ever present. Although there is some protection in complexity, because weakness in one dimension—say, in technology—

may be offset by compensating strength elsewhere—say, in excellent fighting performance and quality of command, it is no less possible that adequate compensation will not be available. Restated, the strategic level comprises the maximum number of factors that can harbor debilitating ambuscades. By extension, moving on to Clausewitz's compound concept of friction, there is just more to go wrong at the strategic level.[37] Next, strategy is difficult because it requires cooperation and some mutual comprehension, if not actual empathy, between the contrasting cultures of the politician and the soldier. Should a particular cohort of senior officers be highly politicized, as, arguably, has happened in the United States since Vietnam, the problems of mutual incomprehension are minimized. However, a politicized military leadership can present other problems. Rather than acting strictly as the servants of the state and its policy, a substantially politicized military can hardly help but become a powerful player in the making of that policy. If Eliot Cohen is to be believed, the traditional or "normal" theory of American civil-military relations as outlined by Huntington has broken down.[38] The country's soldiers are no longer content to behave like political eunuchs, while—for the other side of the coin—political leaders should not automatically trust their professional military advisers, supposedly the experts, to provide reliable military advice. It is not part of my mandate to pursue this important topic beyond simply noting that it is a potential source of trouble for the American sheriff. A straw in this particular wind was the deeply fraught relationship between General Wesley F. Clark, then NATO's Supreme Allied Commander, Europe, and his political superiors, both in Washington and in NATO's European capitals, over the conduct of the war against the former Yugoslavia over Kosovo in 1999.[39] The timely appearance of Eliot Cohen's powerful and elegantly argued book, *Supreme Command,* in 2002, shed significant new light on the inherently tension-prone relationship between the politician and the soldier.

The last of the difficulties to be cited here as an impediment to superior strategic performance is the great problem of so conducting defense planning that one will not be caught short of the needed military capability. Since the future cannot be predicted in detail, the art of good defense planning requires obedience to the golden rule of getting the big things right enough and endeavouring to ensure that most future regrets will concern only secondary matters. This is a tall order. Nonetheless, it is critically important. Fortunately, it is just about feasible, even for a country with a range of probable military needs like the United States, and it is necessary to set the standard this high. Despite the current U.S. endorsement of a relatively proactive security policy, including occasional resort to a strategy of so-called preemption, it is a reasonable bet that by and large the American sheriff will be in response mode. Evil deeds will be committed or threatened quite suddenly, and the United States will have to deter if it can, coerce if it must, and thoroughly defeat as a last resort, using whatever military assets are available that seem likely to fit the case in point.

British Field Marshal Sir Nigel Bagnall probably exaggerates, but he makes a claim of the utmost importance when he observes that "over the centuries identifying a nation's future strategic priorities has proved to be a very imprecise art, and as a result peacetime force structures have seldom proved relevant when put to the test of war."[40] For decades to come, the United States may be militarily so superior to all enemies that virtually any unexpected strategic emergency will be adequately answered by American military power. Alternatively, contemporary American defense planning may be far better than the historical norm, in which case we should repose high confidence in the ability of officials to prepare the military muscle appropriate to the tasks ahead. However, historical experience, respect for tomorrow's enemies, common sense, and a prudent fear of hubris and its likely malign consequences should all incline us to doubt that the future will record much change from the past. American defense planning, and the choice of key assumptions upon which it will be based, must continue to be an imprecise art. Of course, one may believe that a fairly standard American military capability, duly transformed and organized to apply a dominant American style of warfare, will suffice to meet all major needs. Analogously, the United States would be akin to a football team so confident in its ability to impose its style of play on any opponent that it was indifferent to intelligence about the opponent's intentions. Given the current U.S. military lead, it may seem reasonable for Americans to expect to dictate the terms and conditions of future wars. Alas, the paradoxical logic of conflict, in one of its many cunning behaviors, is likely to humble strategic pride. The paradoxical logic virtually guarantees that intelligent and competent, albeit materially inferior, enemies of the United States will pose strategic challenges that American military power is not well designed to meet.[41]

If our defense planners do their job competently, the sheriff's enemies will not succeed, at least not often and certainly not in greatly significant ways, in posing strategic questions for which U.S. military power lacks convincing answers. The American sheriff cannot possibly so improve its skills in prediction, read "guesswork," as to be able to proof itself against surprise. But it can develop a military program that is highly robust and resilient against the effects of surprise. American policymakers cannot know long in advance the precise circumstances in which they may need to threaten or employ military power. But they can make such prudent military preparation, resting on careful, if somewhat generic, analysis of likely threats, that the inability to predict the details of future crises and wars should not be a fatal limitation. For example, it is obvious that the global sheriff of world order cannot function effectively in this twenty-first century unless it is able to protect its homeland, as well as its deployed forces and its friends and allies, against missile attack. If that point is accepted as a non-negotiable element in the sheriff's military story, the inability to predict far in advance exactly when, over what, and by whom American missile defenses might be tested can be regarded simply as a regrettable fact of life. Superior defense planning will enable the United States to ride out future surprises with a fair measure of confidence, even indifference, because a sound defense program will have proofed the country against many, hopefully nearly all, of the potentially bad effects of surprise.

The first essential for superior strategic performance has to be an understanding of strategy's nature and working, as well as of the principal difficulties that are unavoidable. The difficulties that were outlined and discussed immediately above are not occasional harassments; rather, they are structural to, and ineradicable as problems for, strategy and strategic performance. From that extensive discussion, we now turn to a brief identification of those capabilities considered sources of military, and hopefully strategic, effectiveness. In contrast to strategy itself and the difficulties that can impede strategic performance, these desiderata are generally well understood and are not particularly controversial, at least at a general level. This text seeks to avoid becoming embroiled in debate over the ephemeral defense issues of the moment. The burning issues of the hour have a way of burning out, just as fashionable strategic concepts sometimes do when the novelty wears off and they are subjected to more careful appraisal. Although the dynamics of debate in the U.S. defense community award pride of place to those real world events to which Raymond Aron referred, a close second is given to the need of the large advisory industry to have new-sounding ideas to talk about.

To succeed strategically as sheriff of such world order as we enjoy, the United States needs, first and foremost, to understand the nature, workings, and challenges of strategy. Some readers may be a little puzzled or irritated by the attention lavished here on strategy, particularly on the emphatically Clausewitzian approach. I insist on respect for the strategic function because it is the only valid perspective on military power. If the strategic function is neglected, abandoned, even ridiculed by various kinds of strategic nihilists, what are we left with? The threat and use of force for its own sake, or for glory, or because the country could not think of anything else to attempt. History warns us that even strategically experienced, and sometimes gifted, people can find the dynamics of war able to escape their policy control, with the consequence that policy appears to serve war, rather than vice versa. Even if one is vigilant for the authority of strategy, and by extension for that of the outcome of meaningful dialogue between politicians and soldiers, the conduct of war may still be so obedient to war's own "grammar" that the logic of policy becomes a fatal casualty.[42]

U.S. military power needs to provide adaptable and flexible forces, able to contend successfully both in combat and in providing security after combat in all geographical environments against a wide range of regular and irregular enemies. The cost of doing business as sheriff naturally requires global reach with forces able to deter, coerce, and—if need be—defeat, whoever threatens world order. That requirement for global reach is not satisfied simply by the ability to deliver precise firepower over transcontinental distances, but also includes the necessity to provide such logistical support as strategy may need. The character of future war will not always be subject to definition by the United States. A quick and devastating raid from altitude may be the U.S. preference; a fly-by demonstration of godlike potency. But a smart or lucky enemy may take the U.S. measure and so craft the conditions of conflict that the American sheriff will need to sustain a messy and protracted involvement on the ground, very far away from the center of its power. Therefore, the requirement for global reach might encompass very stressful logistical demands. To the requirements for adaptable and flexible forces with a genuinely global reach, we must add, for emphasis, the ability to physically defend the American homeland. Of course homeland protection can never be absolute. However, performance of the sheriff's role in the twenty-first century will not be practicable unless the agents of disorder are denied the military basis for a strategy intended to deter American intervention in their neighborhood. If the Byzantines understood this 1,500 years ago, contemporary Americans ought to have no difficulty grasping the essential logic. Only when the center, the locus of values, is secure against menace, can a country take the initiative far from home. Byzantine armies could campaign on the Euphrates plateau because far behind them, Constantinople was nearly impregnable.[43] Much more recently, Britain could dispatch armies to North America, to Iberia, and to the Middle East only if the home islands were not at serious risk of invasion. Forces cannot be dispatched on world order tasks if American strategy is lacking a convincing answer to the problem posed by missile-borne WMD able to reach North America. This is not to prejudge what the strategic answer should be, but it is to claim that there must be such an answer. Offensive and defensive counterforce must feature prominently in the explanation of why the United States will not find its world ordering strategy paralyzed by the vulnerability of its homeland.

It is important to conclude this explanation of the prospective trials and tribulations of strategic performance with two comments on what has long been the crown jewel of American strategic thought and policy—deterrence. In its demanding guardian role, the United States will need all the deterrent effect that its military power and strategizing can deliver. At the present time the U.S. government seems to be simultaneously discouraged and encouraged about the prospects for deterrence, depending upon the nature of the intended deterree. A proactive, preemptive strategy—that of firing first—is the logical corollary to the belief that some of today's enemies are not deterrable.[44] Post-modern catastrophe terrorists, and possibly some rogue states, pose radically different and, bizarre though it may seem, vastly more difficult challenges for the American deterrer than anything faced during the Cold War. In contrast to official pessimism over the prospects of deterring terrorists and other rogues, official Washington aspires to maintain and extend such a commanding military lead that any state or coalition motivated to compete will be dissuaded from the attempt.[45]

Both the current pessimism and the current optimism over deterrence seem excessive. The American sheriff should be able to improve its strategic performance in deterrence, even in difficult cases, by revising its approach so as to favor a more empirically based theory. To date, American deterrence theory and practice has been dominated by its Cold War legacy.[46] If deterrence has been all but retired prematurely *vis à vis* some terrorists and rogue states, it has been paradoxically elevated to the unrealistic height of a goal to be secured by America's prowess as a military competitor. The U.S. government is not unreasonable in its skepticism about the relevance of deterrence to terrorism or state roguery, or in its hope that major would-be foes will be terminally discouraged from launching bids to compete. The trouble is that those sensible beliefs and aspirations are liable to harden into dogma. Thus it seems that deterrence is all but discounted as a strategy on the one hand, while, as dissuasion, it is the source of immense and unwarranted confidence on the other.

For the specific purpose of this analysis, these two sides of deterrence are linked most significantly by the fact that the United States cannot secure strategic success by its own efforts in either case. The discussion immediately above argued for the American sheriff to maintain adaptable and flexible military forces, which would be logistically sustainable even for truly global reach, and to provide for protection of the homeland. In contrast, this brief review of two aspects of deterrence strategy highlights decisions that Americans cannot force others to make. Because deterrent effect succeeds or fails in the minds of others, it cannot be purchased directly. No military posture is inherently deterring. Whether or not a fearsome warfighting capability, accompanied by a well-deserved reputation for using it to deadly effect, deters in a particular instance is a decision that can only be made by the intended deterree. Of course, we should behave in a way that encourages the adversary to decide to be deterred. But the choice is ultimately his, not ours. Anyone who refers to "the deterrent," even to "the nuclear deterrent," does not understand the subject. Given the scope and scale of strategic performance that is required of the sheriff for world order, American beliefs and strategies regarding deterrence need to be of a high order.

MILITARY TRANSFORMATION AND FUTURE WAR

U.S. military power should be globally dominant for at least the next thirty to fifty years. That claim can be advanced with a fair measure of confidence. But that is not to suggest that the United States will win every conflict in which it participates. The claim is only that its potency in the increasingly joint regular warfare of the future assuredly should bury any enemy. To beat the United States, adversaries will need either to prosecute unusual and irregular forms of combat or to devise cunning plans that succeed in locating and exploiting such vulnerabilities as may lurk beneath the obvious American strengths. Expressions of approval must be qualified because the only conclusive test is the test of actual war. It is important to remember that America's strategic performance in warfare will reflect both the character of the transforming military establishment and the effectiveness of its employment by political leaders.

The great RMA debate of the 1990s is concluded, and by and large a satisfactory outcome appears to have been reached.[47] The George W. Bush administration entered office strongly committed to military transformation. To date, it has met that commitment persuasively in the form of new organizations, a definite vision in the *Quadrennial Defense Review* of September 2001, and in the details of the defense budget for fiscal year 2003. Secretary of Defense Rumsfeld identified six operational goals to provide a focus for transformation efforts. Those goals are as follows:

- Above all, protect critical bases of operations (most importantly, the U.S. homeland) and defeat weapons of mass destruction and their means of delivery;

- Project and sustain power in distant anti-access and area-denial environments;

- Deny enemies sanctuary by developing capabilities for persistent surveillance, tracking, and rapid engagement;

- Leverage information technology and innovative network-centric concepts to link up joint forces;

- Protect information systems from attack; and

- Maintain unhindered access to space—and protect U.S. space capabilities from enemy attack.[48]

It is a sensible program. We do not know what the "right" military posture will be for the United States in the years ahead, let alone in the future decades that are of most interest to this enquiry. The challenge is to develop military forces that are always capable of meeting the demands that foreign policy might place on them. Since long-term U.S. foreign policy calls for a benign hegemonic role in defense of a world order that expresses and advances American interests, the range and scale of threats is sure to be impressive.

The history of defense planning is littered with both new approaches and somewhat refurbished old approaches. Some approaches may have more merit than others, but none of them can solve the basic, endemic problem of how to provide reliable guidance for the efficient and effective preparation of military power for the future. The hegemonic United States will require military capabilities to dissuade, deter, coerce, and, if need be, decisively defeat whoever might pose a seemingly intolerable threat to the world order that it is protecting. With so diffuse and unpredictable a set of possible strategic challenges, the approach to defense planning that is currently in vogue is probably as good as any, though in the opinion of this author it is better than most. We are told that "the new U.S. defense strategy is built around the concept of shifting to a 'capabilities-based' approach to defense."[49] This approach seems to obey the golden rule of trying hard to get the big things right. It recognizes that although we cannot predict the details of future crises and wars, we ought to be able to anticipate the kinds of military power and the strategic style that our enemies may employ against us. As noted above, despite the talk of a preemptive strategy in the context of WMD threats, the sheriff's role is essentially a responsive one. Of course, the United States may need to serve a strategically defensive goal with an offensive operational style. Official Washington notes realistically "that U.S. military forces will need to deter and defeat adversaries who will rely on surprise, deception, and asymmetric warfare to achieve their objectives."[50] Although it may appear unduly pessimistic, even uncharitable, to say it, the evidence of history strongly suggests that we will fail to anticipate the strategic ideas some of our enemies will employ. As a result, we will be embarrassed and, possibly, even defeated occasionally.[51] Such is strategic history.

The American objective cannot be to register a perfect score. Rather, the goal is to conduct fault-tolerant defense planning.[52] We have to plan against the kind of capabilities and strategies that would wreak great harm upon us and our interests and hope that the surprises our more adaptive and competent foes have in store for us fall under the category of actions with lesser consequences. It is probably substantively useful, though not politic, to acknowledge that all approaches to defense planning are doomed to fail. Respect for history and good political judgment are worth far more than apparent sophistication in methodology. It is improbable that America's contemporary defense planners are any wiser than their predecessors, while we know for certain that ever more powerful computing tools cannot reveal the future. However, it is realistic to aspire to conduct defense planning in such a way that when it fails, it fails both relatively gracefully and in respects that do not menace the political or strategic viability of the sheriff's role. The "capabilities-based approach" of the Bush administration, together with a serious official commitment to address the problems of "surprise, deception, and asymmetric warfare," is a superior way to attack an impossible problem.[53] However, the fact that there is no methodology that can pierce the veil concealing the future does not excuse officials from trying. The danger lies in the distinct possibility that they will be overly impressed with their analytical innovations. This peril is especially acute for the United States today, because the relevant historical context is virtually tailor-made for American hubris and, if not nemesis, at least some punishment for the sin of pride. Key features of the context in question are apparent U.S. military dominion; an unpredictable array of foes, both states and others; and the certainty that tomorrow's enemies will seek ways to compete with American power and influence that evade American strengths.

The challenge is to cope well enough with the inconvenient fact that, because the future has yet to occur and time travel is unavailable, defense planning is an exercise in guesswork. Again, for the American sheriff to be successful in its defense planning it can, reasonably, aspire to get most of the big things correct. It can aim to develop military capabilities sufficiently flexible and adaptable to meet policy demands, even though they must operate as a fault-tolerant force. That is to say, over the course of the next several decades the United States will be presented with a strategic problem or two for which its extant forces will be less than perfectly fitted. The defense planning mission, though, is not the impossible one of trying to predict future needs in detail. Instead, it is to so provide against future challenges, generically, that ways can be found to win decisively with the military power, and the options it provides, that happen to be available.[54] In football, great teams find ways to win, even when they are surprised and limited by injuries. So it is in war. For the United

States to be as powerful as it needs to be to sustain the guardian role, it will need to be able to find ways to win—in deterrence, coercion, and war itself—against enemies who will not all be foes of choice from central casting. Moreover, the strategic methods of those enemies may surprise even the more fertile imaginations in the American defense community. More often than not the problem will lie in misassessment of the enemy's fighting prowess, rather than in complete surprise over his combat methods. Americans may be the technical masters of modern warfare, but combat prowess depends on strength of motivation, as well as sophistication of equipment and intensity of training. Clausewitz was crystal clear on this matter.[55]

The first head of the Pentagon's Office of Force Transformation, Vice Admiral Arthur Cebrowski, has offered the sage comment that "transformation is a journey, not a destination—a process, not a goal—a continuum, not an achievement."[56] The U.S. military is naturally seeking to be all that it can be. The idea of military transformation that is currently endorsed with near-religious fervor is generally worthy and sensible. The problem for the American sheriff, however, is going to be more strategic than military, which is why this chapter highlights the strategic rather than the military dimension. The United States has approached the shaping of its defense program with two driving assumptions since the end of the Cold War, and may continue to do so for many years to come. First, it is assumed that the country will consider engagement in wars by discretion—by choice rather than by necessity. Second, it is assumed that, as the military superstate, the United States will be able to dictate the character of its future wars. These assumptions, though imprudent, are by no means foolish. Both have been somewhat shaken by September 11, as one would expect. September 11 and the American reaction to it have revealed the limitations of military transformation, no matter how intelligently conducted. Almost certainly, the American experience as sheriff in every war will reveal the fragility of the assumption that being militarily Number One confers the ability, even the right, to dictate the terms of combat. Events in Iraq after the war was declared to be won also have caused some second thoughts as to the adequacy of the doctrine that accompanies transformation. Foes will vary in their competence and luck, but they will all know that they can only prosper in war against the superstate if they are able to impose a form of conflict that negates many of America's regular military strengths.

Because the United States has stepped up to the sheriff's role, and intends to function as the enforcer of good order for as long as it is able, it cannot plan its future military capabilities with definite enemies and strategic challenges confidently in mind. Obviously, some guesses look better-founded than others, but the possibility, even probability, of major surprises should lead American officials to favor adaptability and flexibility in forces. It can be extraordinarily difficult to persuade those with defense responsibility in a great military power to think in strategic, rather than merely military, terms. Both Imperial and Nazi Germany failed to understand Clausewitz's definition of strategy, with its focus on the use of battle for the object of the war. The United States is at risk to the same peril; it may be so mesmerized by the prospect of its own operational military excellence that it will confuse military effectiveness with strategic effectiveness. This should hardly need saying, considering the lessons that ought to have been learned from the incomplete victory over Iraq in 1991, but the same strategic errors are often repeated over the years, ironically even in the same neighborhood.

It is so easy to be misunderstood on the subject of transformation that I must hasten to explain that, as stated above, the current American commitment to transformation seems well judged and appears thoroughly praiseworthy. As to its general thrust, one commentator penetrates to the heart of the matter when he notes that "since the United States has a high-tech economy, much of the debate on transformation is focused on information technology. The capabilities the military is pursuing are generally designed to take advantage of information that can be moved and analysed on computer."[57] All of which is true to the point of banality and is really beyond argument today. One might as well bid the waves retreat as launch a thoroughgoing assault upon the wisdom of transforming the U.S. armed forces in ways that privilege the effectiveness attainable through information technologies. The problem, perhaps the needed caveat, is context—or, to be more precise, the frequent apparent absence of context.

The contexts that are sometimes absent, or at least faint, are those of war and strategy. It is all too natural to focus on the things we control, rather than those we do not. Hence, discussions of military transformation quite properly emphasize expected improvements in our military performance. But the relative neglect of the pertinent contexts of war and strategy virtually guarantees that the transformation story cannot be assessed properly, no matter how sensible it may be in itself. If one asks what is to be transformed, the answer has to be the character of the American conduct of war, or perhaps American military style. Let there be no misunderstanding, this is important. However, to transform American war-waging—if the enemy and other factors permit—is not to transform war itself, nor is it to change the nature and workings of strategy. The U.S. defense community, with its intelligent pursuit of information-led enhancement of military effectiveness, continues to be far less convincing when it addresses subjects above the tactical and operational levels. Writing more than twenty years ago, Edward Luttwak suggested unkindly "that post-Vietnam America, with its defense planners who are little more than glorified accountants, and its generals who still think that strategy is only logistics, needs Carl von Clausewitz's book much more."[58] I would add to Luttwak's discontents the concern that, in practice, the current process of transformation is unduly inclined to equate the precise delivery of firepower with the successful conduct of war.

Despite the rhetoric to the contrary, war itself is not being transformed by current U.S. efforts to achieve step-level jumps in effectiveness by selective innovation of equipment, practices, organizations, and ideas. War is, and will continue to be, what it has always been. Those theorists and officials who persistently confuse the character of war, which is always changing, with the nature of war, which cannot alter, are responsible for creating confusion and raising false expectations. As the United States "transforms" some of its military establishment over the next several decades, it should gain the ability to do better what it can already do well today. No strategic revolution is in the making.[59] Quite probably, the ability to find highly elusive targets and strike them with great precision will reach new heights of military excellence. I do not mean to dismiss or really criticize in any way the prediction of significant improvements in American military effectiveness. The issue of real importance is not the merit of the American military transformation that has begun, but rather what it can and cannot deliver strategically and politically, given the enduring nature of war and strategy.

The United States has not discovered, and is not in the process of realizing, a style of warfare that will radically improve the country's ability to perform successfully as guardian of world order. While the current approach to transformation may—enemies permitting, of course—help reduce American casualties, which could matter hugely, it also brings its own problems, which I outline briefly below. The argument here, which rests on historical evidence and respect for empirically based strategic theory, is basically that although computer-focused transformation is generally sensible, an enhancement in military effectiveness will not guarantee a parallel improvement in strategic effectiveness. These expectations should be kept in check for reasons that are not hard to find, but that tend not to feature prominently in analyses of military transformation. As stated above, the most fundamental limitations on the scope of transformation's achievements lies in the context of the very nature of war and strategy.

America's program of military transformation may rewrite some of the rules of combat, at least in those conflicts where the enemy can be denied the initiative, but it will not be able to rewrite many of the rules that comprise truths about, or principles of, war. This comment applies at two levels: both the tactical-operational and the structural, which bears directly upon war's basic nature. At the tactical-operational level, history proves the unsurprising conjecture that seemingly revolutionary changes in the conduct of war are almost always condemned to disappoint their parents. The nature of war ensures that naïve aspirations to achieve near total battlespace transparency, to close in upon the elimination of what Clausewitz categorized as friction, or to win through the unparalleled potency of some new "dominant weapon" or operational formula are sure to fail.[60] Of course, even these unsound reductionist approaches to military excellence will succeed if the enemy is truly incompetent. However, sound defense planning cannot assume fatally incompetent enemies. Experience seems to suggest that the high road to military success is opened up by the well-orchestrated actions of combined arms. The outstanding contemporary study of the subject insists that "individual weapons, however powerful, do not win wars. Heavy machine guns, tanks, fighter bombers, tank destroyers, and attack helicopters, at one time or another, have been segregated into separate units and touted as invincible. Once the opponent has time to develop his defenses, however, these weapons lose much of their initial effectiveness."[61] The author of that historically well-supported judgment, Jonathan M. House, explains that "the combined arms concept is the basic idea that different combat arms and weapons systems must be used in concert to maximize the survival and combat effectiveness of the others. The strengths of one system must be used to compensate for the weaknesses of the others."[62] Since the superior merit of combined arms seems to be a military principle of more than 2,000 years standing, it is only sensible to assume that it will continue to hold for the remainder of America's period of ascendancy. When military transformation and new styles of war appear to challenge the continuing authority of the combined arms principle, as has been argued was the case in Kosovo in 1999 and Afghanistan in 2001, it is appropriate to be skeptical.[63]

British historian Jeremy Black holds a holistic and cultural view of war which sharply limits the strategic rewards of military transformations such as the one in which America is currently engaged. Black is worth quoting at some length. I do not read his argument as challenging the logic of transformation, provided that logic is driven by modest expectations and is pursued in broad appreciation of the possible range and certain nature of war. Black argues

> that the notion of the so-called "revolution in military affairs" that sees "smart" weaponry as the driving force in war and military capability is wrong, because it fails to note the multiple contexts of war, not least differing understandings of victory, defeat, loss and suffering. In short, war and success in war are cultural constructs.[64]

Black's final sentence suggests the relevance of an anthropological perspective if we hope to record superior performance in war. This should come as no surprise. After all, as long ago as 1973 Bernard Brodie claimed that "good strategy presumes good anthropology and sociology. Some of the greatest military blunders of all time have resulted from juvenile evaluations in this department."[65] To the best of my knowledge, the merit in Brodie's claim has never been challenged. In fact, the U.S. defense community today is revisiting many aspects of its approach to dissuasion, deterrence, and coercion, paying particular attention to matters culturally specific to possible deterrees. Thus it is plain to see that Black and Brodie have a message for the American sheriff that should not be ignored, no matter how glittering the promise in a transforming military establishment.

Explanations of America's military transformational endeavors, even those that are presented in intentionally broad and inclusive terms, are inevitably narrowly cast. Therefore it is important to underline the ways in which, and the reasons why, the very nature and dynamics of war are likely to constrain the achievements of an improving military machine. These words of Jeremy Black, again, are not at all hostile to military excellence, but they do invite us to take a rounded view of the subject of war. To some of America's enthusiastic, or even just dutiful, transformers, Black's words could be a revelation:

> In its fundamentals, war changes far less frequently and significantly than most people appreciate. This is not simply because it involves a constant—the willingness of organized groups to kill and, in particular, to risk death—but also because *the material culture of war, which tends to be the focus of attention, is less important than its social, cultural and political contexts and enablers.* These contexts explain the purposes of military action, the nature of the relationship between the military and the rest of society, and the internal structures and ethos of the military. Having "high-tech," the focus of much discussion about the future of war, is not the same as winning particular wars, and, anyway, does not delimit the nature of conflict.[66]

If Black's argument is judged plausible, as it is by this author, there is no evading the conclusion that America's efforts at military transformation, meritorious though they may be, can address only some of the problems posed by war, and those are not among the more important. Black probably overstates his case to make his point, but then so do many of the advocates of transformation.

Much as the nature of war, approached holistically in context, is likely to limit the benefit that can be gained from military transformation, so the nature, along with the dynamic workings, of strategy is a potent source of possible constraint. Clausewitz identified five elements of strategy: the moral; physical; mathematical; geographical; and statistical. Michael Howard wrote about four dimensions of strategy in an influential 1979 article: the logistical; operational; social; and technological. I am more than a little embarrassed to acknowledge that my contribution to this long-running stream of analysis has been to specify no fewer than seventeen dimensions of strategy.[67] The preferred number does not matter. What is important is to capture all of the factors that contribute to strategic performance, both positively and negatively. I arrange my seventeen strategic dimensions in three clusters: people and politics; preparation for war; and war proper. Under "people and politics," I list people; society;

culture; politics; and ethics. The category of "preparation for war" includes economics and logistics; organization (defense planning); military administration (recruitment, training, procurement); information and intelligence; theory and doctrine; and technology. Finally, under "war proper"—a Clausewitzian term, as was "preparation for war"—I identify military operations (fighting performance); command (political and military); geography; friction and chance; the adversary; and time.

In case studies of three historical RMAs or transformations—the Napoleonic, the First World War, and the nuclear—I explored the relative salience of my seventeen strategic dimensions.[68] The point in need of clearest appreciation is that strategy, like war itself, functions as a whole. Analysts, defense planners, and military operatives may approach war intending to score heavily for strategic effect, but the realm of strategy wherein they must perform encompasses all the dimensions identified above. And all of strategy's dimensions—be they four, five, seventeen, or however many—are always in play and are always interacting with each other. Not every dimension—say geography or ethics—will be important in every conflict. But a serious shortfall or notable deficiency on literally any of strategy's dimensions could fatally impede strategic performance overall. Naturally enough, no belligerent is blessed with equal excellence on every one of strategy's dimensions. In principle, the very diversity of strategy's constituent elements allows for compensation to be found and applied so that strength can offset weakness. Needless to add, perhaps, there may be so many weak dimensions, or the dimensions that are weak may be so vital (politics, people, society), that adequate compensation is sought in vain. The purpose in outlining this rather theoretical perspective on war and strategy is to provide a context for analysis. American debate over military transformation, and indeed over war as an instrument of the sheriff's policy, tends to be either context-free, or—worse still—only partially alert to contextual elements. When military transformation is bracketed with national security policy and strategy in such a way that it amounts to global guardianship via occasional recourse to expeditionary warfare, it would be reassuring to know that the full contexts of war and strategy are properly appreciated. This may be asking too much, but we can still try.

This treatment of the strategic dimension of the sheriff's role concludes with the brief mention of three particular dangers to which the United States as a strategic actor appears to be characteristically prone.

First, the U.S. armed forces are vulnerable to seduction by the lure of technology. This danger is well recognized. Indeed it is taken sufficiently seriously for the chairman of the Joint Chiefs of Staff (JCS) to include in an article on "Understanding Transformation" a side-bar on "What Transformation Is Not," which opens with the flat statement that "transformation is not just about technology."[69] Since America's love affair with machinery is the better part of two centuries old, and given that the technological dimension of war is a defining strength of the United States, it is all but certain that American officials and soldiers will place a heavier reliance on technology than is wise. After all, they have done so repeatedly in the past. It is scarcely probable that in the context of an ongoing transformation program keyed to information technologies, Americans will suddenly adopt an approach to strategic problems that is notably skeptical of the benefits of technology, and indeed, of material factors in general. Moreover, they should not do so. Americans must be true to their culture. The conduct of a technological style of warfare is mandated by American circumstances and preferences: It is what Americans do well, and it is usually sensible to go with one's strengths. The danger is that America's romance with high technology might distort its understanding of war and strategy. War might be equated with apparently devastating firepower, with impressive mobility, and with wonderful network-centricity in communication flow. Such reductionism, reflecting U.S. technological excellence but strategic naivety, might result in the "social, cultural, and political contexts and enablers" emphasized by Professor Black receiving unduly short shrift by the sheriff.[70]

The second danger to which American strategic endeavor is characteristically prone is the logical corollary of the first: The tendency to rely overmuch on machines is matched by an unwillingness to rely sufficiently on people, especially American people. The armed forces know that people matter most. The danger does not seem to lie in an intellectual failure to grasp how people and machines must work together for excellence in war fighting. Indeed, the essay signed by the chairman of the JCS, from which I have quoted already, contains these arresting and hopeful dicta: "To achieve transformation, the war fighters must understand its intellectual, cultural, and technological elements. The most important breakthroughs will take place between the ears of war fighters and planners."[71] Not elegant prose, but nonetheless a worthy sentiment. Unfortunately, the issue is not only the one to which the chairman refers—that of the vital role people have in effecting transformation. Much more serious is the possibility that the United States is endorsing an approach to combat that is unduly dependent on machines at the expense of the direct human contribution. Eliot Cohen and others have discerned the emergence of a new American way in war, one plainly revealed over Kosovo and then amply reinforced in Afghanistan.[72] This new style of combat privileges high technology, particularly airpower in its several forms, and is characterized by a dearth of Americans on the ground. Due to local political and cultural sensitivities, not to mention the authority of local allies (when extant), there is much to be said for the sheriff's nationals keeping a low, even absentee, profile. The problem is that there are certain to be future conflicts wherein the effect, or lack of effect, of American technology at altitude needs to be augmented by large numbers of American boots on the ground (Iraq 2003, for an obvious example). As we noted earlier, the combined arms approach to warfare is a principle of war with superior authority in all periods and in all material contexts. The trend in the American style of war waging favors American technology, but not large-scale exposure of Americans. When implemented for the right military and political reasons, there is much to be said in praise of a style which hazards our machines rather than our people. Unfortunately, however, not all of the reasons for the contemporary version of the traditional U.S. emphasis upon a technological style of combat stem from military, let alone strategic, logic.

It is something of an open question whether or not a country's armed forces must reflect the attitudes and values of the society from which they derive. The alternative view is that they can stand out, isolated, as an island with attitudes and values at odds with their social context. In two major respects at least, the American sheriff has reason to wonder whether its human assets, professional military and others, have the moral courage that the country's demanding role requires. Specifically, American strategic effectiveness might be threatened by what many commentators, including some participant observers, perceive as a degree of risk aversion which will imperil American global performance. This author is by no means convinced that perception of this danger is sufficiently well founded as to be serious. These comments are highly speculative.

It is possible, so the argument proceeds, that while the U.S. defense establishment has been polishing its high technology and advancing the network-centricity of its joint forces, it has failed to notice that its dominant military culture rewards risk-averse behavior. American soldiers may talk tough, but in practice they behave like the rational careerists that they need to be if they are to advance in an organization that has little time for people—dare one say warriors?—who think and act "outside the box." It is a commonplace observation about the U.S. military profession today that the potential career rewards of boldness are more than balanced by the certain costs of failure. Given the extreme stakes in warfare, I do not intend to praise boldness and risk taking unduly. But, if it is true that the risk aversion so characteristic of American society finds its due reflection in the military establishment, America's armed forces, transformed or not, will not be anywhere near as lethal a strategic policy instrument as the country is sure to need.[73] The other aspect of risk aversion pertains to the issue of casualties. Some observers believe that the parent form of risk aversion is an unwillingness to give orders which are believed likely, let alone certain, to result in American military casualties. If this is true, or even only partially true, then America's glittering armed forces, notwithstanding their high technology dazzle, will not be as potent as they seem. American society may or may not be intolerant of casualties, interpreting them as evidence of incompetence and failure—I am skeptical of this claim—but the professional military does seem to be intolerant of casualties. If that is so, it follows that rational careerists, obedient to the values of a peacetime culture, will eschew operational choices which could involve the loss of American life, and hence the blighting of otherwise promising careers.[74] Whether or not the U.S. sheriff requires a national military strategy all but guaranteed to ensure that heroic performance is not asked of many of its soldiers is a question that this book will not pursue further.[75] It is the view of this (Anglo-American) author that far too much has been made of the alleged casualty-shyness of Americans today. Americans have been sensibly casualty-shy when they feel less than deeply engaged in the political contexts at issue. The Balkans and the horn of Africa are not regions close to American hearts. Nor was Central Asia, prior to September 11, 2001. One need hardly emphasize the point that as guardian of world order, the American sheriff will find occasional need to campaign in regions concerning which domestic opinion is largely indifferent. The connection to

American interests will have to be made very explicit, indeed, if military action is to be justifiable.

Third and finally, as the lone superpower functioning as the sheriff of world order, the United States is at exceptional risk to the machinations of cunning foes who will need to contrive asymmetric styles of warfare if they are to compete at all.[76] While it is true that the role of sheriff exposes the country to particular dangers, it is also true that the world will be increasingly dangerous for a super-wealthy superstate over the next several decades, regardless of its global stance. It is far from clear that Americans will greatly enhance their safety by turning in their sheriff's badge. America's basic offense in the eyes of many is simply what it is and what it represents: it is a kind of existential insult. A danger peculiar to great strength is what has long been known as the victory disease. An America universally acknowledged as unchallengeable in regular forms of war, at least for some time to come, is an America that is likely to exaggerate its military prowess. It is difficult to know how good America's armed forces really are when they have not been tested in combat against a worthy, albeit highly asymmetric enemy, for nearly thirty years.[77] Some of the consequences of that sad, instructive, and contentious episode remain extant even today. It is an all too understandable paradox of great power that serious weaknesses may be hidden by undoubted strength.

Military power and strategic effectiveness are distinctive concepts. If the American sheriff is hoist by its own petard of military dominance, it may not worry very much about the fact that war is a duel, as Clausewitz insisted. In that event, America would be in danger not only of being surprised, which is par for the course in strategic history, but also of being gravely hurt by the effects of some surprises that were not anticipated with due respect. When a succession of easy military victories against third-rate foes is achieved by an American military establishment which is reaching ever greater heights of technological sophistication to effect ever greater military potency, it can be difficult for that establishment to assess itself accurately. It is even more difficult for it to inoculate itself against the danger of holding any and all enemies in contempt. To amend a familiar refrain, those whom the gods would destroy, they first make arrogant! This is not necessarily to accuse the U.S. military establishment of such arrogance, but it is to alert readers to the strong probability of its appearance and effect. In the twentieth century, Germany proved itself to be exceptionally good at fighting. But it repeatedly fell in its inability to translate that combat prowess into an ability to win wars. A world community uneasily dependent upon America's strategic performance as sheriff has to hope that their guardian state will not reveal any like tendency to win battles but lose wars. That community must also hope that America will remember that the purpose of war is not victory, but the achievement of a condition of peace with security superior to the pre-war context. Iraq 2003 has provided some fresh grounds for anxiety on the vital matter.

CHAPTER 5

The Familiar Twenty-First Century

Many books present bold statements of controversial answers to challenging questions. This is not one of those, though some readers may disagree. By calling chapter 1 "The Argument," I risk inadvertently exaggerating the extent to which my nine key points are seriously disputable. A great many people around the world will not like the argument presented here, but that is only to be expected. Furthermore, there are grounds for anxiety lest the role of sheriff should prove unduly demanding on American society. Nonetheless, this author is convinced both that his argument is far more description than it is prescription, and that on balance the United States is capable of performing successfully as required. The most important reason for such confidence is the historical record of American statecraft. In fact, the nine point argument which provides the essential architecture of this text, though necessarily presented and discussed with detailed reference to the international context of the twenty-first century, expresses the beliefs of a classical realist. Adhering to an unfashionably positivist worldview and rejecting as misguided the vagaries of postmodernism and critical theory, I have no difficulty identifying superior, contrasted with inferior, approaches to national and international security.[1] My authority for this confidence lies in the one point among the nine which has yet to be directly discussed. Point nine claims that history offers the best guide to the future. This concluding chapter begins by explaining why history can and should be allowed to provide guidance. The chapter then reflects critically on the principal arguments that have been explored, developed, and to some degree tested throughout the book. But first, what are the strengths, and the weaknesses, of an appeal to history for lessons that have continuing relevance?

FROM THE PAST TO THE FUTURE

History does not tell us what to think, but it does tell us what to think about. The material culture of war is constantly changing, sometimes more and sometimes less rapidly. Episodes of accelerated change are identified as revolutions in military affairs, or transformations.[2] However, war and strategy do not change in nature or function, and neither do the rules for a statecraft that sometimes finds war a necessary instrument of policy. Strategy in the ancient Greece of the city-states, or the ancient China of the Warring States (403–221 B.C.), can be understood and should be analyzed in terms of the same dimensions cited in chapter 4, as can strategy for the American sheriff of the twenty-first century. Thucydides and Sun-tzu wrote works that are timeless and relevant because their subject, statecraft—naturally including the threat and use of force—shows continuities in all essentials through the centuries, indeed the millennia. This distinctly conservative belief will not find favor among those, on the Left and the Right, who believe the historical narrative is the story of human progress in the politics of security, even if such advance is fitful. Undaunted, I believe that the central argument of this book, in both its political and strategic aspects, rests on the authority of history as well as the logic of contemporary geopolitics. Robert Kaplan is persuasive when he asserts that "the greater the disregard of history, the greater the delusions regarding the future."[3]

We have seen the future because we have access to the past. For Americans, the 1990s were a brief interwar period. Bad times always return for international security, and that they did on September 11, 2001. Whether or not it is strategically useful for the United States to consider itself at war, post-September 11, is not really an interesting question.[4] The social dimension of strategy, which can drive the political, afforded American leaders no choice other than to proclaim a condition of belligerency. For Washington, at least, the no-name post–Cold War era definitely ended in September 2001. I argued in chapter 3 that September 11, 2001, accelerated and gave a particular short-term focus to American recognition of its role in the world as the principal agent for the enforcement of order. The ninth point in the argument, outlined briefly in chapter 1, asserts that history is our best guide to the future. In fact, every major thread in the argument either finds impressive historical backing or is an inescapable contemporary reality.

The argument presented and defended throughout this text will not find favor with those who dislike the idea, not to mention the reality, of the United States performing as sheriff of the world community. Such critics will claim, with some justice, that the United States is not a disinterested lawman, but rather is a guardian of its own national interests, first and foremost. They will claim also, in this case unjustly, that there are alternatives to America performing as sheriff. The truth is that in the current global political and strategic contexts there are no alternatives to American guardianship *that would work*. That is a history-based prediction in which this author reposes complete confidence, a rare phenomenon given the uncertainty that shrouds future events. Whether or not, on balance, the United States will succeed as sheriff of world order is very much a matter for speculation, and there is certainly room for debate over just what would warrant description as success. This author is optimistic, again for historically-shaped reasons, but there is a vital sense in which criticism of the United States' sheriff role is irrelevant, and hence foolish. It is irrelevant because there is no alternative to an American sheriff, given the extant, and predictable future, distribution of power. There is no rival sheriff. In 1989 that dangerous context dissolved for at least several decades still to come. Aspirations for a concert diplomacy, necessarily requiring cooperation among the G-8 major industrial polities, are certain to fail both because of American's extraordinary preeminence and because of the natural resentment of its status by the other members. Despite the relatively weak hands they have to play, the G-7 (i.e., the G-8 minus the United States) have shown more inclination to fall into geopolitical rivalry than to function as an oligopoly for world order.

History does not require a sheriff for order, nor does it suggest that a sheriff, or some other policing agency, must succeed. Quite often in modern history, the greatest powers of an era are manifestly unfit to serve as the protectors of international order. Successively, France, Germany, and the Soviet Union prove my point: As great powers, none of them were politically fit to serve in the role of sheriff. Each demonstrated beyond reasonable doubt that it intended to use its extraordinary strength for self-aggrandizement. Those three, when superstates, behaved in such a disorderly, self-promoting manner that they quickly wrought their own demise. The abominable misbehavior of each of them catalyzed the existence of an anti-hegemonic coalition that outmatched the superstate in question.[5]

The United States of the twenty-first century is materially more out-standing in the hierarchy of nations—especially, though certainly not exclusively, in the military realm—than was royal or Napoleonic France, or imperial or Nazi Germany, or Soviet Russia. Nonetheless, it would be the gravest of errors were Americans to come to believe themselves so dominant in the geopolitical hierarchy that they could afford to ride roughshod over the interests of others and to pay no heed to the accepted norms, and conventions of international life. The great challenge to American statecraft is to be able to function effectively as the sheriff of world order, while simultaneously serving its own national interests so that the role remains domestically sus-tainable and also serving the interests of others so they are not mo-tivated to combine for the purpose of humbling the United States.

In the strategic regard quite as much as the political, the United States should allow itself to be educated by "the register of the crimes, follies, and misfortunes of mankind," as Edward Gibbon character-ized our historical experience.[6] Many features of the contemporary scene appear so startling, at least cumulatively so, that respect for history seems to many to be mere antiquarianism. For example, there are apparently unprecedented political events; there is the novelty of a globalized media now able to report world-wide in real-time; we have a considerably globalized economy and financial system; and there is an ongoing military transformation keyed to information technologies which is fueling claims for a new American way of war.[7] Indeed, one could argue that the American RMA and transforma-tion debates have been cast too narrowly, because the terms and conditions of war and the sources of insecurity are well along in a process of transformation.[8] Although the particular changes that bear on international security are indeed great and, in some points, sur-prising, the facts of massive changes and of a widespread sense of liv-ing in a significantly new world are anything but novel. For more than two centuries, since the American, French, and Industrial Revo-lutions, history seems to have been accelerating, particularly in the material sphere. So revolutionary can the political, social, and, above all, scientific and technical developments appear to be, that the thesis that history shows essential continuity in the more important aspects of security is readily dismissed by many. The problem is what I deem the myth of benign transformation.[9]

In its political form, the fallacious belief in benign transforma-tion denies that history is cyclical. Instead, notwithstanding occasional setbacks, history is assumed to be arrow-like.[10] Humankind is believed to be journeying toward perfection, at least in the quality of arrangements it makes for global peace and security. This author is entirely unconvinced that humankind is on a journey to a happy condition of permanent political peace, or at least on a journey at all likely to reach its destination in any timeframe of interest to us today. What we have failed to achieve over the course of the 2,500 years of history that are more or less accessible for our perusal, we will probably not finally achieve in the very near future. The burden of persuasive argument, since one can hardly require evidence, most definitely rests on the shoulders of the optimists. These thoughts are important for the book, because they point to history as a source of significant general guidance for policy and defense planning over the longer term. To those among us who wonder what this new century will be like, the classical realist—this author, for one example—answers that if we are fortunate it will be just another century. The twentieth century was terrible, but it could have been so much worse.[11] By the close of that century, the superstate in a class of its own might have been Nazi Germany or the Soviet Union. Rather more probable than either of those outcomes was that the Soviet Union, perceiving itself to be in competitive decline, might have opted for the imperial German and Austro-Hungarian route, declining to fade quietly.

Grim though the twentieth century was, we can count ourselves lucky that it was not much worse. For the West to have won (or been on the winning side of) three world conflicts in a century, and to have avoided a nuclear war, was probably a better record than the quality of some of our statecraft merited. More to the point, if we are as indifferent in this new century as we were in the previous one to what history can advise us of concerning how best to support world order, we should not assume that our record will continue to be as positive. The argument of this book compactly expresses much of what history should be permitted to tell us. In addition to the master claim that world order has to be policed by someone or by some effective agency (a concert of tolerably like-minded polities, for example), the rich historical experience in military innovation can help save the United States from much gratuitous error in its aspirations for the strategic value of the military transformation that is currently underway.[12]

The dimensions of war and strategy are so numerous, and each can be so important, that any projected military transformation is limited in its probable achievement by those elements of the subject that it cannot reach. This is not to criticize the transformation enterprise. But it is to say that we now have sufficient evidence from historical scholarship, and from social science trying to make cumulative sense of that historical scholarship, to know what to expect of transformation. History tries to tell us that the conduct and exploitation of an RMA is strategic behavior.[13] That means the dynamics and consequences of an RMA will be subject to the play of all the dimensions that shape every case of strategic action. The latest instance of RMA or military transformation has to be understood in the context of all the other RMAs/transformations in history. Similarly, the hopes for using the information technologies at the core of this particular project need to be reviewed in the light of our historical understanding of the important, but limited, role of technology in shaping the course and outcome of conflict. In wars between belligerents who are technically in touch with each other, a technological advantage enjoyed by one side is rarely, if ever, the most significant factor in victory or defeat.[14] This conclusion is well attested from strategic history. The reason is not hard to identify. Given the many dimensions of war and strategy, only the most extraordinary technical shortfall (e.g., we have gunpowder weapons, or the atomic bomb, and you do not) will deny the technically-challenged belligerent any realistic possibility of finding adequate compensation elsewhere. War and strategy have to be studied, planned for, and conducted holistically.

A peril in the contemporary American transformation project is that it tempts a defense community long overly enamored of technology to believe that truly wonderful machines, and genuinely intelligent ideas and organizations to exploit them, are the keys to victory.[15] The historical experience of all periods accessible to us reveals the limited military value of new technology, given that war, and hence strategy for war, is perennially a combined-arms venture. But that nearly axiomatic truth is especially pertinent in the twenty-first century, because at the computerized heart of the American military transformation is a technology that globalization is already making readily available, relatively cheaply, to both friend and foe worldwide. Moreover, the cutting edge of technical excellence in information manipulation is commercial and civilian, rather than official and military. Again, this is not a strike against the transformation project as currently outlined. But it is a reason to be cautious and modest, rather than highly ambitious and arrogant, in the expectations which we attach to a transforming American military. A proper respect for history would, of course, go a long way toward protecting the United States from the folly of believing that it may be in the process of constructing a military machine that will rewrite the timeless lore of war and strategy. These cautionary words in praise of historical experience are well known to many thoughtful people in the defense community. Even some technophiles talk a good deal about the importance of people, ideas, organization, and so on.[16] Nonetheless, words and behavior may not correlate closely. The USSR had an admirable document in Stalin's 1936 Constitution; the problem was that it was entirely ignored in the tyrant's style of governing. The American romance with technology is of such long standing and runs so deep in the culture that even assurances of a sound understanding of technology's limited domain in war and strategy fail to reassure completely.[17]

The United States cannot avoid suffering from the vices of its virtues, a point we have had occasion to register already. As the bearers of a forward-looking, fundamentally optimistic culture, Americans are prepared to undertake the most daunting tasks relatively undismayed by prospective difficulties, to the limited degree to which they are anticipated at all. This willingness to tackle new challenges is a significant social virtue. However, this virtue tends to carry the baggage of the vice of indifference to, though often it is no more than simple ignorance of, what might be learned from historical experience. Given the potential immensity of the project of playing global sheriff, the United States will need all the knowledge that can be gleaned from a careful reading of the history of statecraft and strategy, especially of its own record in those regards. American power and influence today is, of course, historically extraordinary; indeed, this is the fact upon which the argument of this book is founded. But that extraordinary preeminence must function with reference to the essentially unchanging nature of statecraft, strategy, and war. The American cultural bias favoring change is almost bound to come at the cost of undervaluing what remains of value from the past. A defense community firmly set on transforming national military capabilities, especially when it already has the American cultural tilt in favor of the future, is at serious risk of undervaluing strategic continuities. After all, official endorsement of transformation, let alone RMA, can be interpreted as a bold commitment to discontinuity. If this is not so, then military transformation is sorely misnamed.[18] The issue for American defense professionals is not the virtue in military change; rather, it is the need to recognize the context within which that change must occur. That context, as this book seeks to emphasize, is statecraft, strategy, and war, whose natures and workings cannot be redrafted by American prowess, no matter how impressive.

It is true that America's transforming military power is creating for the country an apparently permissive strategic context for performance in the role of sheriff, at least for a while. However, the nature of war and strategy is not to be mocked by American technological achievement. What Clausewitz said about war being the realm of chance, and of friction, and his trinitarian analysis, particularly in its recognition of the role of the people, remains as valid as ever, regardless of the nominal potency of the American sheriff's armament.[19] That novel potency, for all its obvious value as a policy instrument, brings with it an added danger. It may be interpreted by policymakers as offering strategically reliable outcomes to a degree that affronts the very nature of war and strategy. If American society in general, and its defense community in particular, is not prudently respectful of historical experience, it is riding for a fall that will make the mistakes of Vietnam appear minor in comparison.[20] To act as sheriff of world order, the role that the world needs the United States to play, Americans should eagerly seize any source of reasonably well attested wisdom that is available. If treated with respect, the historical record is just such a source. In point of fact, it is the leading such source. Strictly understood, history provides the only source of evidence on what tends to work and what does not in statecraft, strategy, and war.

To close this final appeal in my nine point argument, I offer two quotations that help us see what might be learned from history. The first is from a British admiral, Reginald Custance, writing nearly a century ago in 1907:

> The reader is to observe that the naval mind is divided into two schools—the historical and the *matériel*. The adherents of the one appeal for guidance to the great masters of the art of war by sea and land; they hold that it is very important to study tactics and strategy by the light of history. The disciples of the other do not believe the lessons of the past are applicable to the present; they have neglected the study of tactics and strategy, and have devoted their energies to the development of the *matériel*—ships, guns, armour, etc.[21]

If Admiral Custance's words can be read not so much as an indictment of a current trend, but rather in the spirit of a general warning, the second quotation is unambiguously specific in its criticism. The editors of the outstanding volume of case studies of historical RMAs, Williamson Murray and MacGregor Knox, characteristically pull no punches when they address what they understand to be the ambitions of the current drive for American military transformation.

> Yet even military revolutions have limits: they have not changed in the past—and cannot change in the future—war's underlying nature. Perhaps the most striking claim of contemporary Beltway pundits is that technological innovation, particularly in information technology, will purge the conduct of war of the uncertainties and ambiguities of the past. For those happy powers that set the technological pace, war will become an essentially frictionless engineering exercise. . . . The obsessions of the technological utopians derive equally from the deeply and quaintly American belief that all human problems have engineering solutions, and from the profoundly un-American (to those familiar with the United States' proud and violent history) post-Vietnam search for technological silver bullets that will permit U.S. forces to wage war without suffering—or perhaps even inflicting—casualties.[22]

Like many a powerful critique, this by Murray and Knox is overstated; it is unfair to some of the more thoughtful people who are working on the military transformation project. Nonetheless, they exaggerate for a good cause. The idea is circulating that a new American way of war, which should be realized much more fully as the transformation project gains momentum, will be the vital enabler of the American role as sheriff. If Murray and Knox, two professional historians, are basically correct in their criticism of the American quest for immaculate military performance through technology, then some rude awakenings as to the true nature and workings of war and strategy awaits those policymakers and soldiers who are historically challenged.

CONCLUSIONS

The many threads of argument that have been interwoven through this lengthy discussion lend themselves to presentation as six broad conclusions. Since there is no merit in novelty for its own sake, and these points have generally been well flagged in the body of the text, readers should find little to amaze them in these concluding thoughts. Nonetheless, these are exceptionally important points of argument. It is quite possible that some or all of them might have been so heavily contextualized in the preceding chapters that they either sank from sight or lost the hard edge necessary for clarity.

1. Continuing American domestic support for the role of sheriff cannot simply be assumed.

It is not the case that the United States, the only power currently capable of playing the role of sheriff for a world in need of a well-armed law officer, must fill the need. World politics and international security do not reduce conveniently and reliably to a Toynbee-esque tale of challenge and adequate response. Americans could decide that the challenge of playing the "Dirty Harry" mission, of being the country that gets the job done using whatever means necessary, is not to their liking. Americans might also decide that, notwithstanding loose talk about the essential unity of many security problems in an ever more globalized context of world affairs, a meaningful distinction can be drawn between taking a proactive approach to problems that are emerging for the United States and riding forth actually looking for trouble. For American society to support the performance of the sheriff role, it will need to see plausible, meaning fairly obvious and credible, connections between global U.S. military action and vital, or at least major, American interests.

Domestic tolerance of the sheriff role may not be fragile so soon after September 11, but neither can it be taken for granted. It is a role certain to attract far more foreign criticism than praise. Moreover, it is all but inevitable that the country will occasionally suffer a humiliating defeat that might be physically painful, as well. In Vietnam, Americans stayed the course with remarkable and admirable fortitude, until eventually they chose to snatch certain defeat from the jaws of at least possible victory.[23] Given the high order of incompetence with which the war was conducted, most of American society kept faith with what passed for policy and strategy for much longer than Washington had any right to expect. In a popular democracy, foreign policy must first work at home if it is ever to be tried seriously abroad. This means that the U.S. government will need to keep explaining America's world policing role in terms that find widespread domestic favor. In practice, this requires twin foci of justification, both of which make for additional foreign difficulties. Those difficulties are unavoidable, however, because if American society is not supportive of the sheriff role, the world will lack an effective ordering agent. The twin foci of explanation that are essential for domestic support include, first, a clear assertion, comprised of both a definition and an assessment of importance, of the particular American interest in the case in question. Second, the American interest rationale must be augmented by, or even completely expressed in, an ideological explanation. Generally cynical and pessimistic Europeans typically do not respond warmly to the lofty rhetoric, expression of high ideals, and religiosity with which American leaders speak to domestic audiences.[24] One should not forget that Europe does, after all, contain three other permanent members of the UN Security Council, as well as housing in NATO what, until recently, was frequently described as the most successful, if perennially "troubled," alliance in world history.

Andrew Bacevich makes a powerful existential case for a contemporary American empire.

> Holding sway in not one but several regions of pivotal geopolitical importance, disdaining the legitimacy of political economic principles other than its own, declaring the existing order to be sacrosanct, asserting unquestioned military supremacy with a globally deployed force configured not for self-defense but for coercion; these are the actions of a nation engaged in the governance of empire.[25]

Whether or not Bacevich is eventually judged correct, he advances a story that will not play well, either in Peoria or abroad. Imperial America is a complete non-starter as a public explanation for the American mission in foreign policy. Most, if not all, other countries, by the way, do not have missions in their foreign policy. Indeed, they would find the very idea pretentious and absurd.

The United States truly is not quite an ordinary country, either in its strengths in hard power or in the impossible-to-quantify calculus of influence known as soft power. But to sustain the necessary domestic support for the role of sheriff—a role vastly more acceptable to Americans than that of imperial policeman, even if the practical distinction is hard to discern—the foreign policy discourse must be conducted largely in ideological terms. When combined with a rationale for the acceptance of some risk and pain that emphasizes notably American interests, the foreign policy story may or may not pass muster for the necessary domestic support over the longer term. We should not forget that many of the occasions when the American sheriff will be moved to perform his duty are likely to be wars of choice, rather than of strict necessity. Furthermore, the dangers of such strategic behavior are probably going to increase exponentially as WMD proliferate further. If those two points are found persuasive, it would be rash to assume any automatic, let alone uncritical, domestic tolerance of world ordering duty. When success attends American diplomacy and the occasional exercise of American arms, all—well, most—should be fine at home. But war is always a gamble, no matter how righteous the cause or necessary the action.[26] Domestic support for the role of sheriff could prove fatally fragile in the event, for example, that an American expeditionary force were to suffer a nuclear re-enactment of the Little Big Horn.

Contrary to appearances, perhaps, I am not pessimistic about the willingness of American society to support the foreign policy outlined above, with its implicit military requirements and attendant risks. This first conclusion simply argues that domestic support for the role and its implementing policy and strategy cannot prudently be just assumed.

2. *Although the international authority for the United States to perform as sheriff depends critically upon the country's lone standing at the pinnacle of global power, the way in which the role is played is vital to foreign judgments about its legitimacy, and those judgments do matter.*

On balance, the metaphor of sheriff is appropriate, but it should not be permitted to mislead. For America to perform as sheriff it needs to remain militarily preponderant. The role is feasible only because of the country's strength. That strength has several sources and lends itself to international expression as the ability to coerce, bribe, and persuade. The United States is, of course, the bearer of a candidate universal ideology that can be summarized as a somewhat messianic commitment to democracy and globalized free-market capitalism.

Naturally, it is important to register the potency of American culture, of America as a civilization, and indeed of America as the beneficiary of much soft power. But to play sheriff, the first requirement is to be strong and long of arm, and to be able to shoot straight as often as necessary. In the basically anarchic realm of world politics, when order needs to be maintained or restored, ideas, culture, and civilization follow; they do not precede and enable, let alone substitute for, the hard power of cruise missiles and marines.

This is not to demean, let alone discount, the non-military dimensions of American superpower. I am concerned, though, that America's military strength should not be taken too much for granted. "Peace, democracy, and free markets" may or may not be "the ideas that conquered the world," but America cannot perform as sheriff simply because it is the bearer of an ideology that has extensive, if not quite universal, appeal.[27] Ideas, the attractions of a way of life, and wealth are all vital contributors to the ordering mission. But let there be no confusion: Military preponderance for strategic effectiveness is the most essential enabling agent required for global policing. In the world's rougher neighborhoods, and among its less salubrious political and cultural leaders, America's soft power is not a front-line contributor in the struggle for order.[28] Civilization follows—it does not precede—muscular manifestation of the prowess of the stars and stripes.

This second conclusion adds the recognition of international uncertainty to the domestic uncertainty already flagged as the first conclusion. Authority is legitimized power, and it is important that America's exercise of power on behalf of what it sees as world order should be widely regarded as legitimate. However, it is necessary to be clear about the basis of such legitimacy.

There is a sense in which power creates authority; it is self-legitimating. That overly simple point needs prompt correction by two amending judgments. Power loses authority if it is exercised either ineffectively or in ways blatantly disdainful of the interests of other security communities. It is not easy to grasp the true relationship between power and authority, and it is still less easy for the United States to behave in such a way that its power will yield the authority necessary for the world ordering role to be practicable and long lasting. America's right to act globally in protection of its definition of world order derives strictly from its unmatched military power. It has the authority that derives from strength. Undeniably, authority can be eroded by the manifest failure of policy and strategy, or by behavior that is unduly self-serving and is pursued with an obvious indifference to non-American interests. Nonetheless, America's authority as the principal guardian of world order rests most critically upon its extraordinary status as a polity in a class of its own across all the dimensions of national power. Although American behavior will affect foreign attitudes toward the legitimacy of its actions, that legitimacy rests significantly upon the authority bequeathed by perceptions of capability. If the role of sheriff is considered a duty, it is a duty that falls to Americans only because of the country's solitary material preeminence. To perform well enough as sheriff, the hard power of potential economic and military command requires assistance from the soft power of political persuasion and influence. But that soft power is relevant, and indeed exists, only because it rides on the back of the world's most productive economy and most formidable military machine.[29]

For many years to come, the United States could probably police its understanding of a tolerable world order virtually regardless of foreign hostility. America should be strong enough, and sufficiently potent a provider of security and other benefits for some allies of conviction and others of convenience, to be able to enforce its will without appearing to be truly isolated. However, only limited comfort should be taken from this judgment. Of course there will be instances, hopefully rare, when the United States should threaten or take action out of duty to its own interests and on behalf of what it believes is in the best interest of the world community, even if the sheriff has to stand and perform quite alone. From time to time a leader, in this context America as the only possible leader, should do what it believes to be right, regardless of the opinions of others. But, as students of the history of statecraft we know from Thucydides that "fear, honor, and interest" are "three of the strongest motives" that influence behavior.[30] If the American sheriff polices world order in the teeth of opposition from yesterday's great powers, and perhaps tomorrow's, it should be able to enforce its will. But polities great and small whose honor is thus affronted, though unable to thwart the sheriff directly, will assuredly be more than capable of raising the costs of the guardian role. If the costs of performing as sheriff are high, even when the mission seems to be conducted successfully, the vital American domestic support for the role will grow perilously fragile. We need to remember that in most cases of potential military action, the American sheriff will confront wars of discretion, not of strict necessity. It would be unwise for Americans to be strongly disdainful of the honor and interests of those abroad who voice what will often appear to be hypocritical and self-regarding criticism of the sheriff's efforts. Americans may be right on the issues, but they will needlessly stimulate a wealth of harassing opposition that must endanger performance of the policing role that world order requires.

3. *There are many reasons, including those just cited, why American performance of the sheriff role may prove untenable. That would be unfortunate, because the need for world order to be effectively policed is greater than ever.*

It would be nice to be able to consider alternatives to the American role presented and discussed in these pages. Instead of an American sheriff leading, first on its own behalf and, as a secondary bonus, on behalf of the whole world, what alternative agents or mechanisms for the maintenance of order are on offer? A deafening silence is the realistic answer. Surely there are several cooperative multilateralist alternatives to American guardianship. Is not the UN Security Council functionally a potential war (and peace) cabinet for humankind? Or, if that possible option is deemed a little too exclusive with respect to its five permanent members, and rather too indiscriminate with regard to the rotating members, could not the G-8 Powers institutionalize the practice of a new form of concert statecraft on behalf of world order? Neither of these notions is entirely ridiculous. The problem is that neither would work. Paradoxically, perhaps, American power is a principal problem as well as the unavoidable solution.

The United States today is too powerful to participate simply as one among the small crowd of G-8's greater polities. America's economic, and more importantly its military, strength means that it must dominate multilateral debate over policy and strategy in defense of world order. Indeed, it must dominate debate over the definition of the proper meaning of order. The enormous disparities in wealth and ready military power between America and any candidates for concert partners, whether in the institutional context of the G-8 or the UN, translates in practice as an American authority born of physical strength. That is the way things are in world politics. If a country contributes disproportionately to a multilateral enterprise, it will insist on a suitably disproportionate say in decisions about what is to be done and how it is to be done. Critics of the American policing role that I have endorsed will need to be careful that they do not succumb to the undoubted attractions of liberal institutionalist fantasies. As this book has outlined in some detail, there are several reasons why America might not perform well as sheriff, and many serious problems must attend attempted conduct of the role. However, the fundamental case for America as sheriff is not that it is judged by this author to be the superior alternative. Rather, the case is that if world order is to be policed, hopefully effectively, there is simply no alternative to America as sheriff.

A malign synergism between foreign and domestic opposition could well abort the sheriff project. Unfortunately, there are no other options on the menu for protecting world order when dangerous, difficult, and expensive strategic behavior is required. The alternatives to American leadership and, necessarily, dominance, are either a complete absence of any enforcement agency, or a process of endless debate among states certain to find a rich brew of reasons for delay, compromise, and—in consequent effect—inaction. My argument is that America must perform as sheriff, if there is to be a sheriff that can provide the needed maintenance and periodic restoration of world order. As an old-fashioned positivist, and a classical realist to boot, I insist that there is literally no practicable alternative to an American trusteeship over the world order of the next several decades. Whether or not the United States has the political, cultural, and economic fortitude, not to mention the wisdom, to perform the duty well enough is, of course, quite another matter.

A good number of the commentators who are, or profess to be, appalled by what they see as evidence of American unilateralism, are sadly deficient in their grasp of the workings of world politics. There are no grounds for argument against the strong desirability of the American sheriff operating with as much explicit and tacit international consent, as well as actual foreign assistance, as can be garnered—as long as it is consistent with the integrity of the ordering mission. The basic problem, which is to say the plot that many critics have never unravelled, is that the means for protecting world order cannot be understood as a challenge that people of goodwill from different countries and cultures can resolve in a thoroughly constructive, multilateral spirit. The conduct of world politics is not an academic seminar. Politicians are not seeking truth, they are looking both for advantage and to avoid disadvantage. Whether the nominal security issue of the hour is addressed effectively can be very much a secondary consideration.

There can be no ignoring the self-regarding imperatives that dominate states' security policies, just as there can be no denying the vast differences in capabilities among states. For at least several decades into the twenty-first century, the tougher cases of actual or potential international disorder will have to be met by the United States if they are to be met by any agency other than the interplay of local forces. If the American sheriff is wise, it will ride out only rarely; will seek, listen to, and be prepared to accept advice from those who are well informed about the region at issue; will be willing to pay some modest price in compromised control in return for international cooperation; and will protect most jealously its invaluable reputation for strategic effectiveness. Too much of the debate about the United States' role in the world, including the discussion among scholars, allows itself to be sidetracked by second-order topics. It is a first-order conclusion of this discussion, if I may test readers' impatience with the repetition, that the United States must perform as sheriff if such world order as we enjoy is to be protected. There are no workable alternatives. It is possible that Americans will not perform effectively, but if they do not, we are all in serious trouble because there is no deputy sheriff capable of stepping into the breach, nor is there some institutionalized multilateral alternative. Needless to add, perhaps, the style of U.S. performance of the guardian role—which is comprised of a basket of second-order matters—can facilitate or hinder, possibly fatally, the prospects for success. As an overall judgment, analyses of international peace and security that are not composed in the context of the historical realities of world politics are worse than a waste of time. They mislead the uneducated and, as a consequence, endanger the performance of the guardian mission by its only feasible current agent, the United States.

4. *The role of sheriff must serve a clear foreign policy; it should not simply express, or appear to express, military preponderance.*

The role of principal protector of world order is politically sensitive, not to mention controversial, because as a general rule the sanction it enjoys from international and domestic law will be eminently challengeable, at least legally. As sheriff of world order, the United States performs duties to which it is self-appointed. That self-appointment rests on the authority of unequalled economic and, especially, military strength. Given the centrality of America's military power to the guardianship mission, it is extraordinarily important that foreign policy should be seen guiding national security behavior. Two closely linked issues need to be given parallel treatment. On the one hand, American military behavior genuinely should be instrumental in support of foreign policy. On the other hand, that behavior must appear instrumental, with foreign policy providing the guiding direction.

This fourth conclusion may seem obvious to some readers; unfortunately it is not so. There is a two-way relationship between political goals and military power; this is the realm of strategy. People unfriendly toward an American sheriff may be inclined to suspect that military prowess feeds political ambition to an unhealthy degree. In other words, they suspect the United States may do what it believes it can do militarily, with foreign policy justification trailing in the wake of strategic feasibility. Since policy goals are apt to expand to meet what the military is believed capable of delivering, Americans need to police their decision making to guard against the appearance of undue strategic opportunism.

Justly or otherwise, the United States has a reputation abroad for being ready to reach for its guns when most of the rest of the world would prefer noncoercive, certainly nonviolent, statecraft. The differences in attitude toward the relevance of force between, say, Europe and America, are easily explained with reference to culture and geopolitics.[31] However, foreign charges that Americans are a little too quick, if not quite actually eager, to flex their military muscles merit a considered answer. By its very nature, effective performance of the sheriff's role critically depends on America's reputation for strategic excellence. But there is a need to guard against the strategy bridge between policy and military favoring traffic from the military side. It follows that U.S. policymakers must explain the role of sheriff of world order with much more regard to the needs of international security than to the exciting options now enabled by the transforming military establishment.

Because policy aspiration can, and indeed usually does, grow with perceived capability, Americans will have to carefully maintain the proper relationship between policy and military power and not permit the latter to encroach beyond its proper sphere. The connection is complex because foreign policy choices for the American sheriff must be influenced by judgments regarding what is, and what is not, militarily practicable for the necessary strategic effect.

Although clear statement of American foreign policy intentions can be reassuring to those at home and abroad who worry about the perils of military opportunism, such clear statement can also advertise that which might better be left in obscurity. Performance of the self-appointed role of sheriff of world order is a fact reflecting contemporary geopolitics. Many foreigners can accept, even occasionally welcome, America performing global protection duty. They find that duty much less palatable if they must confront an almost embarrassingly clear American foreign policy explanation of what the country is about and why. The case for being led by foreign policy rather than strategic behavior is overwhelming. However, some of the geopolitical realities of practical inequalities in world affairs are best left understated.

5. *Military transformation can be a snare and a delusion if it is not approached and exploited in the context of strategy.*

The prosecution of a military transformation needs to be understood as strategic behavior.[32] The idea has gained ground that the role of sheriff is critically enabled by the new military potency yielded by the transformation that is underway and by a new style of joint warfare that the transformation enables. The argument of this fifth conclusion is not that transformation will fail in significant military respects. Rather is the claim that the process of transformation encourages focus upon, and undue celebration of, the excellence of the American military instrument at the risk of neglecting the purpose of it all. It is understandable why the military superpower, at present supremely confident in its effectiveness, should be disinclined to think strategically. The more powerful a country judges itself to be *vis à vis* potential foes, the less likely it is to be strongly motivated to reason strategically. If America is sufficiently strong militarily, so the argument might proceed, strategic effect will take care of itself.

A somewhat engineering-minded superstate, committed to a proactive security policy supported by a transforming military establishment, is liable to miss the full potential strategic rewards from its undoubted military prowess. As we have had occasion to mention in earlier discussion, the U.S. defense community has several impressive strengths, but sophisticated and holistic approaches to war and strategy are not prominent among them. An undue focus on the military instrument, rather than on its purpose or its needed performance for strategic effect, is all but guaranteed by the contemporary political and military contexts. On the one hand, the role of sheriff requires opposition to whoever would disturb the *pax Americana*. On the other hand, the strong American commitment to military transformation cannot help but place an exceptionally heavy emphasis on what American military power might do to others. This is not so much wrong as it is incomplete.

Whether or not a transforming American military establishment can support the role of sheriff as it may need to be supported will depend on the full and relevant contexts of war and strategy. America's unilateral military prowess is not an issue. The issues are the kinds of conflicts with which the sheriff will have to cope. In addition, it is vital to recognize that strategy's several dimensions can offer some potent sources of compensation for enemies who are categorically overmatched in most aspects of military power. For example, the long-standing American habit of referring to its nuclear forces as the nuclear *deterrent* prejudges that which only trial-by-crisis can demonstrate to be probably true. Just as near-habitual reference to the nuclear deterrent presumes a strategic effectiveness that U.S. forces may or may not achieve, so a defense community apparently obsessed with the transformation project is likely to focus unduly on its own prospective potency at the expense of imaginative consideration of the choices that others might exercise.[33]

It has been necessary to register this conclusion, but the problem to which I have been referring is probably not capable of being addressed effectively. The United States may be militarily too powerful, and culturally too deeply imbued with an engineering spirit, to systemically adopt a holistic approach to war and strategy. Nonetheless, one can but do one's duty and try. The role of sheriff will have to be pursued despite weaknesses that are really the consequences of extraordinary material strengths.

6. *There are persuasive grounds for believing that the United States will be able to succeed well enough as sheriff of the new world order.*

This book has pulled no punches in citing and discussing the problems that will, or might, seriously impede U.S. performance in defense of world order. Paradoxically, the strength of some of the actual and predictable difficulties provides grounds for optimism about the American role. The challenges are all too real, as recent events have affirmed. It is possible, though not probable, that the country will choose to forego the duty of guarding world order, save only for cases with the most direct of connections to American national security. However, the grounds for optimism are neither ephemeral nor trivial.

World order needs to be policed. Such strict necessity is no guarantee of performance, of course, but in the U.S. superstate there is a polity, indeed the only polity, capable of performing the mission. The role of sheriff will be performed by the United States or it will not be performed at all. The practical alternative to American leadership in guarding the world order of the twenty-first century is an absence of guardianship. If the United States does not step up to this mission, recognizing it as a duty both to itself and the world, the job will not be done. The more recent public debate over American policy might give the misleading impression that major alternative approaches to the maintenance of world order can be considered. This would be desirable, but alas it is not so. Let there be no misunderstanding on this most vital of matters. The alternative to America in the sheriff role is a vacancy. Aside from the United States, there is no country, coalition, or institution capable of taking the lead in protecting world order over the next several decades. Americans may not perform well. They might retire from all except the most directly self-serving of strategic behavior in the face of some obvious failures and much criticism at home and abroad. As we have noted, performance of the sheriff role cannot prudently be taken for granted. However, our final conclusion is that there are persuasive grounds to be optimistic about the prospects for American success.

A substantial stream of European opinion—or at least "Old European" opinion—may well dissent from this judgment, but the recent and contemporary historical record of U.S. statecraft is truly impressive. After all, the United States did play either a leading or the leading role in achieving decisive victories in no fewer than three great wars in the twentieth century. Furthermore, following an understandable shake-down period of an interwar kind in the 1990s, the country responded to the events of September 11, 2001, not only with a strategy to address that particular class of peril, but also with a tolerably clear vision of America's global duty on behalf of order. As Huntington and others have long observed, the United States is a very large country that tends to perform best when it undertakes tasks suitable to its preeminence.[34]

Americans can be impatient, as one might expect from the members of a powerful country that believes it has the ability to force the pace of events. But, time and again, American statecraft and strategy have demonstrated an impressive absence of haste. During the long Cold War, American outlasted, outwaited, and helped push to self-destruction the evil empire of the heirs of Lenin. There was much that could be criticized about the U.S. mission in Vietnam, but excessive strategic impatience could not be cited in the indictment. On balance, and granting that the role of sheriff assuredly will meet with only mixed success, there are strong grounds to be confident that the duty will be performed well enough. Possibly most important among them is the American recognition that from time to time it will need to act militarily, whether or not there is a loud chorus of international approval. Americans appear to understand that the policing role, though bound to benefit from foreign approval, is not an ongoing exercise in popularity. They recognize both that most people will always favor peace over war, if policy choice is thus crudely reduced, and that the American exercise of its supreme military power will inevitably attract resentment and hostility. That is just the way of the world.

The argument developed in these pages ought to be valid. I claim in this concluding discussion not only that the world needs the United States to act as sheriff of world order, but also that it is likely to perform well enough. Victory is not only possible; it is probable. The United States has an impressive national history of rising to monumental challenges and of finding ways to succeed in meeting them. I may be wrong, but the smart money is on America performing as the world requires in protection of international security and civilized values.

*   *   *   *

By way of the necessary Parthian shot to this lengthy analysis, it is important to remind people that the United States is the only possible candidate for the world policing role. The United Nations, the

G-8, NATO, international law, and international governance—a slippery concept favored by many academics[35]—are none of them plausibly adequate agents for world order without active American participation. American statecraft will certainly and perennially have to contend with contentious arguments regarding its authority for strategic behavior in protecting world order. If it is prudent, America will demonstrate a decent respect for the opinions and interests of others. But, again if it is prudent, it will not permit those opinions to divert it from performing coercively as sheriff when it deems such strategic behavior essential. The United States has the authority of unmatched power, of unmistakeable success, and of observably acting in ways that benefit the world community as well as itself. Root-and-branch critics of this American role, whatever their motives, quite literally have nothing constructive to offer in place of a temporary American global guardianship. If Americans should decline the honor and responsibility of protecting world order, there is no one, and nothing, else capable of attempting the mission, at least not for many decades to come.

NOTES

CHAPTER 1
THE ARGUMENT

1. Gray, *Strategy for Chaos.*
2. Bull, *Anarchical Society,* and Clark, *Hierarchy of States,* are fundamental; while Hartmann and Heuser, eds., *War, Peace and World Orders,* provides historical and cultural depth; and Mead, *Special Providence,* esp. ch. 8, provides an American context for international order.
3. Howard has argued plausibly that "it has to be said that a high proportion of states that have come into existence since 1945 have not developed as nations at all, for one basic reason. They have not experienced that essential rite of passage: fighting, or at least showing a credible readiness to fight, for their independence." *Invention of Peace,* pp. 98–9.
4. By which they meant, narrowly, the calculable balance between the strategic nuclear forces of the United States and the Soviet Union.
5. The administration of George W. Bush has appreciated this point clearly enough, but political realities at home and abroad have obliged it to pretend that there is a bilateral strategic nuclear "balance" which can and should be subject to negotiation for mutual reductions. The vital documents are the "U.S.-Russia Strategic Offensive Reductions Treaty" and the "U.S.-Russia Joint Declaration," both signed in Moscow on May 24, 2002. The political significance of these documents is as great as their military-strategic implications are near trivial.
6. Kagan, *On the Origins of War,* p. 570. In contrast to collective defense, collective security rests on the principle that any aggressor will be opposed by the collectivity of states, regardless of the identity of the malefactor or the intensity of interest of individual states in the issues immediately at stake.
7. Blainey, *Causes of War,* emphasizes the role of uncertainty over the distribution of power. Blainey summarizes his argument thus: "War began when two countries had contradictory ideas of their own bargaining positions and therefore could not solve peacefully an issue which vitally affected them" (p. 241). Also see in particular two more recent studies: Van Evera, *Causes of War,* and Copeland, *Origins of Major War.*
8. Mead, *Special Providence,* illustrates well the persistence of competing impulses in American attitudes toward the outside world.
9. Soft power is a concept all but patented by Nye. In his most recent book-length disquisition on the subject, he tells us that soft power is the power to co-opt people rather than coerce them. It is an indirect form of power, unlike the hard power that typically is military or economic. *Paradox of American Power,* esp. pp. 8–9.
10. Kissinger, *Does America Need a Foreign Policy?* p. 17 (emphasis added).
11. Kagan, *On the Origins of War,* p. 568.
12. See Bacevich, "Steppes to Empire," p. 52, and *American Empire,* for the full story.

13. Donnelly, "Past as Prologue," p. 165. Donnelly is reviewing Boot's excellent study of *Savage Wars of Peace*. Boot has borrowed his major title from Rudyard Kipling's 1899 poem, "The White Man's Burden" (or "The United States and the Philippine Islands").

14. See Billington, *America's Frontier Heritage*, and Slotkin, *Gunfighter Nation*.

15. Historian Paul Kennedy, who warned of the perils of "imperial overstretch" in his best-seller, *Rise and Fall of the Great Powers*, p. 515, reminds us now of just how wide the U.S. defense economic margin is over everyone else, severally and combined. Writing prior to recent large increases in the Pentagon budget (for FY2003), Kennedy notes that "the Pentagon's budget in the year 2000 was equivalent to the combined defense spending of the next nine largest military powers. There exists no equal in history to such a disproportionate share, even if we went back to the time of the Roman Empire. Indeed, American strategic power is even greater than the statistics suggest, since it is buttressed by an unrivalled technological and scientific base." "Maintaining American Power," p. 59.

16. Books by the usual suspects who are right, up to a point, press the case for the benefits of pursuing influence in a multilateral, and institutionalized, framework. See Ikenberry, *After Victory*, and Nye, *Paradox of American Power*.

17. Boot, *Savage Wars of Peace*, is useful. His closing advice is particularly so. "Yes, there is a danger of imperial overstretch and hubris—but there is an equal, if not greater, danger of undercommitment and lack of confidence. America should not be afraid to fight 'the savage wars of peace' if necessary to enlarge the 'empire of liberty.' It has done it before" (p. 352).

18. Aron spoke for all players and all periods when he advised that "prudence is the statesman's supreme virtue." *Peace and War*, p. 585. He contrasted prudence not with idealism, but rather with "*idealist illusion*, whether that illusion is juridical or ideological" (emphasis in the original).

19. Mandelbaum, "Inadequacy of American Power," pp. 61–73, reminds Americans that their power, of all kinds, cannot readily and swiftly transform the world so that "peace, democracy, and free markets" (p. 73) will characterize global conditions. See also Mandelbaum, *Ideas that Conquered the World*.

20. Murray and Knox are fairly persuasive in arguing that "revolutions in military affairs have emerged from evolutionary problem-solving directed at specific operational and tactical issues in a specific theatre of war against a specific enemy. Successful innovators have always thought in terms of fighting wars against *actual* rather than *hypothetical* opponents, with *actual* capabilities, in pursuit of *actual* strategic and political objectives" (emphasis in the original). "Conclusion: The Future Behind Us," p. 192.

21. As usual, Clausewitz offers a potent thought relevant to this phenomenon: "So long as no acceptable theory, no intelligent analysis of the conduct of war exists, routine methods will tend to take over even at the highest levels." *On War*, ed. and trans. Michael Howard and Peter Paret (1832; Princeton, N.J.: Princeton University Press, 1976), p. 154.

22. Vickers, "Revolution Deferred," p. 189.

23. For one prominent, and unquestionably cogent, example, see Ikenberry, "America's Imperial Ambition," pp. 44–60.

24. The latest major contribution to the neorealist canon is Mearsheimer, *Tragedy of Great Power Politics*, which offers this gem: "Structural factors such as anarchy and the distribution of power, I argue, are what matter most for explaining international politics. The theory pays little attention to individuals or domestic political considerations such as ideology. It tends to treat states like black boxes or billiard balls" (pp. 10–11). In some contrast, I am a classical realist who finds the world of rational choice of the neorealists of American political science thoroughly unconvincing. The poverty of American political science in its neorealist guise has been exposed mercilessly by Payne in his revisionist writings on deterrence. Payne demonstrates how important those local domestic details, including individual psychology, can be. See his book, *Fallacies of Cold War Deterrence*.

25. As exemplified in Bush, *National Security Strategy of the United States* (2002).

26. Three major statements issued under the signature of the Secretary of Defense tell a fairly clear and consistent story. Rumsfeld: *Quadrennial Defense Review Report;* "Transforming the Military"; and *Annual Report* (2002). For a reasonable assessment of Rumsfeld's transformation plan, insofar as it has been revealed to date, see O'Hanlon, "Rumsfeld's Defense Vision."

27. In 2002, in his State of the Union address on January 29, in a graduation speech at West Point delivered on June 1, and in the master policy document, *National Security Strategy of the United States* (2002), Bush announced, explained, and elaborated on the new doctrine of preemption. In the last mentioned of those citations, the President said: "To forestall or prevent such hostile acts by our adversaries, rogue states or terrorists who may use weapons of mass destruction (WMD), the United States will, if necessary, act pre-emptively" (p. 15). Recall that preemption means to attack first in the last resort. When one is seriously at risk to WMD, the last resort could well imply too long a delay for comfort. Prudence, that prime virtue in statecraft, suggests the wisdom of preventive, not literally preemptive, action.

28. Amid a vast literature, and for this particular dimension of the Vietnam experience, see Krepinevich, *Army and Vietnam;* Buzzanco, *Masters of War;* and McMaster, *Dereliction of Duty.*

29. Those peacetime errors include the choice of commanders who intellectually, physically or morally prove unequal to the unique burdens of wartime command.

30. Luttwak, "Towards Post-Heroic Warfare," and Cohen, "Kosovo and the New American Way of War."

31. Kissinger, *Does America Need a Foreign Policy?* pp. 79–80.

32. The concept and practical meaning of victory merit more attention than is usually allocated. Two attempts to probe its mysteries are Bond, *Pursuit of Victory;* and Gray, *Defining and Achieving Decisive Victory.*

33. President George W. Bush is not confused on this vital point. "We must build and maintain our defenses beyond challenge"; and, lest the point had not been made with sufficient clarity, "our military must dissuade future military competition." *National Security Strategy of the United States* (2002), p. 29.

34. I am much indebted to Liddell Hart, who wrote that "the point, and the distinction between actual surprise and surprise effect, are of significance to the theory of war." He was describing the surprise effect of the British bombard-

ment of the Messines Ridge, and the use of mines, in May 1917. *History of the First World War,* p. 325.

35. See Gooch, *Plans of War,* esp. ch. 6. It should be needless to say that after 1870 France had its eyes fixed more firmly on the Rhine than on the Channel.

36. For classic statements of the problem, see Spykman, *Geography of the Peace* and *America's Strategy in World Politics.*

37. My analysis focuses on *strategic* threats, which is to say threats that involve the actual or prospective use of force. This is not to deny that world order can also be menaced by other kinds of threats; for example, by economic disruption or sudden environmental degradation.

38. Walter Laqueur offers a ray of hope when he argues that "movements inspired by religious and radical fanaticism do not last forever. Past experience shows that the original fanaticism tends to peter out, whether because of internal quarrels, external setbacks, or the rise of a new generation with different priorities." So much for the good news. The less good news is that the capacity of terrorists to inflict truly catastrophic damage is here to stay, even as their motivation changes. "Left, Right, and Beyond," esp. pp. 80–2.

39. Kagan, "Power and Weakness," p. 15. The article attracted so much notice that Kagan was moved to expand its message to short book-length: *Paradise and Power.*

40. But Cohen offers a plausible analysis keyed to the global imperial role, in "Defending America in the Twenty-first Century."

41. I borrow the phrase from the title of chapter 10 in Brodie, *Strategy in the Missile Age.* See also Brodie's earlier analysis, "Strategy as a Science."

42. Brooks and Wohlforth, "American Primacy in Perspective," p. 21.

43. See the characteristically colorful argument in Peters, *Fighting for the Future,* pp. 70–83.

44. Sun-tzu, *Art of War,* p. 219. With apologies, I am adapting Sun-tzu, not employing him exactly. "Fatal terrain" is too evocative a concept to be confined strictly to Sun-tzu's use of it. "Where if one fights with intensity he will survive but if he does not fight with intensity he will perish, it is 'fatal terrain.'"

45. Laqueur explains that "[n]o society can protect all its members from terrorist attack, but all societies can reduce the risk by taking the offensive, by keeping terrorists on the run rather than concentrating on defense alone." "Left, Right, and Beyond," p. 81.

46. Recognition of this need lies behind the creation of the officially supported Deterrence Analysis Center, at the National Institute for Public Policy in Fairfax, Virginia. The center is addressing the challenges identified by Payne in his book, *Fallacies of Cold War Deterrence.* Payne's reasoning bears more than a casual resemblance to some elements in the argument developed a generation earlier in Booth, *Strategy and Ethnocentrism.*

47. This principle was outlined and explained with exemplary clarity a century ago in Callwell, *Small Wars,* ch. 7.

48. See Crane, ed., *Transforming Defense;* Binnendijk, ed., *Transforming America's Military;* and esp. Rumsfeld, *Annual Report* (2002), ch. 6, "Transforming the Force."

49. The traditional American way of war, which has tended to privilege attrition, is well presented in Weigley, *American Way of War,* and Huntington, *American Military Strategy.*

50. Howard, "When Are Wars Decisive?" p. 130. Also see Bond, *Pursuit of Victory.*

51. Clausewitz, *On War,* p. 607. "At the highest level the art of war turns into policy—but a policy conducted by fighting battles rather than by sending diplomatic notes."

52. Cohen, *Supreme Command.*

53. See Jablonsky, "Why Is Strategy Difficult?"; Gray, "Why Strategy Is Difficult"; and Betts, "The Trouble with Strategy."

54. This point is pressed hard in Gray, *Strategy for Chaos,* ch. 9, "Strategy as a Duel: RMA Meets the Enemy."

55. In Huntington's timeless judgment: "The U.S. military establishment is a product of and reflects American geography, culture, society, economy, and history." *American Military Strategy,* p. 13.

56. John Keegan startled the world of military scholarship a generation ago when he placed the human dimension center stage in his path-breaking study, *Face of Battle.* Evidence of his influence is widespread, but is exceptionally direct in Hanson, *The Western Way of War,* and in Goldsworthy, *Roman Army at War.*

57. Binnendijk, ed., *Transforming America's Military.*

58. Vandergriff, *Path to Victory,* may overstate the indictment, but still it is a troubling sign of the times. Also see Wong, *Stifling Innovation.* Cohen's *Supreme Command* carries the message that the American military profession is not to be trusted to be willing to behave boldly, when boldness is needed. Whether Cohen and other critics are, on balance, correct in their suspicions, there is merit in the maxim that a society has the defense establishment it deserves. I am grateful to Stephen Cimbala of Pennsylvania State University for reminding me of the significance of this ancient truth. We should not be unduly surprised if the American forces today carry attitudes strongly characteristic of the society from which they spring.

59. This was an exceptionally transparent message in the famous, or notorious, "Weinberger doctrine," first articulated on November 28, 1984. Secretary Weinberger's first test for the suitability of U.S. military action was as follows: "(1) FIRST, the United States should not commit forces to *combat* overseas unless the particular engagement is deemed vital to our national interest or that of our allies." Reprinted in Handel, *Masters of War,* p. 310 (emphasis in the original). It should be needless to say that an imperial power, enjoying global military preponderance, is unlikely to find many occasions for possible military intervention wherein its vital national interests will be engaged beyond scope for serious question.

60. *Mea culpa* for Gray, *Modern Strategy.* I acknowledge the inspiration of Kaplan for these words, though not for the thought: "There is No 'Modern' World," *Warrior Politics,* the title of ch. 1.

61. For a first-rate and mercifully terse guide to the basics and more, see Sarkesian, Williams, and Cimbala, *U.S. National Security.*

62. For example, see the careful critical analyses in O'Hanlon, *Defense Policy Choices for the Bush Administration,* and Williams, ed., *Holding the Line.*

63. Sun-tzu, *Art of War,* p. 179.

64. Ikenberry, "America's Imperial Ambition."

CHAPTER 2
PROTECTING WORLD ORDER

1. The concept of the "strategic moment" is more than a little ambiguous, which is probably a useful quality given the extensive range of historical phenomena it can be obliged to characterize. Ikenberry makes minimalist and uncontentious use of the term when he writes: "Major postwar junctures are rare strategic moments when leading or hegemonic states face choices about how to use their newly acquired power." *After Victory,* p. 4. By way of contrast, the case studies in Murray, Knox, and Bernstein, eds., *Making of Strategy,* though barely using the concept explicitly, rest on the proposition that states can have particular strategic moments of extraordinary influence and highly variable duration.

2. See the discussion of strategy in ch. 4.

3. For definitions and other basics, see Gray, *Modern Strategy,* esp. pp. 17–23. I understand strategy to mean the use that is made of force and the threat of force for the ends of policy. This is an elementary adaptation from Clausewitz (*On War,* p. 128).

4. In one of the clearest illustrations of this malady, Murray and Millett, writing about the German triumphs of 1940, observed that "for the Germans, the victory over France suggested that everything was possible for the Third Reich." *War to be Won,* p. 89.

5. Those determined to burrow into the literature on world order could do worse than attempt the following: Kissinger, *A World Restored;* Bull, *Anarchical Society;* Williams, *Failed Imagination?;* Knutsen, *Rise and Fall of World Orders;* Hartmann and Heuser, eds., *War, Peace and World Orders;* and Ikenberry, *After Victory.* Those who favor a more biographical approach should appreciate Knock, *To End All Wars.*

6. Friedman expresses the matter neatly, yet accurately, when he writes that "[t]he United States now faces mainly wars of choice, not compulsion." *Seapower as Strategy,* p. 98.

7. Strassler, ed., *The Landmark Thucydides;* Sun-tzu, *Art of War.*

8. See Kennedy, *Rise and Fall of the Great Powers,* esp. pp. 360, 514–35. He titles a section, "The United States: The Problems of Number One in Relative Decline" (p. 514). If history could serve as a reliable guide, he should have been right. As it was, his error proved to be embarrassingly large. The moral of this tale may be that historians are better at history than they are at using history to inspire ventures in futurology.

9. A well-balanced and hugely expert long view of the pace of technological change is provided in Falls, *A Hundred Years of War,* ch. 1. Falls is usefully skeptical of the idea that military-technical advance proceeds by occasional and sudden transformational lurches. I discuss his important perspective in *Strategy for Chaos,* pp. 51–6.

10. Aron, "Evolution of Modern Strategic Thought," p. 25. It would be even more accurate to claim that strategic thought draws its inspiration at each moment of history from the problems and opportunities flagged by officials acting as opinion leaders. See Gray, *Strategy for Chaos*, p. 1.

11. Brodie, *War and Politics*, p. 452.

12. Rosen, "Vietnam and the American Theory of Limited War"; Payne, *Fallacies of Cold War Deterrence;* and Gray, *House of Cards*. Payne's critique of American deterrence theory and attempted practice can be supplemented usefully by a classic of scholarship from yesteryear: George and Smoke, *Deterrence in American Foreign Policy*.

13. See Rathjens, "Dynamics of the Arms Race."

14. According to the highly placed Soviet sources used by Odom, the ABM treaty was welcomed in Moscow as being of great assistance to their bid for competitive success with ICBMs. Odom, *Collapse of the Soviet Military*, p. 436 n. 25.

15. Wohlstetter, *Legends of the Arms Race*.

16. There are a few glimmers of light in the darkness. See Flournoy, ed., *QDR 2001*, and Kugler and Binnendijk, "Choosing a Strategy."

17. For a convenient comparison of defense expenditures and related vital statistics, see The International Institute for Strategic Studies, *Military Balance, 2002–2003*, table 26, pp. 332–37.

18. For exemplars, see Waltz, *Theory of International Politics*, and Mearsheimer, *Tragedy of Great Power Politics*.

19. Gray, "Clausewitz Rules, OK?" Theorists of a neorealist, Waltzian persuasion have a tough time explaining the demise of the USSR.

20. Payne, *Fallacies of Cold War Deterrence*.

21. For example, Nye chose to advertise his new book, *Paradox of American Power*, with an article titled, "The new Rome meets the new barbarians."

22. Clausewitz, *On War*, p. 85.

23. ibid., p. 119.

24. Goldsworthy, *Roman Army at War*, p. 67.

25. I have borrowed the phrase with gratitude from Graves and Hodge, *Long Weekend*.

26. President Bush's speech, delivered at the Aspen Institute on August 2, 1990, bore the title, "United States Defenses: Reshaping Our Forces." See Cohen, *Cambridge History of American Foreign Relations: Vol. IV*, esp. p. 244. Henry Kissinger somewhat cruelly lumped together the do-good impulses of both the Bush and Clinton administrations, observing that "for the third time in this century, America thus proclaimed its intention to build a new world order by applying its domestic values to the world at large. And, for the third time, America seemed to tower over the international stage" (p. 805).

27. Mackinder, *Democratic Ideals and Reality;* and Spykman, *America's Strategy in World Politics*. Sloan, *Geopolitics in United States Strategic Policy*, provides valuable theoretical and historical perspectives.

28. I developed these geostrategic thoughts in some detail in the 1970s and 1980s. Gray: *Geopolitics of the Nuclear Era; Maritime Strategy, Geopolitics;* and *Geopolitics of Super Power*.

29. The two key documents outlining the containment thesis, both drafted by American diplomat George F. Kennan, are reprinted conveniently in Etzold and Gaddis, eds., *Containment,* pp. 50–63, "Moscow Embassy Telegram No. 511: 'The Long Telegram'" (February 22, 1946), and pp. 84–90, "The Sources of Soviet Conduct" (excerpted from *Foreign Affairs,* July 1947).

30. Howard, "Mistake to Declare this a 'War'"; and Freedman, "Third World War?" offer thoughtful analyses of the phenomenon at issue.

31. The new dismal science of strategic analysis has long recognized the scale of the problem that was approaching in the form of catastrophe terrorists armed with WMD. See Laqueur, "Postmodern Terrorism"; Shubik, "Terrorism, Technology, and the Socioeconomics of Death"; and Betts, "New Threat of Mass Destruction," all of which rang the warning bell years before September 11, 2001.

32. Westad, ed., *Reviewing the Cold War,* offers a rich haul for the dedicated quarrier. Scholarship on the Cold War, including on the quality of U.S. policy and strategy therein, is going to be a deeply contested academic field for centuries to come.

33. I am delighted to record that the Professor of Modern History at Cambridge University shares my disdain for "virtual history." Evans, "Telling it like it wasn't." Evans believes, as I do, that "altering one part of the kaleidoscope of history shakes up all the others in ways that are so unpredictable as to make either medium or long-term alternative scenarios completely unconvincing" (p. 25).

34. Ikenberry offers a list of postwar settlements as Appendix One in *After Victory,* p. 275.

35. One of the reasons I am reluctant to criticize Western policymakers for missing a rare window of opportunity for creative statecraft in the 1989–91 period, is because of the problem of hindsight-foresight. At least until the failure of the right-wing coup against Mikhail Gorbachev in August 1991, and the consequent rise of Boris Yeltsin, it was by no means certain that the new Russia would be a generally cooperative player in world security politics. At the beginning of the 1990s, Western statecraft did not really know what it was attempting to deal with in Russia.

36. In the early post–Cold War years, few audiences were comfortable being told that the present was an interwar period. I was an agent of such discomfort with an inaugural lecture I delivered in January 1994. See Gray, "Villains, Victims, and Sheriffs."

37. Friedman, *Fifty-Year War,* offers a balanced judgment that allows Gorbachev his due as the inadvertent instrument of destruction that the Soviet Union could not survive. For uninhibited attribution of credit to the authors of cunning plans hatched in Washington, see Schweizer, *Victory.*

38. See Clinton: *National Security Strategy of Engagement and Enlargement* (1994); *National Security Strategy for a New Century* (1997); and *National Security Strategy for a New Century* (1999).

39. Kissinger, *Does America Need a Foreign Policy?* p. 19.

40. ibid., p. 283. It may be important to note that the book was published just prior to September 11, 2001.

41. ibid., p. 158.

42. Bull, "Theory of International Politics," p. 39.

43. Fukuyama, "End of History?" He wrote that "what we may be witnessing is not just the end of the Cold War, or the passing of a particular period of post-war history, but the end of history as such; that is, the end point of mankind's ideological evolution and the universalization of Western liberal democracy as the final form of human government" (p. 4). At the time of its publication I regarded this view as pretentious nonsense, an opinion that I see no good reason to alter today. See also Fukuyama, *End of History and the Last Man.*

44. Bush, *National Security Strategy of the United States* (2002).

45. Amid the flood of instant wisdom after September 11, see Lewis, *What Went Wrong?;* and Booth and Dunne, eds., *Worlds in Collision.*

46. Quoted in Clayton, *British Empire as a Superpower,* p. 18.

47. See Owen, ed., *Deliberate Force.*

48. See Bacevich and Cohen, eds., *War over Kosovo,* and Lambeth, *NATO's Air War for Kosovo.*

49. The worldview of the Clinton administration is best appreciated via the pages of Nolan, ed., *Global Engagement.*

50. See Peden, *British Rearmament and the Treasury,* esp. pp. 109–13.

51. Knutsen, *Rise and Fall of World Orders,* p. 1.

52. ibid., pp. 1–2.

53. Bull, *Anarchical Society,* pp. 21–2.

54. ibid., p. 22.

55. I have yet to stumble across much of value in the theoretical literature on the causes of war, or wars. A truly outstanding skeptical review of theories is Blanning, *Origins of the French Revolutionary Wars,* ch. 1, "The Origins of Great Wars." Howard, *Invention of Peace,* also is exceptionally useful.

56. The salience, indeed the allegedly growing salience, of extrastrategic menaces to order is emphasized in two books written a decade apart: Buzan, *People, States and Fear,* and Nye, *Paradox of American Power.*

57. See the inspired German explanation of American cunning in Joffe, "How America Does It."

58. A careful treatment of this subject is provided in Handel, *Masters of War,* Appendix E, pp. 353–60, "The Problems of the Level of Analysis and the 'Tacticization of Strategy.'"

59. Overy, *Why the Allies Won,* performs a useful service by reminding us just how great a power Germany was in 1942, when it ruled in Europe from the Pyrenees to the Volga. Stepping back a generation, it is worth recalling that imperial Germany defeated Russia, fought the French and British to a standstill, and made Americans pay a high price for their education in modern warfare.

60. The United States was informed fairly brusquely in the early 1990s that its services for order would not be required in the former Yugoslavia. Apparently, a European Union feeling its oats would cope with "the Balkans" as a European complex of problems. For a while, at least, Washington was delighted to comply, and leave the former Yugoslavia to the tender ministrations of the EU and the UN. The result was catastrophic. Only the American-led air campaign, Operation Deliberate Force—carried out from August 30 to September 20,

1995—restored some balance on the ground against the Bosnian Serbs, while U.S. intervention to help arm and train the Croats similarly dealt dire blows to Serbs in the north. Needless to add, perhaps, moral culpability was spread generously among all belligerent parties. The Serbs appeared more bestial than the rest, but that may well have spoken more to circumstance and opportunity than to inherent moral failings. The unmistakeable U.S. reluctance to become involved in the former Yugoslavia was prudent, if unfortunately ultimately impractical.

61. Kagan, *Origins of War,* p. 570.
62. The importance of the inexorability of Roman justice is well explained in Santosuosso, *Storming Heavens,* esp. p. 148.
63. See Nye, *Bound to Lead* and *Paradox of American Power.*

CHAPTER 3
STAYING NUMBER ONE

1. Bacevich, *American Empire,* offers a more generous view of U.S. policy in the 1990s than do I. He finds evidence of a consistency of generally admirable purpose. And what is that purpose? "That purpose is to preserve and, where both feasible and conducive to U.S. interests, to expand an American imperium. Central to this strategy is a commitment to global openness—removing barriers that inhibit the movement of goods, capital, ideas, and people. Its ultimate objective is the creation of an open and integrated international order based on the principles of democratic capitalism, with the United States as the ultimate guarantor of order and enforcer of norms" (p. 3). It is more than thirty years since the imperial theme featured noticeably in American policy commentary. In the 1960s, as today, the leading theorists of empire have been affiliated with the School of Advanced International Studies of Johns Hopkins University in Washington, D.C. Bacevich's worthy predecessor was George Liska, who wrote *Imperial America* in 1967, which was a distinctly active year for American ordering behavior.
2. Kagan, *Origins of War,* p. 570.
3. Not all scholars concur. Hegemonic stability theory finds scant approval in Copeland, *Origins of Major War.* Of the theory, Copeland advises us that "contrary to its predictions, in five of the six major wars that began in conditions of multipolarity from 1600 to 1945, war was brought on by a state with marked military superiority. Moreover, in every one of the thirteen major wars or major crises across the ten historical periods covered in this book, conflict was initiated by a state fearing decline. This challenges the hegemonic stability assertion that rising states are typically the instigators of conflict" (p. 2). I have quoted Copeland in order to show that there are some grounds for contention, even as to the basics of what should encourage a condition of peace with security. Were this a venture in the theory or the history of International Relations, I would detain the reader with a critical examination of Copeland's evidence and reasoning. As it is, Kagan's dictum can serve well enough.
4. Gray and Sloan, eds., *Geopolitics, Geography, and Strategy,* may be regarded as a long overdue step on the path to rehabilitation.

5. Respectively, these definitions are offered in Cohen, *Geography and Politics*, p. 24; and Gray, "Inescapable Geography," p. 164. My definition is an adaptation from the excellent study by Parker, *Geopolitics*, p. 7.

6. Libicki, "Emerging Primacy of Information," is a classic statement of this view.

7. For a superior analysis of the somewhat rival traditions in the history of American foreign policy, see Mead, *Special Providence*.

8. John Mueller has established a brave record of voicing opinions that challenge prevailing dogmas. His has been a somewhat lonely voice daring to suggest that September 11 might presage nothing very much. "Harbinger or Aberration?"

9. Bush, *National Security Strategy* (2002), p. 26.

10. Political culture can nurture some atavistic corners in societies that are not entirely reconciled to the radical demotion of their state. The periodic unpleasantness in Franco-American relations stems nontrivially from French unhappiness with their international standing. If the national failures of 1815 and 1870 were difficult to absorb and cope with, that of 1940 was to prove an impossibility.

11. For 2001, the GDP of China and Japan were US$1.2 trillion and US$4.1 trillion, respectively.

12. In case any readers are wondering what meaning might attach to the great power ascription today, I will quote the advice offered by a leading realist theorist. Mearsheimer tells us that "to qualify as a great power, a state must have sufficient military assets to put up a serious fight in an all-out conventional war against the most powerful state in the world. The candidate need not have the capability to defeat the leading state, but it must have some reasonable prospect of turning the conflict into a war of attrition that leaves the dominant state seriously weakened, even if that dominant state ultimately wins the war." *Tragedy of Great Power Politics*, p. 5. Mearsheimer's formula is far from entirely satisfactory, but the subject is, admittedly, a distinctly slippery one today.

13. Although I remain skeptical of their analyses, I am grateful for the clarity and insight shown in Creveld, *Transformation of War*, and Kaldor, *New and Old Wars*.

14. Bush, *National Strategy to Combat Weapons of Mass Destruction (WMD)*, p. 1.

15. Joffe, "Of Hubs, Spokes and Public Goods," p. 17.

16. See Gray, *Second Nuclear Age*, ch. 3.

17. Bush, *National Strategy to Combat Weapons of Mass Destruction (WMD)*, p. 1.

18. ibid., p. 2.

19. Clausewitz, *On War*, p. 101.

20. See Lambakis, Kiras, and Kolet, "Understanding Asymmetric Threats," for thoughtful treatment of a concept that is more often repeated than understood, let alone explained.

21. See Mack, "Why Big Nations Lose Small Wars"; Ion and Errington, eds., *Great Powers and Little Wars*; and Arreguin-Toft, "How the Weak Win Wars."

22. Gray, "Thinking Asymmetrically," takes a fairly cool and skeptical look at the concept.

23. Bush, *National Security Strategy* (2002), p. 30.

24. The phrase, indeed the concept, of shock and awe was first introduced to the world at large at Iraq's expense in 2003, but the notion of a paralyzingly effective aerial blitzkrieg has been in professional circulation for many years. See Ullman and Wade, *Shock and Awe*. It is hoped that the shock of the precise firepower will be at least as psychological as military in its effect—hence the "awe."

25. "Cultural thoughtways—myths as well as reason—form the core of societies and play a central role in the affairs of men." Booth, *Strategy and Ethnocentrism*, p. 14. See also Harrison and Huntington, eds., *Culture Matters*.

26. See Marquis, *Unconventional Warfare*.

27. Joffe, "Of Hubs, Spokes and Public Goods."

28. Gentry, "Doomed to Fail," probably overstates the danger.

29. A commitment to network-centric operations is a vital pillar in the architecture of transformation. See Cebrowski and Garska, "Network-Centric Warfare," for a relatively early statement of the concept. Naval analysts have taken the lead in developing this idea. Cebrowski has explained the concept as follows: "Network-centric warfare looks at war as a complex, adaptive system wherein nonlinear variables continuously interact. Physical forces play a part, but so do cognitive and behavioral factors. Within the constant dimensions of war (force, space, and time), the domains of belief, knowledge and the physical world must be portrayed. Lanchestrian models emphasize the physical, but warriors since Sun-tzu have known intuitively the importance of belief and reason to victory in war. Network-centric warfare captures these aspects by using a systems-based approach having war in toto as its object." "President's Notes," p. 6. The center of gravity has attained the dubious honor of being a contested concept. Readers can usefully augment Clausewitz, *On War*, pp. 595–600, with Echevarria, *Clausewitz's Center of Gravity*.

30. Fontenot, book review, p. 159.

31. Rumsfeld, *Annual Report* (2002), p. 3.

32. Quinlan, *Thinking about Nuclear Weapons*, p. 19.

33. Bush, *National Strategy to Combat WMD*, p. 19.

34. See Cohen, "Technology and Warfare," esp. p. 244.

35. The reputation of the "principles of war" has never quite recovered from Brodie's withering sarcasm in his *Strategy in the Missile Age*, ch. 1. He performed too complete a demolition exercise, slaying guilty and innocent alike. See Alger, *Quest for Victory*.

36. Clausewitz, *On War*, p. 77 (emphasis in the original).

37. Mearsheimer, *Tragedy of Great Power Politics*, pp. 10–11.

38. ibid., p. 11.

39. For example, Layne, "Unipolar Illusion"; and Krauthammer, "Unipolar Moment Revisited."

40. For 1995, see Owen, *Deliberate Force*; for 1999, Lambeth, *NATO's Air War for Kosovo*.

41. Booth and Dunne, "Worlds in Collision," would be a useful place for Americans to start.

42. Mearsheimer, "False Promise of International Institutions," offers a robust indictment.

43. Howard, *Invention of Peace,* p. 124.

44. See Gray, "Clausewitz Rules, O.K.?" and Kaplan, *Warrior Politics,* for recent examples of reaffirmation of this creed.

45. Tyler, "U.S. Strategy Plan," p. 14.

46. ibid., p. 1.

47. ibid.

48. "Excerpts from Pentagon's Plan."

49. Bush, *National Security Strategy* (2002), p. 29. Kugler, "Dissuasion," announces the arrival, or at least the newly fashionable status, of a relatively unfamiliar strategic concept.

50. "Excerpts from Pentagon's Plan."

51. The commander's-eye view is well presented in Clark, *Waging Modern War.* For a very different perspective, Bacevich and Cohen, eds., *War over Kosovo,* is indispensable.

52. Keaney and Cohen, *Revolution in Warfare?,* was a significant sign of the times. It was a 1995 revised edition of the summary volume of the USAF's Gulf War Air Power Survey, originally published in 1993. See also Cohen's 1996 article, "A Revolution in Warfare." After 1995 the question mark tended to be dropped from the titles to discussions of RMA.

53. Betts, "Should Strategic Studies Survive?" and Builder, "Keeping the Strategic Flame," can be read as pleas in mid-decade (1996–97) from a profession that felt itself under severe pressure. Even as late as 2000, there was a distinctly defensive edge to Betts' superb analysis which was organized admirably to demolish the question he posed, "Is Strategy an Illusion?"

54. Bush, *National Security Strategy* (2002), p. 15.

55. See Rice, "Promoting the National Interest." The *National Security Strategy* document of 2002 promised that "the U.S. national security strategy will be based on a distinctly American internationalism that reflects the union of our values and our national interests" (p. 1).

56. Gray, *Modern Strategy,* p. 17.

57. Freedman, "Third World War?"

58. Howard, "Mistake to Declare this a 'War'" and "What Friends Are For."

59. Henrick, *Crimson Tide,* p. 97.

60. For an effective critique of those who would make too much of "the Afghan model," see Biddle, *Afghanistan and the Future of Warfare.*

61. See Gray, *Defining and Achieving Decisive Victory,* p. 21.

62. Mearsheimer, *Tragedy of Great Power Politics,* reminds us why it is that competition for influence is a law of international life.

63. The "Melian Dialogue" would not play well with the global media market of today. Whatever an American proconsul or diplomat might think privately, he would not hold his position for long were he to speak as did the proud and superpower Athenians to the wretched Melians in 416 B.C. "You know as well as we do that right, as the world goes, is only in question between equals in

power, while the strong do what they can and the weak suffer what they must." Strassler, ed., *Landmark Thucydides*, p. 352.

64. Ikenberry, *After Victory*, p. 271.

65. ibid.

66. ibid., p. 273.

67. Scales, *Future Warfare*, is outstandingly prescient.

68. Bacevich, *American Empire*, p. 3.

69. ibid.

70. See Campen, Dearth, and Goodden, eds., *Cyberwar;* Campen and Dearth, eds., *Cyberwar 2.0;* and Campen and Dearth, eds., *Cyberwar 3.0,* for useful analyses of the problem.

71. Kagan, *Origins of War,* p. 407.

72. See Gray, *Defining and Achieving Decisive Victory.*

73. George, "Role of Force in Diplomacy," is persuasive in its insistence on the potency of positive, as well as negative, inducements.

74. Clausewitz, *On War,* p. 85.

75. ibid., p. 605.

76. "We also found that the belief that the U.S. public is especially casualty-shy, widely accepted by policymakers, civilian elites, and military officers, is a myth." Feaver and Kohn, "Conclusion: The Gap," p. 467.

77. Kagan, "Power and Weakness," p. 15.

CHAPTER 4
THE STRATEGIC DIMENSION

1. Vasquez, *Power of Power Politics;* Donnelly, *Realism and International Relations;* and Haslam, *No Virtue Like Necessity,* are superior analyses.

2. Cohen, *Supreme Command,* pp. 234–39. See also Betts, "Is Strategy an Illusion?" Creveld presents a different point of view in "What is Wrong with Clausewitz?"

3. Nye, *Bound to Lead* and *Paradox of American Power.*

4. It is in the very nature of maritime powers to foster a commercial culture keyed to trade, to be tolerant of political liberties, and to pose less than deadly threats to the interests of other, especially continental, states. Britain could be rather overbearing in her long period of preeminence—never a "unipolar moment" after the model of Rome or, in the future, the United States—but the Royal Navy posed less than a deadly menace to continental enemies. Padfield, *Maritime Supremacy,* emphasizes the historical fact that "freedom" is a "distinguishing mark of merchant power" (p. 3); while Lambert, *Crimean War,* shows and argues that British sea-based power was not as impotent as is often assumed in conflicts between maritime and continental powers.

5. "Rumsfeld Interview."

6. Coercion is not particularly well-travelled country by strategic theorists. Useful contributions over a thirty-five-year period include: Schelling, *Arms and Influence;* George, Hall, and Simons, *Limits of Coercive Diplomacy;* Craig and

George, *Force and Statecraft*, ch. 15; George, "Role of Force in Diplomacy";
Cimbala, *Coercive Military Strategy;* and Freedman, ed., *Strategic Coercion.*

7. See Gray, *Weapons for Strategic Effect.*

8. Clausewitz, *On War,* p. 605 (emphasis in the original).

9. See Scales, *Future Warfare;* and Matthews, ed., *Challenging the United States.*

10. In the case of nuclear-powered aircraft carriers (CVNs), the designed service
life is significantly longer, in fact up to fifty years. Friedman, *Seapower as Strategy,* p. 275.

11. Clausewitz, *On War,* p. 101.

12. ibid., p. 75.

13. This argument is amply illustrated in Macksey, *Why the Germans Lose at War.*

14. This thesis is the central insight underpinning Luttwak, *Strategy.*

15. See House, *Combined Arms Warfare.* The spirit, and much of the logic- and
history-based argument of House, appears very effectively in Biddle, *Afghanistan and the Future of Warfare.*

16. Keegan is a brilliant military historian who rejects the Clausewitzian dictum in
the most forthright of terms. He believes that "the success with which it [the
First French Republic] waged ideological war prompted the Prussian soldier,
Carl von Clausewitz, to promulgate the most pernicious philosophy of
warmaking yet conceived. War, he said, is nothing more than the continuation
of politics by means of force—he may have meant policy, the German word
Politik obscures the point—and it is to be limited only by the calculation of
the political interest in which it was undertaken in the first place. War, in short,
is a value-free activity, outside the moral sphere; but the implication is that
politics is too." There is more in the same vein, including the somewhat extravagant charge that "Clausewitz was polluting civilized thought about how
wars could and should be fought." *War and Our World,* pp. 41–2, 43. Keegan's
anti-Clausewitzian blasts may also be sampled in his short review essay, "Peace
by other means?" as well as in his most ambitious work, *History of Warfare.*
Needless to say, I disagree with Keegan and find myself aligned solidly with
Betts, "Is Strategy an Illusion?" and Cohen, *Supreme Command,* pp. 234–39.
See Gray, "In Praise of Strategy."

17. See Jablonsky, "Why Is Strategy Difficult?"; Gray, "Why Strategy Is Difficult";
and Betts, "The Trouble with Strategy."

18. If it is any consolation to Americans today, the globally dominant British navy
of the nineteenth century faced exactly the situation that I specify in the text.
The Royal Navy had to be responsive to the actual and potential demands of
foreign policy, while satisfying certain domestic criteria (bearing mainly on
demands for economy, navies are always hideously expensive). In addition, the
Navy had to remain preeminent in combat power, innovating prudently (transforming) in a period of rapid technological change. The outstanding study
remains Bartlett, *Great Britain and Sea Power.*

19. Clausewitz, *On War,* p. 607.

20. See Wylie, *Military Strategy,* ch. 2, and Gray, *Modern Strategy,* ch. 1.

21. Panofsky, "Mutual Hostage Relationship," and Kahan, *Security in the Nuclear
Age,* did not understate the condition. It is probably fair to say that these

authors spoke eloquently for the school of thought which regarded the mutual hostage relationship as a regrettable necessity.

22. Huntington, *The Soldier and the State*, p. 11. See the thought-provoking revisionist analysis in Cohen, *Supreme Command*.

23. They do so in large part due to the admittedly unsatisfactory portmanteau concept of strategic culture. Gray, *Modern Strategy*, ch. 5. See Desch, "Culture Clash," for a skeptical review of the claims made for culturalist theories.

24. The standard text is Weigley, *American Way of War*.

25. For the outline of a new American way of war, one at some variance with the Powell doctrine of "overwhelming force," see Cohen, "Defending America in the Twenty-First Century"; Bacevich and Cohen, eds., *Wars over Kosovo*; and Bacevich, *American Empire*.

26. Huntington, *American Military Strategy*, p. 13.

27. ibid., p. 16.

28. Scales, "Adaptive Enemies," and Luttwak, *Strategy*, should be required reading in the Pentagon.

29. Huntington, *American Military Strategy*, p. 13.

30. Cohen, "Tale of Two Secretaries," p. 39.

31. See Feaver and Kohn, "Conclusion: The Gap," p. 467.

32. Clausewitz, *On War*, p. 128 (emphasis in the original). I recommend to readers the following judgment by Christopher Bassford: "Many criticisms of Clausewitz boil down to accusations that he was no more able than any of the rest of us to encapsulate all of reality in a single, pithy phrase. His work survives as a living influence because his approach, overall, comes closer to capturing the complex truth about war than any writer since." "Book review," p. 99. Gray, *Modern Strategy*, chs. 3–4, follows Bassford's opinion entirely.

33. See Payne, *Fallacies of Cold War Deterrence*.

34. Clausewitz, *On War*, p. 610.

35. Chandler, *Military Maxims of Napoleon*, p. 81.

36. I am indebted to Builder, "Keeping the Strategic Flame."

37. Clausewitz, *On War*, pp. 119–21. Also see Watts, *Clausewitzian Friction and Future War*; and Cimbala, *Clausewitz and Chaos*.

38. Cohen, *Supreme Command*. I am painfully aware of the violence I am doing to the subtlety of Cohen's analysis. Huntington's formula, following Harold Lasswell, which specified "the management of violence" as "the central skill" of the military profession, is not only correct but also can be understood as an ideal type. Nonetheless, it is important, indeed essential, to remember that "the function of a military force is successful armed combat." *Soldier and the State*, p. 11.

39. See Clark, *Waging Modern War*; Bacevich and Cohen, eds., *War Over Kosovo*; and Lambeth, *NATO's Air War for Kosovo*.

40. In the foreword to Hobkirk, *Land, Sea or Air?* p. x.

41. See the inspired analysis in Luttwak, *Strategy*.

42. Clausewitz, *On War*, p. 605, draws the crucial distinction between the "grammar" and the "logic" of war.

43. But Constantinople could never be sufficiently siege-proof as to cause an emperor no anxiety, if, for example, he was campaigning in distant Armenia while an Avar horde was rampaging through the Balkans. See Haldon, *Byzantium in the Seventh Century,* pp. 45–7. Also see Stratos, *Byzantium in the Seventh Century.*

44. Bush, *National Strategy to Combat WMD,* p. 3

45. Bush, *National Security Strategy* (2002), p. 29. Kugler explains that "dissuasion arises in a different, less confrontational place along the spectrum from peace to war" than does deterrence. "Dissuasion as a Strategic Concept." If dissuasion is effective, there should be no need for deterrence.

46. Payne, *Fallacies of Cold War Deterrence,* offers a constructive critique.

47. Those seeking reading material from the RMA debate could occupy themselves for many years. See Hindley, *Past Revolutions;* Metz, *Armed Conflict in the 21st Century;* Knox and Murray, eds., *Dynamics of Military Revolution;* Crane, ed., *Transforming Defense;* Gray, *Strategy for Chaos;* Sloan, *Revolution in Military Affairs;* Binnendijk, ed., *Transforming America's Military;* and Owens, "Once and Future Revolution in Military Affairs."

48. Rumsfeld, *Annual Report* (2002), p. 3. Also see Rumsfeld, "Transforming the Military."

49. Rumsfeld, *Annual Report,* p. 19.

50. ibid., p. 20.

51. There is much of value in Barnett, *Asymmetrical Warfare,* particularly for those Americans who are in danger of being overly impressed with their country's military prowess.

52. Gray, *Weapons Don't Make War,* ch. 5.

53. Rumsfeld, *Annual Report* (2002), p. 20.

54. This was part of my message in *Defining and Achieving Decisive Victory.*

55. Clausewitz, *On War,* p. 77.

56. Cebrowski, "President's Forum," p. 8.

57. Norquist, "Defense Budget," p. 98.

58. Luttwak, *Strategy and Politics,* p. 263.

59. My distinctly conservative view is almost certainly a minority position among my fellow American defense professionals. I respect the alternative view, which sniffs and detects military revolution in the wind, but I disagree. Owens, *Lifting the Fog of War,* is a fairly extreme statement of the view from which I dissent. See my *Strategy for Chaos,* esp. ch. 9.

60. For the classic statement of the "dominant weapon" thesis, see Fuller, *Armament and History.* Watts, *Clausewitzian Friction,* can be read as a devastating critique of the worldview of Owens, *Lifting the Fog of War.*

61. House, *Combined Arms Warfare,* p. 281.

62. ibid., p. 4.

63. John Keegan, one of Britain's leading military historians, was a convert to the theory of "victory through airpower," by NATO's air campaign over Kosovo. See his newspaper article, "How We Beat Milosevic." Bacevich and Cohen, eds., *War Over Kosovo,* develops the proposition that the 1990s witnessed the emergence of a new American way of war. That way is keyed to the ever more

precise potency of American airpower, and it is conducted in a manner that holds few Americans at risk. Lambeth, *Transformation of American Air Power*, is a first-rate analysis by a friend of airpower. For some useful historical perspective, see Gentile, *How Effective is Strategic Bombing?*; and Cox and Gray, eds., *Air Power History*. With regard to Afghanistan in 2001, see Biddle, *Afghanistan and the Future of Warfare*.

64. Black, *War in the New Century*, pp. vii–viii. For example, Saddam Hussein was convinced that he was victorious in 1991. Given the odds against him, one can see his point.

65. Brodie, *War and Politics*, p. 332.

66. Black, *War in the New Century*, p. 114 (emphasis added).

67. Clausewitz, *On War*, p. 183; Howard, "Forgotten Dimensions of Strategy"; and Gray, *Modern Strategy*, ch. 1. For a summary of the three sets of elements or dimensions, see Gray, *Strategy for Chaos*, p. 123.

68. Gray, *Strategy for Chaos*.

69. Myers, "Understanding Transformation," p. 40.

70. Black, *War in the New Century*, p. 114.

71. Myers, "Understanding Transformation", p. 38.

72. Cohen, "Kosovo and the New American Way of War."

73. Referring to the American military approach to Kosovo in 1999, Eliot Cohen offers this troubling judgment: "The unthinking recitation of the requirement for 'force protection' as the first mission for American soldiers, ahead of any objective for which they might be put in harm's way, reflects an unwillingness to come to terms with what the use of force means." "Unequal Dialogue," p. 456.

74. By way of an extreme example of my argument, on April 1, 2001, a U.S. Navy EP-3 on a routine surveillance flight off the Chinese coast was damaged in a collision with a Chinese fighter. The fighter crashed, and the EP-3 successfully executed a difficult emergency landing on Hainan Island. Evidently, it was acceptable to American military culture and discipline for a plane crammed with highly sensitive technology to be placed under Chinese control. This is not to belittle the undoubted skill of the crew in saving the aircraft, or the effort expended to destroy as much of the on-board equipment as proved feasible in the short time available. However, the crew obviously believed that their first duty was to their own safety, not to safeguarding the secrets on board their EP-3.

75. See Luttwak, "A Post-Heroic Military Policy."

76. See Metz and Johnson, *Asymmetry and U.S. Military Strategy*, and Barnett, *Asymmetrical Warfare*.

77. Cohen has made the related point that the American debate over RMA-transformation must remain inconclusive, pending validation under fire in warfare involving enemies more challenging than the United States faced in the 1990s. "Technology and Warfare," p. 243. It would seem to be the case that the country is beginning its career in the twenty-first century in a manner calculated to provide at least some of the evidence Cohen demands.

CHAPTER 5
THE FAMILIAR TWENTY-FIRST CENTURY

1. Terriff and others, *Security Studies Today*, ch. 5, "The Post-Positivist Turn," is as clear as it is mercifully brief. Those who seek a deeper understanding of some recent intellectual fashions could do worse than consult Krause and Williams, eds., *Critical Security Studies*, and Jones, *Security, Strategy, and Critical Theory*.

2. McInnes argues that the RMA and transformation debates have been distinctive, with the former "focusing largely upon the impact of technology, especially information technology, upon military means." In some contrast, "the transformation of war debate looks at broader changes in the international system and in society, as well as changes in technology, upon the character and experience of war." "A Different Kind of War?" p. 165 n. 3. Also see McInnes, *Spectator-Sport War*. The truth of the matter is that there are two transformation debates: the one that is a continuation of the old RMA debate, and the much broader one to which McInnes correctly refers.

3. Kaplan, *Warrior Politics*, p. 39.

4. Though it was a question posed, and answered, bravely and to an unpopular conclusion by Howard, "Mistake to Declare this a 'War.'" His argument was out of step with domestic realities in the United States, if not necessarily with the actual character of the security challenge.

5. See Schroeder, "Napoleon's Foreign Policy"; Overy, *Why the Allies Won;* Friedman, *Fifty-Year War;* and Gray, *Strategy for Chaos*.

6. Gibbon, *Decline and Fall*, I, p. 84.

7. Cohen, "Kosovo and the New American Way of War." By way of a reality check which supports my impressions, I note that the XIV Annual Strategy Conference of the U.S. Army War College, April 8–10, 2003, was on the theme of "The 'New' American Way of War." Needless to add, perhaps, another kind of reality check simultaneously was being played out in the Gulf.

8. See Creveld, *Transformation of War;* Kaldor, *New and Old Wars;* and McInnes, *Spectator-Sport War*. There is no question but that these thoughtful authors have interesting and even sometimes valid points to make. But, how important and plausible are their arguments that war has been, or is being, transformed politically, socially, and culturally? And even if one finds their transformational theses persuasive, the basic strategist's question remains, "so what?"

9. See Gray, "Clausewitz Rules, OK?"

10. See Gould, *Time's Arrow, Time's Cycle*.

11. I strive to make this point as forcefully as I dare, given the undeniable horrors of the century just past, in my article, "In Praise of Strategy."

12. Knox and Murray, eds., *Dynamics of Military Revolution*, is indispensable.

13. At least, so I believe. Gray, *Strategy for Chaos*, tells the story as I see it.

14. Showalter has summarized the evidence thus: "The conviction that machines, rather than men, are the decisive factor in modern warfare has grown even stronger in this age of the black box and the automated weapons system. On closer examination, however, some startling discrepancies emerge. In particular, soldiers and scholars agree that even in the wars of industrial societies,

anything more than marginal technical advantages are rare. What is loosely described as technological superiority usually means either greater skill at employing roughly equivalent means, or simply greater numbers. Where it does exist, superiority in the quality of weapons and equipment in land warfare is marginal and ephemeral, seldom remaining long with any army." *Railroads and Rifles*, p. 13. The current American military-technical lead is historically most unusual, but it cannot guarantee easy victories over all comers. That advantage obliges America's enemies to wage war "in the round," holistically (as I keep insisting), if they are to compete with any prospect of success.

15. This fundamental error is well represented in Ullman and Wade, *Shock and Awe*, and Owens, *Lifting the Fog of War.*

16. I am grateful to Cohen, as so often in these pages, for the concepts of the technophile and the technophobe. "Technology and Warfare," esp. p. 236.

17. What has been termed "cultural instinct" has a lot to answer for. Bathurst, *Intelligence and the Mirror*, is a work of rare perception. Cultural instinct appears on p. 25.

18. Biddle, "Past as Prologue," is a potent critique of much RMA thinking.

19. Clausewitz, *On War*, p. 89. Also see Villacres and Bassford, "Reclaiming the Clausewitzian Trinity."

20. But what should the American experience in Vietnam be permitted to teach? See the contrasting analyses: Record, *Wrong War*, and Walton, *Myth of Inevitable U.S. Defeat in Vietnam.*

21. "Barfleur (pseud. for Custance), *Naval Policy*, pp. vii–viii.

22. Murray and Knox, "Future Behind Us," pp. 178, 179.

23. Such, at least, is the plausible argument in Woodruff, *Unheralded Victory*, and Walton, *Myth of Inevitable U.S. Defeat in Vietnam.*

24. Kagan, *Paradise and Power*, exaggerates a fairly sound argument. He tends to overemphasize the significance of the differences in power between America and its European allies, but still he is essentially correct in pointing to the depth and width of the transatlantic divide.

25. Bacevich, *American Empire*, pp. 243–44.

26. These sources should be regarded as supplements to those already cited on the subject of why strategy is difficult: Cohen and Gooch, *Military Misfortunes;* Strauss and Ober, *Anatomy of Error;* and Beyerchen, "Clausewitz, Nonlinearity, and the Unpredictability of War."

27. Mandelbaum, *Ideas that Conquered the World.*

28. Peters, *Fighting for the Future* and *Beyond Terror*, are strongly recommended.

29. For a somewhat different view, perhaps more a different style in explanation, see Nye, *Paradox of American Power*, esp. pp. 8–9.

30. Strassler, ed., *Landmark Thucydides*, p. 43.

31. Kagan, *Paradise and Power.*

32. This argument is central to Gray, *Strategy for Chaos.*

33. See the outstanding discussion in Scales, *Future Warfare*, ch. 3, "Adaptive Enemies."

34. Huntington, *American Military Strategy.*

35. Governance is the term that has been invented to fill the space between international government, which we do not enjoy, and international anarchy, which in its pejorative sense would be a considerable exaggeration of the amount of mayhem in world politics. Although it is undoubtedly useful to have a concept that means less than government but more than anarchy, it is important to remember that its very vagueness is key to its utility. See Evans, *Penguin Dictionary of International Relations,* p. 209.

BIBLIOGRAPHY

Alger, John I. *The Quest for Victory: The History of the Principles of War.* Westport, Conn.: Greenwood Press, 1982.

Aron, Raymond. *Peace and War: A Theory of International Relations.* Garden City, N.Y.: Doubleday, 1966.

———. "The Evolution of Modern Strategic Thought." In *Problems of Modern Strategy,* edited by Alastair Buchan, 13–46. London: Chatto and Windus, 1970.

Arreguin-Toft, Ivan. "How the Weak Win Wars: A Theory of Asymmetric Conflict." *International Security* 26 (2001): 93–128.

Bacevich, Andrew J. *American Empire: The Realities and Consequences of U.S. Diplomacy.* Cambridge, Mass.: Harvard University Press, 2002.

———. "Steppes to Empire." *The National Interest* 68 (2002): 39–53.

"Barfleur" (pseud. for Reginald Custance). *Naval Policy: A Plea for the Study of War.* Edinburgh: William Blackwood and Sons, 1907.

Barnett, Roger W. *Asymmetrical Warfare: Today's Challenge to U.S. Military Power.* Washington, D.C.: Brassey's, 2003.

Bartlett, C. J. *Great Britain and Sea Power, 1815–1853.* Oxford: Clarendon Press, 1963.

Bassford, Christopher. "Book Review." *RUSI Journal* 148 (2003): 97–9.

Bathurst, Robert B. *Intelligence and the Mirror: On Creating an Enemy.* London: SAGE Publications, 1993.

Betts, Richard K. "Is Strategy an Illusion?" *International Security* 25 (2000): 5–50.

———. "The New Threat of Mass Destruction." *Foreign Affairs* 77 (1998): 26–41.

———. "Should Strategic Studies Survive?" *World Politics* 50 (1997): 7–33.

———. "The Trouble with Strategy: Bridging Policy and Operations." *Joint Force Quarterly* 29 (2001–02): 23–30.

Biddle, Stephen. *Afghanistan and the Future of Warfare: Implications for Army and Defense Policy.* Carlisle, Pa.: Strategic Studies Institute, U.S. Army War College, November 2002.

———."The Past as Prologue: Assessing Theories of Future Warfare." *Security Studies* 8 (1998): 1–74.

Billington, Ray Allen. *America's Frontier Heritage.* Albuquerque, N.M.: University of New Mexico Press, 1974.

Binnendijk, Hans, ed. *Transforming America's Military.* Washington, D.C.: National Defense University Press, 2002.

Black, Jeremy. *War in the New Century.* London: Continuum, 2001.

Blainey, Geoffrey. *The Causes of War.* London: Macmillan, 1973.

Blanning, T. C. W. *The Origins of the French Revolutionary Wars.* London: Longman, 1986.

Bond, Brian. *The Pursuit of Victory: From Napoleon to Saddam Hussein.* Oxford: Oxford University Press, 1996.

Boot, Max. *The Savage Wars of Peace: Small Wars and the Rise of American Power.* New York: Basic Books, 2002.

Booth, Ken. *Strategy and Ethnocentrism.* London: Croom, Helm, 1979.

Booth, Ken, and Tim Dunne. "Worlds in Collision." In *Worlds in Collision: Terror and the Future of Global Order,* edited by Booth and Dunne, 1–23. Basingstoke, U.K.: Palgrave Macmillan, 2002.

Brodie, Bernard. "Strategy as a Science." *World Politics* 1 (1949): 479–88.

——. *Strategy in the Missile Age.* Princeton, N.J.: Princeton University Press, 1959.

——. *War and Politics.* New York: Macmillan, 1973.

Brooks, Stephen G., and William C. Wohlforth. "American Primacy in Perspective." *Foreign Affairs* 81 (2002): 20–33.

Builder, Carl H. "Keeping the Strategic Flame." *Joint Force Quarterly* 14 (1996–7): 76–84.

Bull, Hedley. *The Anarchical Society: A Study of Order in World Politics.* New York: Columbia University Press, 1977.

——. "The Theory of International Politics, 1919–1969." In *The Aberystwyth Papers: International Politics, 1919–1969,* edited by Brian Porter, 30–55. London: Oxford University Press, 1972.

Bush, George W. *The National Security Strategy of the United States of America.* Washington, D.C.: The White House, September 2002.

——. *National Strategy to Combat Weapons of Mass Destruction.* Washington, D.C.: The White House, December 2002.

Buzan, Barry. *People, States and Fear: An Agenda for International Security Studies in the Post–Cold War Era,* 2d ed. Boulder, Colo.: Lynne Rienner Publishers, 1991.

Buzzanco, Robert. *Masters of War: Military Dissent and Politics in the Vietnam Era.* Cambridge: Cambridge University Press, 1996.

Callwell, Charles E. *Small Wars: A Tactical Textbook for Imperial Soldiers,* 3d ed. London: Greenhill Books, 1990.

Campen, Alan D., Douglas H. Dearth, and R. Thomas Goodden, eds. *Cyberwar: Security, Strategy and Conflict in the Information Age.* Fairfax, Va.: AFCEA International Press, 1996.

Campen, Alan D., and Douglas H. Dearth, eds. *Cyberwar 2.0: Myths, Mysteries and Reality.* Fairfax, Va.: AFCEA International Press, 1998.

———, eds. *Cyberwar 3.0: Human Factors in Information Operations and Future Conflict.* Fairfax, Va.: AFCEA International Press, 2000.

Cebrowski, Arthur K. "President's Forum." *Naval War College Review* 53 (2000): 5–8.

———. "President's Notes." *Naval War College Review* 52 (1999): 4–7.

Cebrowski, Arthur K., and John J. Garstka. "Network-Centric Warfare: Its Origins and Future." *U.S. Naval Institute Proceedings* 124 (1998): 28–35.

Chandler, David G. *The Military Maxims of Napoleon.* New York: Macmillan, 1988.

Cimbala, Stephen J. *Clausewitz and Chaos: Friction in War and Military Policy.* Westport, Conn.: Praeger Publishers, 2001.

———. *Coercive Military Strategy.* College Station: Texas A and M University Press, 1998.

Clark, Ian. *The Hierarchy of States: Reform and Resistance in the International Order.* Cambridge: Cambridge University Press, 1989.

Clark, Wesley K. *Waging Modern War: Bosnia, Kosovo, and the Future of Combat.* New York: Public Affairs, 2002.

Clausewitz, Carl von. *On War.* Edited and translated by Michael Howard and Peter Paret. Princeton, N.J.: Princeton University Press, 1976.

Clayton, Anthony. *The British Empire as a Superpower, 1919–39.* Athens: University of Georgia Press, 1986.

Clinton, William J. *A National Security Strategy of Engagement and Enlargement.* Washington, D.C.: The White House, July 1994.

———. *A National Security Strategy for a New Century.* Washington, D.C.: The White House, May 1997.

———. *A National Security Strategy for a New Century.* Washington, D.C.: The White House, December 1999.

Cohen, Eliot A. "Defending America in the Twenty-First Century." *Foreign Affairs* 79 (2000): 40–56.

———. "Kosovo and the New American Way of War." In *War over Kosovo: Politics and Strategy in a Global Age,* edited by Andrew J. Bacevich and Cohen, 38–62. New York: Columbia University Press, 2001.

———. "A Revolution in Warfare." *Foreign Affairs* 75 (1996): 37–54.

———. *Supreme Command: Soldiers, Statesmen, and Leadership in War-time.* New York: Free Press, 2002.

———. "A Tale of Two Secretaries." *Foreign Affairs* 81 (2002): 33–46.

———. "Technology and Warfare." In *Strategy in the Contemporary World: An Introduction to Strategic Studies,* edited by John Baylis and others, 235–53. Oxford: Oxford University Press, 2002.

———. "The Unequal Dialogue: The Theory and Reality of Civil-Military Relations and the Use of Force." In *Soldiers and Civilians: The Civil-Military Gap and American National Security,* edited by Peter D. Feaver and Richard H. Kohn, 429–58. Cambridge, Mass.: MIT Press, 2001.

Cohen, Eliot A., and John Gooch. *Military Misfortunes: The Anatomy of Failure in War.* New York: Free Press, 1990.

Cohen, Saul B. *Geography and Politics in a Divided World.* London: Methuen, 1964.

Cohen, Warren I. *The Cambridge History of American Foreign Relations: Vol. IV, America in the Age of Soviet Power, 1945–1991.* Cambridge: Cambridge University Press, 1993.

Copeland, Dale C. *The Origins of Major War.* Ithaca, N.Y.: Cornell University Press, 2000.

Cox, Sebastian, and Peter Gray, eds. *Air Power History: Turning Points from Kitty Hawk to Kosovo.* London: Frank Cass, 2002.

Craig, Gordon A., and Alexander L. George. *Force and Statecraft: Diplomatic Problems of Our Time,* 3^d ed. New York: Oxford University Press, 1995.

Crane, Conrad, ed. *Transforming Defense.* Carlisle, Pa.: Strategic Studies Institute, U.S. Army War College, December 2001.

Creveld, Martin van. "What Is Wrong with Clausewitz?" In *The Clausewitzian Dictum and the Future of Western Military Strategy,* edited by Gert de Nooy, 7–23. The Hague: Kluwer Law International, 1997.

———. *The Transformation of War.* New York: Free Press, 1991.

Desch, Michael C. "Culture Clash: Assessing the Importance of Ideas in Security Studies." *International Security* 23 (1998): 141–70.

Donnelly, Jack. *Realism and International Relations.* Cambridge: Cambridge University Press, 2000.

Donnelly, Thomas. "The Past as Prologue: An Imperial Manual." *Foreign Affairs* 81 (2002): 165–70.

Echevarria, Antulio J., II. *Clausewitz's Center of Gravity: Changing Our Warfighting Doctrine–Again!* Carlisle, Pa.: Strategic Studies Institute, U.S. Army War College, September 2002.

Etzold, Thomas H., and John Lewis Gaddis, eds. *Containment: Documents on American Policy and Strategy, 1945–1950*. New York: Columbia University Press, 1978.

Evans, Graham, and Jeffrey Newnham. *The Penguin Dictionary of International Relations*. London: Penguin Books, 1998.

Evans, Richard J. "Telling it like it wasn't." *BBC History Magazine* 3 (2002): 22–5.

Evera, Stephen Van. *Causes of War: Power and the Roots of Conflict*. Ithaca, N.Y.: Cornell University Press, 1999.

"Excerpts from Pentagon's Plan: 'Prevent the Re-Emergence of a New Rival.'" *The New York Times*, March 8, 1992.

Falls, Cyril. *A Hundred Years of War*. London: Gerald Duckworth, 1953.

Feaver, Peter D., and Richard H. Kohn. "Conclusion: The Gap and What It Means for American National Security." In *Soldiers and Civilians: The Civil-Military Gap and American National Security*, edited by Feaver and Kohn, 459–73. Cambridge, Mass.: MIT Press, 2001.

Flournoy, Michèle A., ed. *QDR 2001: Strategy-Driven Choices for America's Security*. Washington, D.C.: National Defense University Press, 2001.

Fontenot, Gregory. Book review. *Parameters* 32 (2002–03): 158–59.

Freedman, Lawrence. *The Revolution in Strategic Affairs*, Adelphi Paper 318. London: International Institute for Strategic Studies, April 1998.

———. "The Third World War?" *Survival* 43 (2001): 61–87.

———, ed. *Strategic Coercion: Concepts and Cases*. Oxford: Oxford University Press, 1998.

Friedman, Norman. *The Fifty-Year War: Conflict and Strategy in the Cold War*. Annapolis, Md.: Naval Institute Press, 2000.

———. *Seapower as Strategy: Navies and National Interests*. Annapolis, Md.: Naval Institute Press, 2001.

Fukuyama, Francis. "The End of History?" *The National Interest* 16 (1989): 3–18.

———. *The End of History and the Last Man*. New York: Free Press, 1992.

Fuller, J. F. C. *Armament and History*. London: Eyre and Spottiswoode, 1946.

Gentile, Gian P. *How Effective Is Strategic Bombing? Lessons Learned from World War II to Kosovo*. New York: New York University Press, 2001.

Gentry, John A. "Doomed to Fail: America's Blind Faith in Military Technology." *Parameters* 32 (2002–03): 88–103.

George, Alexander L. "The Role of Force in Diplomacy: A Continuing Dilemma for U.S. Foreign Policy." In *The Use of Force after the Cold War,* edited by H. W. Brands, 59–92. College Station: Texas A and M University Press, 2000.

George, Alexander L., David K. Hall, and William E. Simons. *The Limits of Coercive Diplomacy: Laos, Cuba, Vietnam.* Boston: Little, Brown, 1971.

George, Alexander L., and Richard Smoke. *Deterrence in American Foreign Policy: Theory and Practice.* New York: Columbia University Press, 1974.

Gibbon, Edward. *The History of the Decline and Fall of the Roman Empire, I.* Edited by J. B. Bury. London: Methuen, 1909.

Goldsworthy, Adrian Keith. *The Roman Army at War, 100 B.C.–A.D. 200.* Oxford: Clarendon Press, 1996.

Gooch, John. *The Plans of War: The General Staff and British Military Strategy, c. 1900–1916.* London: Routledge and Kegan Paul, 1974.

Gould, Stephen Jay. *Time's Arrow, Time's Cycle: Myth and Metaphor in the Discovery of Geological Time.* Cambridge, Mass.: Harvard University Press, 1987.

Graves, Robert, and Alan Hodge. *The Long Week-end: A Social History of Great Britain, 1918–1939.* London: Faber and Faber, 1940.

Gray, Colin S. "Clausewitz Rules, OK? The Future is the Past—with GPS." In *The Interregnum: Controversies in World Politics, 1989–99,* edited by Michael Cox, Ken Booth, and Tim Dunne, 161–82. Cambridge: Cambridge University Press, 1999.

———. *Defining and Achieving Decisive Victory.* Carlisle, Pa.: Strategic Studies Institute, U.S. Army War College, April 2002.

———. *The Geopolitics of the Nuclear Era: Heartland, Rimlands, and the Technological Revolution.* New York: Crane, Russak, 1977.

———. *The Geopolitics of Super Power.* Lexington: University Press of Kentucky, 1988.

———. *House of Cards: Why Arms Control Must Fail.* Ithaca, N.Y.: Cornell University Press, 1992.

———. *Maritime Strategy, Geopolitics, and the Defense of the West.* New York: Ramapo Press, 1986.

———. *Modern Strategy.* Oxford: Oxford University Press, 1999.

———. "In Praise of Strategy." *Review of International Studies* 29 (2003): 285–95.

———. *Strategy for Chaos: Revolutions in Military Affairs and the Evidence of History.* London: Frank Cass, 2002.

————. "Thinking Asymmetrically in Times of Terror." *Parameters* 32 (2002): 5–14.

————. "Villains, Victims, and Sheriffs: Strategic Studies and Security for an Interwar Period." *Comparative Strategy* 13 (1994): 353–69.

————. *Weapons for Strategic Effect: How Important is Technology?* Occasional Paper 21. Maxwell AFB, Ala.: Center for Strategy and Technology, Air War College, January 2001.

————. "Why Strategy Is Difficult." *Joint Force Quarterly* 22 (1999): 6–12.

Gray, Colin S., and Geoffrey Sloan, eds. *Geopolitics, Geography and Strategy.* London: Frank Cass, 1999.

Haldon, J. F. *Byzantium in the Seventh Century: The Transformation of a Culture.* Cambridge: Cambridge University Press, 1990.

Handel, Michael. *Masters of War: Classical Strategic Thought,* 3^d ed. London: Frank Cass, 2001.

Hanson, Victor Davis. *The Western Way of War: Infantry Battle in Classical Greece.* London: Hodder and Stoughton, 1989.

Harrison, Lawrence E., and Samuel P. Huntington, eds. *Culture Matters: How Values Shape Human Progress.* New York: Basic Books, 2000.

Hartmann, Anja V., and Beatrice Heuser, eds. *War, Peace and World Orders in European History.* London: Routledge, 2001.

Haslam, Jonathan. *No Virtue Like Necessity: Realist Thought in International Relations since Machiavelli.* New Haven, Conn.: Yale University Press, 2002.

Henrick, Richard P. *Crimson Tide.* New York: Avon Books, 1995.

Hindley, Richard O. *Past Revolutions, Future Transformations: What Can the History of Revolutions in Military Affairs Tell Us about Transforming the U.S. Military?* Santa Monica, Calif.: RAND, 1999.

Hobkirk, Michael D. *Land, Sea or Air? Military Priorities, Historical Choices.* London: Macmillan, 1992.

House, Jonathan M. *Combined Arms Warfare in the Twentieth Century.* Lawrence: University Press of Kansas, 2001.

Howard, Michael. "The Forgotten Dimensions of Strategy." *Foreign Affairs* 57 (1979): 975–86.

————. *The Invention of Peace and the Reinvention of War.* London: Profile Books, 2002.

————. "Mistake to Declare This a War." *RUSI Journal* 146 (2001): 1–4.

————. "What Friends Are For." *The National Interest* 69 (2002): 8–10.

————. "When Are Wars Decisive?" *Survival* 41 (1999): 126–35.

Huntington, Samuel P. *American Military Strategy*. Chester W. Nimitz Memorial Lecture. Policy Papers in International Affairs 28. Berkeley: Institute of International Studies, University of California, Berkeley, 1986.

―――. *The Soldier and the State: The Theory and Politics of Civil-Military Relations*. New York: Vintage Books, 1964.

Ikenberry, G. John. *After Victory: Institutions, Strategic Restraint, and the Rebuilding of Order after Major Wars*. Princeton, N.J.: Princeton University Press, 2001.

―――. "America's Imperial Ambition." *Foreign Affairs* 81 (2002): 44–60.

International Institute for Strategic Studies. *The Military Balance, 2002–2003*. London: Oxford University Press, 2002.

Ion, A. Hamish, and E. J. Errington, eds. *Great Powers and Little Wars: The Limits of Power*. Westport, Conn.: Praeger Publishers, 1993.

Jablonsky, David. "Why Is Strategy Difficult?" In *The Search for Strategy: Politics and Strategic Vision*, edited by Gary L. Guertner, 3–45. Westport, Conn.: Greenwood Press, 1993.

Joffe, Joseph. "How America Does It." *Foreign Affairs* 76 (1997): 13–27.

―――. "Of Hubs, Spokes and Public Goods." *The National Interest* 69 (2002): 17–20.

Jones, Richard Wyn. *Security, Strategy, and Critical Theory*. Boulder, Colo.: Lynne Rienner Publishers, 1999.

Kagan, Donald. *On the Origins of War and the Preservation of Peace*. New York: Doubleday, 1995.

Kagan, Robert. "Power and Weakness." *Policy Review* 113 (2002): 3–28.

―――. *Paradise and Power: America and Europe in the New World Order*. London: Atlantic Books, 2003.

Kahan, Jerome H. *Security in the Nuclear Age: Developing U.S. Strategic Arms Policy*. Washington, D.C.: Brookings Institution, 1975.

Kaldor, Mary. *New and Old Wars: Organized Violence in a Global Era*. Cambridge: Polity Press, 1999.

Kaplan, Robert D. *Warrior Politics: Why Leadership Demands a Pagan Ethos*. New York: Random House, 2002.

Keaney, Thomas A., and Eliot A. Cohen. *Revolution in Warfare? Air Power in the Persian Gulf*. Annapolis, Md.: Naval Institute Press, 1995.

Keegan, John. *The Face of Battle*. London: Pimlico, 1991.

―――. *A History of Warfare*. London: Hutchinson, 1993.

————. "How We Beat Milosevic." *The Daily Telegraph*, July 12, 1999.

————. "Peace by Other Means?" *The Times Literary Supplement*, December 11, 1992: 3–4.

————. *War and Our World*. The Reith Lectures, 1998. London: Hutchinson, 1998.

Kennedy, Paul M. "Maintaining American Power: From Injury to Recovery." In *The Age of Terror: America and the World after September 11*, edited by Strobe Talbott and Nayan Chanda, 55–79. New York: Basic Books, 2001.

————. *The Rise and Fall of the Great Powers: Economic Change and Military Conflict from 1500 to 2000*. New York: Random House, 1987.

Kissinger, Henry A. *Diplomacy*. New York: Simon and Schuster, 1994.

————. *Does America Need a Foreign Policy? Toward a Diplomacy for the 21ˢᵗ Century*. New York: Simon and Schuster, 2001.

————. *A World Restored: The Politics of Conservatism in a Revolutionary Age*. New York: Grosset and Dunlop, 1964.

Knock, Thomas J. *To End All Wars: Woodrow Wilson and the Quest for a New World Order*. New York: Oxford University Press, 1992.

Knutsen, Torbjorn L. *The Rise and Fall of World Orders*. Manchester, U.K.: Manchester University Press, 1999.

Krause, Keith, and Michael C. Williams, eds. *Critical Security Studies: Concepts and Cases*. London: UCL Press, 1997.

Krauthammer, Charles. "The Unipolar Moment Revisited." *The National Interest* 70 (2002–03): 5–17.

Krepinevich, Andrew F. *The Army and Vietnam*. Baltimore: Johns Hopkins University Press, 1986.

Kugler, Richard L. "Dissuasion as a Strategic Concept." *Strategic Forum* 196 (2002).

Lambakis, Steven, James Kiras, and Kristin Kolet. "Understanding 'Asymmetric' Threats to the United States." *Comparative Strategy* 21 (2002): 241–77.

Lambert, Andrew D. *The Crimean War: British Grand Strategy, 1853–56*. Manchester, U.K.: Manchester University Press, 1989.

Lambeth, Benjamin S. *NATO's Air War for Kosovo: A Strategic and Operational Assessment*. Santa Monica, Calif.: RAND, 2001.

————. *The Transformation of American Air Power*. Ithaca, N.Y.: Cornell University Press, 2000.

Laqueur, Walter. "Left, Right, and Beyond: The Changing Face of Terror." In *How Did This Happen? Terrorism and the New War*, edited by James F. Hoge Jr. and Gideon Rose, 71–82. Oxford: Public Affairs, 2001.

———. "Postmodern Terrorism." *Foreign Affairs* 75 (1996): 24–36.

Layne, Christopher. "The Unipolar Illusion: Why New Great Powers Will Rise." *International Security* 17 (1993): 5–51.

Lewis, Bernard. *What Went Wrong? Western Impact and Middle Eastern Response.* London: Phoenix, 2002.

Libicki, Martin C. "The Emerging Primacy of Information." *Orbis* 40 (1996): 261–74.

Liddell Hart, Basil. *History of the First World War.* London: Pan Books, 1972.

Liska, George. *Imperial America: The International Politics of Primacy,* Studies in International Affairs 2. Washington, D.C.: The Washington Center of Foreign Policy Research, School of Advanced International Studies, The Johns Hopkins University Press, 1967.

Luttwak, Edward N. *Strategy and Politics: Collected Essays.* New Brunswick, N.J.: Transaction Books, 1980.

———. *Strategy: The Logic of War and Peace.* Cambridge, Mass.: Harvard University Press, 2002.

———. "Towards Post-Heroic Warfare." *Foreign Affairs* 75 (1996): 33–44.

Mack, Andrew J. R. "Why Big Nations Lose Small Wars: The Politics of Asymmetric Conflict." *World Politics* 27 (1975): 175–200.

Mackinder, Halford J. *Democratic Ideals and Reality.* New York: W. W. Norton, 1962.

Macksey, Kenneth. *Why the Germans Lose at War: The Myth of German Military Superiority.* London: Greenhill Books, 1999.

Mandelbaum, Michael. *The Ideas that Conquered the World: Peace, Democracy, and Free Markets in the Twenty-First Century.* Oxford: Public Affairs, 2002.

———. "The Inadequacy of American Power." *Foreign Affairs* 81 (2002): 61–73.

Marquis, Susan L. *Unconventional Warfare: Rebuilding U.S. Special Operations Forces.* Washington, D.C.: Brookings Institution Press, 1997.

Matthews, Lloyd J., ed. *Challenging the United States Symmetrically and Asymmetrically: Can America Be Defeated?* Carlisle, Pa.: Strategic Studies Institute, U.S. Army War College, July 1998.

McInnes, Colin. "A Different Kind of War? September 11 and the United States' Afghan War." *Review of International Studies* 29 (2003): 165–84.

———. *Spectator-Sport War: The West and Contemporary Conflict.* Boulder, Colo.: Lynne Rienner Publishers, 2002.

McMaster, H. R. *Dereliction of Duty: Lyndon Johnson, Robert McNamara, the Joint Chiefs of Staff, and the Lies that Led to Vietnam.* New York: HarperCollins, 1997.

Mead, Walter Russell. *Special Providence: American Foreign Policy and How It Changed the World.* New York: Routledge, 2002.

Mearsheimer, John J. "The False Promise of International Institutions." In *Theories of War and Peace: An International Security Reader,* edited by Michael E. Brown and others, 329–83. Cambridge, Mass.: The MIT Press, 1998.

———. *The Tragedy of Great Power Politics.* New York: W. W. Norton, 2001.

Metz, Steven. *Armed Conflict in the 21ˢᵗ Century: The Information Revolution and Post-Modern Warfare.* Carlisle, Pa.: Strategic Studies Institute, U.S. Army War College, April 2000.

Metz, Steven, and Douglas V. Johnson II. *Asymmetry and U.S. Military Strategy: Definition, Background, and Strategic Concepts.* Carlisle, Pa.: Strategic Studies Institute, U.S. Army War College, January 2001.

Mueller, John. "Harbinger or Aberration? A 9/11 Provocation." *The National Interest* 69 (2002): 45–50.

Murray, Williamson. "Thinking about Revolutions in Military Affairs." *Joint Force Quarterly* 16 (1997): 69–76.

Murray, Williamson, and MacGregor Knox. "Conclusion: The Future behind Us." In *The Dynamics of Military Revolution, 1300–2050,* edited by MacGregor Knox and Williamson Murray, 175–94. Cambridge: Cambridge University Press, 2001.

Murray, Williamson, MacGregor Knox, and Alvin Bernstein, eds. *The Making of Strategy: Rulers, States and War.* Cambridge: Cambridge University Press, 1994.

Murray, Williamson, and Alan R. Millett. *A War to Be Won: Fighting the Second World War.* Cambridge, Mass.: Harvard University Press, 2000.

Myers, Richard B. "Understanding Transformation." *U.S. Naval Institute Proceedings* 129 (2003): 38–41.

Nolan, Janne E., ed. *Global Engagement: Cooperation and Security in the 21ˢᵗ Century.* Washington, D.C.: The Brookings Institution, 1994.

Norquist, David L. "The Defense Budget: Is It Transformational?" *Joint Force Quarterly* 31 (2002): 91–9.

Nye, Joseph S., Jr. *Bound to Lead: The Changing Nature of American Power.* New York: Basic Books, 1990.

————. "The New Rome Meets the New Barbarians." *The Economist*, March 23, 2002: 23–5.

————. *The Paradox of American Power: Why the World's Only Super-power Can't Go It Alone*. Oxford: Oxford University Press, 2002.

Odom, William E. *The Collapse of the Soviet Military*. New Haven, Conn.: Yale University Press, 1998.

O'Hanlon, Michael. *Defense Policy Choices for the Bush Administration, 2001–05*. Washington, D.C.: Brookings Institution Press, 2001.

————. "Rumsfeld's Defense Vision." *Survival* 44 (2002): 103–17.

Overy, Richard. *Why the Allies Won*. London: Jonathan Cape, 1995.

Owen, Robert C., ed. *Deliberate Force: A Case Study in Effective Air Campaigning, Final Report of the Air University Balkans Air Campaign Study*. Maxwell AFB, Ala.: Air University Press, January 2000.

Owens, Bill. *Lifting the Fog of War*. New York: Farrar, Straus and Giroux, 2000.

————. "The Once and Future Revolution in Military Affairs." *Joint Force Quarterly* 31 (2002): 55–61.

Padfield, Peter. *Maritime Supremacy and the Opening of the Western Mind: Naval Campaigns that Shaped the Modern World, 1588–1782*. London: John Murray, 1999.

Panofsky, Wolfgang K. H. "The Mutual Hostage Relationship between America and Russia." *Foreign Affairs* 52 (1973): 109–18.

Parker, Geoffrey. *Geopolitics: Past, Present and Future*. London: Pinter, 1998.

Payne, Keith B. *The Fallacies of Cold War Deterrence and a New Direction*. Lexington, Ky.: University Press of Kentucky, 2001.

Peden, G. C. *British Rearmament and the Treasury, 1932–1939*. Edinburgh: Scottish Academic Press, 1979.

Peters, Ralph. *Beyond Terror: Strategy in a Changing World*. Mechanicsburg, Pa.: Stackpole Books, 2002.

————. *Fighting for the Future: Will America Triumph?* Mechanicsburg, Pa.: Stackpole Books, 1999.

Quinlan, Michael. *Thinking about Nuclear Weapons*, RUSI Whitehall Paper. London: RUSI, 1997.

Rathjens, George W. "The Dynamics of the Arms Race." *Scientific American* 220 (1969): 15–25.

Record, Jeffrey. *The Wrong War: Why We Lost in Vietnam*. Annapolis, Md.: Naval Institute Press, 1998.

Rice, Condoleezza. "Promoting the National Interest." *Foreign Affairs* 79 (2000): 45–62.

Rosen, Stephen Peter. "Vietnam and the American Theory of Limited War." *International Security* 7 (1982): 83–113.

"Rumsfeld Interview." *The Times*, February 10, 2003: 13.

Rumsfeld, Donald H. *Annual Report to the President and the Congress.* Washington, D.C.: Department of Defense, 2002.

———. *Quadrennial Defense Review Report.* Washington, D.C.: Department of Defense, September 30, 2001.

———. "Transforming the Military." *Foreign Affairs* 81 (2002): 20–32.

Santosuosso, Antonio. *Storming the Heavens: Soldiers, Emperors, and Civilians in the Roman Empire.* Boulder, Colo.: Westview Press, 2001.

Sarkasian, Sam E., John Allan Williams, and Stephen J. Cimbala. *U.S. National Security: Policymakers, Processes and Politics*, 3ᵈ ed. Boulder, Colo.: Lynne Rienner, Publishers, 2002.

Scales, Robert H., Jr. *Future Warfare: Anthology.* Carlisle, Pa.: U.S. Army War College, May 1999.

Schelling, Thomas C. *Arms and Influence.* New Haven, Conn.: Yale University Press, 1966.

Schroeder, Paul W. "Napoleon's Foreign Policy: A Criminal Enterprise." *Journal of Military History* 54 (1990): 147–61.

Schweizer, Peter. *Victory: The Reagan Administration's Secret Strategy that Hastened the Collapse of the Soviet Union.* New York: Atlantic Monthly Press, 1994.

Showalter, Dennis E. *Railroads and Rifles: Soldiers, Technology and the Unification of Germany.* Hamden, Conn.: Archon Books, 1986.

Shubik, Martin. "Terrorism, Technology, and the Socioeconomics of Death." *Comparative Strategy* 16 (1997): 399–414.

Sloan, Elinor C. *The Revolution in Military Affairs.* Montreal: McGill-Queen's University Press, 2002.

Sloan, Geoffrey R. *Geopolitics in United States Strategic Policy, 1890–1987.* Brighton, U.K.: Wheatsheaf Books, 1988.

Slotkin, Richard. *Gunfighter Nation: The Myth of the Frontier in Twentieth Century America.* New York: Athenaeum, 1992.

Spykman, Nicholas J. *America's Strategy in World Politics: The United States and the Balance of Power.* Hamden, Conn.: Archon Books, 1970.

———. *The Geography of the Peace.* New York: Harcourt, Brace, 1944.

Stratos, A. N. *Byzantium in the Seventh Century, I, 602–34.* Amsterdam: Adolf M. Hakkert, 1968.

Strassler, Robert B., ed. *The Landmark Thucydides: A Comprehensive Guide to "The Peloponnesian War."* Translated by Richard Crawley, rev. ed. New York: Free Press, 1996.

Strauss, Barry S., and Josiah Ober. *The Anatomy of Error: Ancient Military Disasters and Their Lessons for Modern Strategists.* New York: St. Martin's Press, 1990.

Sun-tzu. *The Art of War.* Translated by Ralph D. Sawyer. Boulder, Colo.: Westview Press, 1994.

Terriff, Terry, et al. *Security Studies Today.* Cambridge: Polity Press, 1999.

Tyler, Patrick E. "U.S. Strategy Plan Calls for Insuring No Rivals Develop." *The New York Times,* March 8, 1992.

Ullman, Harlan, and James Wade Jr. *Shock and Awe: Achieving Rapid Dominance.* Washington, D.C.: National Defense University Press, November 1996.

"U.S.-Russia Strategic Offensive Reductions Treaty" (May 24, 2002). *Comparative Strategy* 21 (2002): 337–38.

"U.S.-Russia Joint Declaration" (May 24, 2002). *Comparative Strategy* 21 (2002): 338–43.

Vandergriff, Donald. *The Path to Victory: America's Army and the Revolution in Human Affairs.* Novato, Calif.: Presidio Press, 2002.

Vasquez, John A. *The Power of Power Politics: From Classical Realism to Neotraditionalism.* Cambridge: Cambridge University, 1998.

Vickers, Michael G. "Revolution Deferred: Kosovo and the Transformation of War." In *War over Kosovo: Politics and Strategy in a Global Age,* edited by Andrew J. Bacevich and Eliot A. Cohen, 189–209. New York: Columbia University Press, 2001.

Villacres, Edward J., and Christopher Bassford. "Reclaiming the Clausewitzian Trinity." *Parameters* 25 (1995): 9–19.

Walton, C. Dale. *The Myth of Inevitable U.S. Defeat in Vietnam.* London: Frank Cass, 2002.

Watts, Barry D. *Clausewitzian Friction and Future War,* McNair Paper 52. Washington, D.C.: National Defense University Press, October 1996.

Westad, Odd Arne, ed. *Reviewing the Cold War: Approaches, Interpretations, Theory.* London: Frank Cass, 2000.

Weigley, Russell F. *The American Way of War.* New York: Macmillan, 1973.

Williams, Andrew. *Failed Imagination? New World Orders of the Twentieth Century.* Manchester, U.K.: Manchester University Press, 1998.

Williams, Cindy, ed. *Holding the Line: U.S. Defense Alternatives for the Early 21st Century.* Cambridge, Mass.: MIT Press, 2001.

Wohlstetter, Albert. *Legends of the Arms Race.* USSI Report 75–1. Washington, D.C.: United States Strategic Institute, 1975.

Woodruff, Mark W. *Unheralded Victory: Who Won the Vietnam War?* New York: HarperCollins, 1999.

Wong, Leonard. *Stifling Innovation: Developing Tomorrow's Leaders Today.* Carlisle, Pa.: Strategic Studies Institute, U.S. Army War College, April 2002.

Wylie, J. C. *Military Strategy: A General Theory of Power Control.* Annapolis, Md.: Naval Institute Press, 1989.

INDEX